ULI–the Urban Land Institute
1090 Vermont Avenue, N.W.
Washington, D.C. 20005

ACPL ITEM
DISCARDED

SO-BWV-507

333.33 C265c
Casazza, John.
Condominium conversions   7072437

DO NOT REMOVE
CARDS FROM POCKET

ALLEN COUNTY PUBLIC LIBRARY

FORT WAYNE, INDIANA 46802

You may return this book to any agency, branch,
or bookmobile of the Allen County Public Library.

DEMCO

Condominium Conversions

John A. Casazza

About ULI–the Urban Land Institute ▬▬▬

ULI–the Urban Land Institute is an independent, nonprofit research and educational organization incorporated in 1936 to improve the quality and standards of land use and development.

The Institute is committed to conducting practical research in the various fields of real estate knowledge; identifying and interpreting land use trends in relation to the changing economic, social, and civic needs of the people; and disseminating pertinent information leading to the orderly and more efficient use and development of land.

ULI receives its financial support from membership dues, sale of publications, and contributions for research and panel services.

Allen County Public Library
Ft. Wayne, Indiana

Ronald R. Rumbaugh
Executive Vice President

ULI Staff ▬▬▬▬▬▬▬▬

Frank H. Spink, Jr.	Senior Director, Publications
Nadine Huff	Editor
Robert L. Helms	Staff Vice President, Operations
Regina P. Agricola	Production Manager
Jeffrey Hughes	Art Director
Rosalyn Migdal	Artists
Carolyn deHaas	

© 1982 by ULI–the Urban Land Institute, 1090 Vermont Avenue, N.W., Washington, D.C. 20005.

All rights reserved. Reproduction or use of the whole or any part of the contents without written permission of the copyright holder is prohibited. This report was funded in part by the United States Department of the Interior, Office of Water Research and Technology, but does not necessarily reflect their views and policies.

ISBN-0-87420-607-3
Library of Congress Catalog Number 82-70139
Printed in the United States of America

Acknowledgments

7072437

The process of real estate development requires the participation and interaction of many parties. A single individual can rarely take sole credit for the successful completion of a development project. Similarly, the preparation of this book required the participation, cooperation, and assistance of many individuals who are worthy of recognition.

Thanks go first to the case study participants and to the ULI staff. The frankness and cooperation of the case study participants were essential in compiling the individual case studies and in preparing the chapter on the conversion process. A special note of thanks to Chris Carley of CTC Associates, Inc. in Chicago. ULI staff members Frank Spink and Paul O'Mara made valuable suggestions during the preparation of the manuscript, Lois Steinberg identified research materials, and Jane Lynas and Karen Rice typed the manuscript.

Secondly, thanks go to the Steering Committee for their guidance during the initial stages of the book's preparation and for their review of the manuscript.

Thirdly, Deborah Johnson of Taylor-Johnson Associates, Hinsdale, Illinois, provided photos for use in the book, and the staff of HUD's Division of Policy Studies provided information on a variety of conversion projects. To each a note of thanks.

Finally, thank you to my wife Liz for her interest, understanding, and encouragement throughout the book's preparation.

John A. Casazza

Steering Committee

John (Jack) Bloodgood
President
John D. Bloodgood Architects, P.C.
Des Moines, Iowa

William F. Caldwell
President
Caldwell Equity Corporation
Troy, Michigan
ULI Second Vice President

Mitchell Durland-Blumberg
President
David Mitchell Companies
Houston, Texas

Robert E. Engstrom
President
Robert Engstrom Associates, Inc.
Minneapolis, Minnesota

James D. Klingbeil
President
The Klingbeil Management
Group, Inc.
Columbus, Ohio

George A. Smith
Chairman of the Board
George Smith Financial Corporation
Los Angeles, California

James W. Todd
President
Mobil Land Development
Corporation—Eastern Division
Reston, Virginia

Contents

Chapter 1   The Conversion Phenomenon

Chapter 2   The Conversion Process

Chapter 3   Case Studies

Appendices

List of Illustrations

Foreword

Condominium conversions, or more accurately, the conversion of rental dwelling units to condominium ownership dwelling units, is a current phenomenon that elicits many responses—good, bad, emotional, practical—when the subject is mentioned. It was only a few years ago that conversions were little more than a novel idea taking place in a few highly selective markets. Then a series of events occurred which resulted in a dramatic growth in the activity of conversion. Changes in tax laws and rising operating costs have made investment in rental properties less attractive. Single-family housing became less and less available at an affordable price, particularly for the first buyer. Thus, market acceptance of other forms of ownership housing, including townhouses, duplexes and quadruplexes, condominiums in low-, mid-, and high-rise configuration, and even the all but moribund cooperative, grew dramatically. Changing attitudes about living in cities, fuelled by the energy crisis, made close-in sites attractive. Coupled with these trends were our changing demographics—a decline in household sizes due to declining birth rates but an increase in the number of households due to an increase in single-person and empty-nester households. In various combinations, these events gave birth to and nourished condominium conversion activity.

The concept of condominium conversion is not without its critics, both in the development community and within the public sector and community at large. Foremost among these are the consumers of rental housing. They have been faced with the rising costs of rental housing due to inflation and reduced housing stock, displacement as a result of the disinterest or inability to convert to ownership, and fears of neighborhood decline or gentrification in varying circumstances. As a result of public attention, the public sector enacted laws which regulated, prohibited, or imposed moratoria on conversions while a determination of the public interest was made.

In the early stages, even professional developers were slow to accept the concept of conversion. There were few, if any, professional developers involved in condominium conversions. There was no experience to draw upon in selection, design, marketing, management of the conversion process, tenant relations and tenant relocations, and a myriad of other elements necessary to successful condominium conversions both from a development business standpoint and from marketplace consumer experience.

Today it is clear that the conversion phenomenon is neither temporary nor limited to a few housing markets. Because most of the literature on conversions has dealt with the social problems of condominium conversions or with the simple legal mechanics and not with good development practices, this publication seeks to provide an objective, balanced look at successful condominium conversions through a general discussion of conversions as well as through case studies of conversions. Its intent is also to share good development practices, to identify problems that have occurred and how they have been managed, and to describe ways to ameliorate if not eliminate some of the problems arising from conversions, resulting in the betterment of the community as a whole.

Frank H. Spink, Jr.
Senior Director,
Publications

Introduction

Perhaps no aspect of the real estate development industry has received more attention in recent years than condominium conversions. And, indeed, this attention is well justified. The growth of the condominium conversion phenomenon, often referred to by the mass media as "condoversions" or "condomania," has been staggering. During the 1970s, 366,000 rental apartment units in the United States were converted to condominiums, with 71 percent of these conversions occurring during the last three years of the decade.[1] It is projected that from 1980 through 1985 approximately 1.1 million additional rental units will be converted to condominiums. Conversions have clearly become an integral part of the land development industry.

The conversion phenomenon has been accompanied by considerable controversy and debate over the causes, the impacts, and the regulation of conversions. And, in many jurisdictions throughout the United States, condominium conversions have become a sensitive and highly emotional issue.

A number of publications have provided detailed discussions of the pros and cons of conversions. The purpose of this book, however, is not to debate the merits of conversions, but instead to provide an overview of condominium conversions—that is, where and to what extent are conversions occurring, what are the reasons for and impacts of conversions, and what has been and is being done in response to conversions. Secondly, and most importantly, the book is intended to serve as a practical "how to" manual for those who are interested in undertaking conversion projects but who are relatively unfamiliar with the conversion process. A detailed review of the conversion process has been provided and is accompanied by a series of in-depth case studies on condominium conversion projects.

While acknowledging some of the problems related to conversions, the book's focus is on how to undertake conversions in a responsible, professional, and profitable manner, thereby avoiding problems inherent in conversions. Much of the material on the conversion process and all of the case study material was obtained from meetings and discussions with experienced professionals. These individuals have undertaken numerous conversions which have been successful not only financially, but also socially. Their professionalism, which is reflected in a concern for individuals as well as for the "bottom line," has helped to advance the state-of-the-art for condominium conversions.

---

[1] This statistic and most of the facts and figures in the following chapter are from *The Conversion of Rental Housing to Condominiums and Cooperatives* (Washington: U.S. Department of Housing and Urban Development, Office of Policy Development and Research, Division of Policy Studies, June 1980).

John A. Casazza
Associate,
Publications

The Conversion Phenomenon

Condominium is a Latin word meaning joint ownership or control. Condominium ownership refers to ownership of a single unit in a multiunit building or complex of buildings, along with an individual share of the common areas and facilities. The buyer of a condominium unit purchases cubic air space and interior unit surfaces, as well as a proportion of the common elements. Condominium units are individually mortgaged and assessed for property taxes just as if they were single-family detached homes. Condominium unit owners are part of a condominium association which governs the common elements, prepares a budget, and assesses a monthly fee for each unit owner to cover maintenance of the common elements and to maintain a reserve fund for repairs.

A condominium is legally created through a master deed or declaration which formally dedicates a piece of real estate to the condominium form of ownership. The deed includes a description of the land, the building, the common areas, the individual units, the percentage of interest of each unit, and the owners' rights and obligations. A condominium also has bylaws which govern the operation of the project.

Although condominiums are a relatively new concept in the United States, their origins can, in fact, be traced back to ancient Babylon (approximately 4,000 years ago) and ancient Rome (approximately 2,000 years ago). Condominiums have been prevalent in Europe since the Middle Ages and in Latin America for half a century. Brazil enacted legislation to permit development of these "horizontal properties" in 1928.

The condominium form of ownership first acquired legal status in the United States and its possessions in 1951 with the passage of a law in Puerto Rico. This was followed by another Puerto Rican law in 1958, the Horizontal Property Act, which governed the ownership of property under the condominium category. In 1961 the United States Congress enacted Section 234 of the National Housing Act, extending government insurance of mortgages to condominiums. By 1968, all 50 states had enacted their own enabling legislation for condominiums.

Condominium conversion is the process of changing a multiunit rental property from single ownership to condominium ownership. Typically, the term condominium conversion is associated with the conversion of a rental apartment building or complex to condominium ownership. However, the conversion phenomenon has also involved the conversion of nonresidential structures or complexes, such as office, retail, or industrial uses, to condominium ownership, either with a change to residential use or with their original use.[1]

The conversion movement also involves the conversion of rental properties to the cooperative form of ownership rather than to condominiums. The cooperative is a form of housing ownership which differs in several respects from condominium ownership. A resident in a cooperative does not own the unit but instead owns a share of stock in the nonprofit corporation which owns the building or complex. Under cooperative ownership, title to land and buildings is vested in a nonprofit corporation, and the ownership of shares of stock or a membership certificate in the corporation entitles the residents to the rights and privileges of a proprietary lease for a specific unit. To purchase a unit membership representing a specific unit and to take occupancy of the unit, a transfer of stock or membership certificate must take place subject to the approval of the cooperative's board of directors. The corporation generally obtains a blanket mortgage for the property and cooperative members contribute toward its repayment as well as pay a proportional share of operating and maintenance expenses.[2]

While the owner of a condominium unit may default on the unit mortgage without directly affecting the legal rights and solvency of other owners, this is not the case in a cooperative. If a cooperative member fails to make payments toward the blanket mortgage, other members are responsible for that member's contribution. If a number of cooperative members fail to make payments toward the blanket mortgage, there is a significant risk of foreclosure on the property, possibly causing solvent members to lose their units.

---

[1] Figures cited on conversion volumes include conversions of rental apartments to either condominiums or cooperatives. However, conversions of nonresidential buildings or complexes to either residential or nonresidential condominiums or cooperatives are not included in these figures.

[2] Throughout the book the term condominium conversions refers to the conversion of rental properties to cooperatives as well as to condominiums (unless otherwise indicated).

1-1 and 1-2   The Prince Spaghetti Building in Boston is an example of the conversion of a nonresidential structure (opposite page) to residential condominiums (below).

The Extent and Location of Conversions ■■■

As mentioned earlier, between 1970 and 1979 366,000 rental units in the United States were converted to condominium ownership.[3] A majority of these conversions took place during the last few years of the decade. While only 86,000 rental units were converted during the first five years of the decade, the number of units converted between 1976 and 1979 increased dramatically to 280,000, with significant increases occurring in each of these four years. Converted units numbered 20,000 in 1976, 45,000 in 1977, 80,000 in 1978, and 135,000 in 1979.

Table 1—Number of Rental Units Converted Per Year

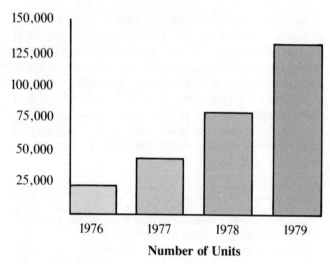

Number of Units

Source: HUD Report, p. IV-5.

Despite their increasing numbers and the extensive publicity which they have received, conversions are not yet a nationwide phenomenon. Rather, they have been concentrated in the nation's major housing markets. Seventy-six percent of the nation's conversions during the 1970s (265,191 units) occurred in the 37 largest Standard Metropolitan Statistical Areas (SMSAs) and 59 percent (136,902 units) took place in just 12 of the nation's SMSAs.[4] Thirty-one percent of the nation's conversions during the decade were concentrated in the Chicago and Washington, D.C. SMSAs, with 70,000 units (20 percent of the nation's total) converted in Chicago and 39,000 units (11 percent of the nation's total) converted in Washington, D.C.

During the 1970s only 23.5 percent of the nation's conversions (59,874 units) took place outside of the 37 largest SMSAs. Thus far, conversions have tended to occur in large metropolitan areas where the condominium form of ownership has been established for some time. However, a closer analysis of the data on conversion volumes during the 1970s indicates that a trend

1-3 Carl Sandburg Village is a 2,610-unit conversion in Chicago, housing a population of approximately 6,000. Chicago was the nation's major conversion market during the 1970s.

may be emerging leading away from a concentration of conversion activity in large urban areas.

Between 1970 and 1976, 63 percent of all converted units were located in the nation's 12 most active SMSAs. Between 1977 and 1979 the percentage of the nation's conversions which occurred in the 12 most active SMSAs had fallen slightly to 57 percent. At the same time, the conversions taking place outside the nation's 37 largest SMSAs had increased from 20 percent of the nation's total during the 1970–1976 period to 25 percent of the total conversions during the 1977–1979 period. More significantly, in 1979 nearly half of all conversions took place in areas outside the 37 largest SMSAs. Fifty-one percent of those conversions occurring in the 37 largest SMSAs between 1970 and 1979 were in suburban jurisdictions, while the remaining conversions in these SMSAs took place in central cities. Suburban conversions typically involved garden apartment or townhouse complexes, while the central city conversions typically involved high-rise and midrise structures. The distribution of conversions between the central cities and the suburbs has varied significantly from one market to the next. For example, in

---

[3] This includes 18,000 units which were converted to cooperative ownership, representing seven percent of all conversion activity during the decade. Most cooperative conversions have been located in the metropolitan areas of New York City, Washington, D.C., and San Francisco-Oakland. Seventy percent of the nation's cooperative conversions have taken place in the New York City SMSA.

[4] The 12 SMSAs which have been the most active conversion markets are: Boston; Chicago; Denver-Boulder; Houston; Los Angeles-Long Beach; Miami; Minneapolis-St. Paul; New York City; San Francisco-Oakland; Seattle-Everett; Tampa-St. Petersburg; and Washington, D.C.

Chicago, Pittsburgh, Atlanta, Baltimore, Milwaukee, and Miami, conversions during the 1970s were about evenly divided between the central city and the suburbs. In other metropolitan areas (such as Minneapolis-St. Paul, Hartford, Los Angeles-Long Beach, Detroit, San Francisco, Cleveland, and Washington, D.C.) suburban conversions during the 1970s greatly outnumbered those in the central city. Finally, there were markets where central city conversions were predominant during the decade. These included Denver-Boulder, San Diego, Dallas-Fort Worth, San Antonio, and Houston.[5]

The Converters

Most condominium conversions, particularly those conversions in the central cities and in prime suburban locations, are undertaken by professional converters. In most markets, there are also lenders, attorneys, and property managers who become experts in conversions. A majority of the professional converters are locally based developers, although there are converters who operate on the regional or national levels. Most of the regional or national converters got their start on the local level and then expanded gradually into other markets.

Few of the original owners of rental apartments undertake their own conversions. The property is nearly always sold to a developer for conversion. This is done for tax purposes, as well as to obtain the expertise of a professional converter. Under federal tax laws, owners of rental buildings or complexes who convert and sell individual units are considered dealers in real estate and the profits earned are treated as ordinary income and taxed at a relatively high rate. However, if the owner sells the property to a developer who undertakes the conversion, the owner's profits are considered a capital gain and are taxed at a much lower rate than ordinary income.

Despite these tax advantages, there are owners who undertake conversions directly instead of selling the building or complex to a developer. This has been more frequent with cooperative conversions than with condominiums. With a cooperative conversion it is sometimes possible for the owner to receive capital gains tax treatment of his profits by selling the converted project to the cooperative corporation which, in turn, sells shares representing individual units.

---

[5] Central city conversions are defined as those which fall within the city limits. This definition, together with the annexation policies in Texas, accounts for the large number of central city conversions in the major Texas markets.

Table 2—Condominium and Cooperative Conversions

	1970–75	1976	1977	1978	Three Quarters of 1979	Total 1970–79	Total 1977–79	Total (%) 1970–79	Total (%) 1977–79
Total U.S.	85,746	19,976	45,527	80,334	114,493	346,476	240,754	100.0	100.0
Condominium	82,540	19,452	43,546	74,462	108,370	328,370	226,378	94.8	94.0
Cooperative	3,206	524	1,981	5,872	6,523	18,106	14,376	5.2	6.0
37 Largest Metro Areas									
12 High Conversion Activity SMSAs	55,916	10,679	31,670	50,886	54,346	203,497	136,902	58.7	56.9
Condominium	54,099	10,175	30,050	45,521	48,108	187,953	123,679	54.2	51.4
Cooperative	1,817	504	1,620	5,365	6,238	15,544	13,223	4.5	5.5
Remaining 25 SMSAs	14,308	3,408	8,761	14,996	20,221	61,694	43,978	17.8	18.3
Condominium	13,188	3,408	8,441	14,509	20,084	59,630	43,034	17.2	17.9
Cooperative	1,120	0	320	487	137	2,064	944	0.6	0.4
Balance of U.S.	15,522	5,889	5,096	14,452	40,326[1]	81,286	59,874	23.5	24.9
Condominium	15,253	5,869	5,055	14,432	40,178	80,778	59,656	22.3	24.8
Cooperative	269	20	41	20	148	498	209	0.2	0.1
Percent Rental Converted Total U.S.	0.32	0.08	0.17	0.30	0.43	1.31	0.91		
Percent Rental Converted 12 High Activity SMSAs[2]	0.75	0.14	0.42	0.68	0.72	2.71	1.83		
Percent Rental Converted 25 Moderate Activity SMSAs[3]	0.30	0.07	0.18	0.32	0.43	1.30	0.93		
Percent Rental Converted Balance of U.S.[4]	0.11	0.04	0.04	0.10	0.28	0.57	0.42		

[1] For all 12 months of 1979.
[2] The 12 SMSAs accounted for 28.3 percent of U.S. occupied rentals in the 1977 Annual Housing Survey by the Bureau of the Census.
[3] The 25 SMSAs accounted for 17.9 percent of U.S. occupied rentals in the 1977 Annual Housing Survey by the Bureau of the Census.
[4] The balance of the U.S. accounted for 53.8 percent of U.S. occupied rental in 1977, by subtraction.

Source: HUD Report, p. IV-6.

In some areas conversions have been carried out successfully by tenants. In order to undertake a conversion the tenants must incorporate as a nonprofit corporation which is legally capable of holding real estate. Although a developer usually is hired by the tenants to actually undertake the conversion, the tenants have the overall responsibility for the conversion process. When the conversion is completed the tenants' nonprofit organization disbands and a condominium association is formed (made up of tenant purchasers as well as any outside buyers).

Structures Being Converted

The structures and complexes which have been and are being converted vary considerably in several ways. Converted buildings include high-rise and mid-rise buildings, garden apartments, and townhouses as well as nonresidential structures such as hotels, warehouses, schools, or factories. They may be as much as 50 or 100 years old or they may be relatively new. They may be in good to excellent condition and require very little repair work and renovation, or they may be in comparatively poor condition and require extensive repairs and renovation. They may be large complexes, such as the 2,610-unit Carl Sandburg Village in Chicago or the 1,684-unit Parkfairfax project in Alexandria, Virginia, or they may be structures containing only a few units.

Thus, conversions are not limited to buildings or complexes of a particular type, size, age, or condition. However, there are certain characteristics which a majority of converted buildings and complexes have in common. For instance, most conversions in central cities tend to involve high-rise buildings 11 to 20 years old which are usually in good condition. In most cases, the renovation required is relatively minor and of a cosmetic nature. In the suburbs, most conversions involve buildings which are newer than those in the central city (more than half of the suburban buildings are five to 10 years old). The buildings tend to be low-rise structures (primarily garden apartments and rental townhouses) in sound condition. The repair and renovation work required is usually minimal.

Nonresidential buildings which are converted tend to be older structures. Their age, together with the change in use, often makes it necessary for the converter to undertake major repairs and renovation. Frequently, kitchens and bathrooms and plumbing, electrical, heating, and air conditioning systems must be replaced or installed. Such nonresidential conversions have taken place primarily in the northeastern United States, particularly in New York and Boston, although they are becoming more prevalent in other areas of the country, such as Washington, D.C., Seattle, and Chicago.

1-4 and 1-5 Both large apartment complexes, such as the 1,684-unit Parkfairfax complex (left), and small individual structures, such as this 13-unit building in San Francisco (right), have been part of the conversion phenomenon.

Table 3—Age and Type of Converted Buildings as Perceived by Current Residents

Age of Building (years)	Central City (%)	Suburbs (%)
Less than 5	1	6
5 to 10	23	53
11 to 20	50	25
21 to 30	4	3
31 to 40	2	6
41 to 50	9	2
Over 50	11	5
Total	100	100
Number	381	335

Type of Structure	(%)	Suburbs (%)
High-rise	55	11
Mid-rise	19	13
Low-rise	26	68
Townhouse	0	5
Other	0	3
Total	100	100
Number	455	396

Source: HUD Report, p. VIII-29, Survey of Current and Former Residents

Reasons for Conversions

There have been four factors which, more than any others, have fueled the condominium conversion phenomenon: an increasing demand for home ownership; the increasing unaffordability of most forms of ownership housing; the rapidly declining profitability of owning and operating rental property; and changing social and demographic forces. Taken separately, none of these four factors could have accounted for the conversion phenomenon; however, occurring concurrently they have been directly responsible for the large number of conversions. Examining each of these factors in more detail helps to provide a better understanding of the reasons for conversions.

The Increasing Demand for Home Ownership

Home ownership is an American tradition. As of 1980, 65 percent of American households owned their own homes, compared to 40 percent of the nation's households in 1940. During the 1980s, 42 million people in the United States will turn 30 years old (a result of the 1950s baby boom), creating an estimated 17 million new households during the decade. It is expected that a majority of these new households, following the home ownership tradition, will want to become homeowners during the 1980s.

However, economics and not tradition is the major impetus for ownership. High inflation rates greatly enhance the advantage of owning a home rather than renting. Whereas a renter collects nothing but the receipts from the monthly rent payments, a homeowner has a significant investment which generally will keep up with the rate of inflation as well as provide shelter.

Public policy, through federal income tax laws, also encourages home ownership. Homeowners can deduct mortgage interest on their federal income tax returns. As stated by economist Anthony Downs of the Brookings Institution, "the economics of home ownership are now more attractive than the economics of renting."[6]

The Increasing Unaffordability of Ownership Housing

Inflation, the rising cost of new construction, rising interest rates, and increasing land and energy costs have made both new and used single-family homes and new condominiums unaffordable to many who wish to take advantage of the investment opportunities and the security of owning rather than renting. The cost of refurbishing rental apartments to make them marketable is much less than replacing them with new units; thus, conversions represent one of the few affordable home ownership opportunities for a large portion of the population, particularly for the first time and middle-income homebuyer.

The Declining Profitability of Rental Property

Rising operating costs have made it extremely difficult for a rental apartment building or complex to generate sufficient cash flow and a reasonable return on investment. Owners of many rental properties have found themselves in the middle of a cost-rent squeeze. As measured by the Consumer Price Index, in the time that the cost of owning and operating rental property has doubled, rents have increased, on the average, by about 60 percent. Thus, conversions have presented an opportunity to dispose of unprofitable rental property. However, the profit picture for converters has frequently been overstated. While it is true that some converters have made significant profits, a generally accepted return for most converters is 10 to 12 percent of gross sales, and it is not unheard of for a converter to break even on a project.

[6] *Business Week* (February 18, 1980), p. 90.

In general, the worsening operating margins and the declining return on investment from rental properties are not associated solely with depressed housing markets which have high vacancy rates and low rent levels. Even in a healthy rental market, it has become difficult to operate a rental property profitably. In fact, conversions tend to be associated with healthy, tightening rental markets characterized by strong demands for home ownership and by higher-than-average rent levels.

Rent control generally is not necessary for conversions, nor does it appear to be a leading cause of conversions. Although 76 percent of the nation's conversions during the 1970s occurred in the 37 largest SMSAs, only seven of these SMSAs include jurisdictions which have enacted some form of rent control. Nationally, less than seven percent of local officials in jurisdictions with some conversion activity have reported enactment of local rent control ordinances. While some of the jurisdictions which have enacted rent control have had some of the highest numbers of conversions (New York, Boston, and Washington, D.C.), neither Chicago (with the greatest number of conversions of any city) nor Denver and Houston (both cities with high conversion volumes) have had any form of rent control. Thus, in general, there does not appear to be a correlation between rent control and the high volume of conversion activity. Rather, conversions tend to be more directly related to the overall decline in the profitability of owning and operating rental properties, whether or not rent control is in existence.

Changing Social and Demographic Forces

In recent years there has been a significant decline in the size of the average American household, with one- and two-person households now representing a substantial portion of the American population. The increase in smaller households has been the result of a number of trends including an increase in the number of singles, due both to later marriages and a sharply increasing divorce rate; an increase in the percentage of persons over 55 years of age (due in part to better health care), resulting in an abundance of one- and two-person, "empty-nester" households; and a declining birth rate, leading to an overall decrease in household size. Changing social trends in recent years include a new lifestyle with more leisure time, a preference for maintenance-free dwellings with amenities, and a demand for urban residential locations. These changing social and demographic forces have made condominiums (both conversions and new construction) a desirable housing type.

1-6   The 20-unit Airy View conversion in Washington, D.C., was built in 1911 as a luxury rental apartment building.

8

Conversion Impacts

The impacts of conversions have probably received more publicity and discussion than any other aspect of the conversion phenomenon. And this attention is indeed warranted. Conversions have had a number of significant impacts. Probably the most important of these is the increase in opportunities for affordable housing. Rapidly rising development costs have simply made new housing, whether single-family detached homes or attached units, unaffordable to many prospective homeowners, particularly the first-time and middle-income buyer. Although precise data for sales prices on a national basis is unavailable at this time, it is readily apparent that conversions are priced below both new and used single-family detached homes and new condominium units. As a general rule, suburban conversion costs average about $40 to $45 per square foot, compared to an average cost of about $60 per square foot for newly constructed suburban condominiums. In downtown areas, conversions cost about $100 a square foot compared to an average cost of $110 a square foot for a new condominium.[7] Thus, in some markets the sales price for a small (700-square-foot) converted unit may be less than $30,000.

Nevertheless, the affordability of condominium conversions is limited in a couple of cases. Some conversions are aimed at a luxury market, which reduces the opportunities for first-time or middle-income buyers. Secondly, conversions for the most part have not been aimed at the nation's low-income population, who normally cannot afford to buy.

Impact on Tenants

The impact of conversions on tenants has no doubt been one of the most emotional aspects of the conversion phenomenon. The coverage of conversions by the mass media has typically emphasized the displacement of tenants, particularly the poor and the elderly, with little or no relocation assistance provided and with no concern by the converter for those being uprooted. However, in reality, this is usually not the case for a variety of reasons.

Tenants living in projects being converted are not always displaced. Nationally, approximately 22 percent of tenants in projects undergoing conversion purchase their units. In some projects, the majority of tenants purchase their units. Horizon House, a high-rise conversion in Fort Lee, New Jersey, had 1,132 out of 1,263 units purchased by tenants.[8] Parkfairfax, a 1,684-unit, garden apartment complex in Alexandria, Virginia, had 70 percent of the tenants purchase units. It is usually in the best interest of converters to encourage a high percentage of tenant purchases, since existing tenants

1-7 Rapidly rising development costs have made single-family detached homes and new condominiums unaffordable to many prospective homeowners.

offer a ready-made market for the converter and, therefore, help to minimize marketing costs and increase the likelihood of a rapid sell-out. A common way to encourage a high rate of tenant purchases is to offer sales price discounts to tenants. This is a widespread practice, with approximately 90 percent of tenant buyers receiving discounts. Also, in some cases, converters offer tenants the option of buying units in "as is" condition, further lowering the sales price.

Other tenants continue to live in the project following the conversion, not as homeowners but as renters. With many conversions, a significant number of units are sold to investors, who then lease the unit rather than live in it. For example, with the Parkfairfax conversion, 10 percent of the project's 1,684 units were sold to investors and then were leased on a fixed-rent basis to existing tenants who could not afford to buy or did not want to buy. It is a policy of many converters to make units which are purchased by investors available to the existing tenants in the project, particularly the elderly and the handicapped, on a preferential basis. In other conversions, developers do not sell all of the units but retain a small number of them to rent to certain tenants. When these continuing renters are considered together with the tenant purchasers, nationally the percentage of tenants who are not displaced in a conversion project is increased to 34 to 42 percent.

[7] "Shortfall of Affordable Housing Fuels Condo Demand," *Professional Builder* (September 1979), p. 76.

[8] *Multi-Housing News* (June 1981), p. 18.

Although in certain instances the poor and the elderly are displaced or inconvenienced as a result of conversions, in a majority of conversions the poor and the elderly are not affected. Most conversions involve successful, strategically located rental buildings which are generally occupied by nonelderly, middle- and upper-income households. Approximately 20 percent of those tenants relocating as a result of conversions have incomes under $12,500 and approximately 20 percent are over 65 years of age.

For most tenants, relocation as a result of conversion does not present a significant problem. Those tenants who are displaced by conversions generally are able to obtain comparably priced units in the same neighborhoods. In fact, 90 percent of all former tenants of converted buildings reported in a HUD survey that they are satisfied with their new apartments and buildings.[9] In addition, many tenants who relocate as a result of conversion would very likely have moved shortly even if the conversion had not taken place. Nationally, at least 40 percent of all renters move at least once each year. Further, many tenants who relocate as a result of conversion do so out of choice and not because they cannot afford to purchase their unit. Of those tenants who moved as a result of conversion, about 42 percent, nationally, moved because they could not afford to purchase their unit.

In addition to providing discounts on sales prices in order to encourage a high percentage of tenants to purchase units, converters have provided relocation assistance to those tenants who relocate. Such assistance, which is provided by developers either voluntarily or in compliance with local or state conversion regulations, has often been an important factor in alleviating the impact of conversions on poor, elderly, or handicapped tenants. This assistance may consist of counseling and assistance in finding a new apartment, as well as the payment of moving costs and related relocation expenses.

The Arlington, a 518-unit garden apartment complex in the Washington, D.C. metropolitan area, is one example of a conversion in which the developer provided considerable relocation assistance. An ombudsman was hired by the developer to handle tenant relations and to assist with relocation and was available to tenants 24 hours a day. Relocation assistance consisted of the early refund of security deposits (and, in some cases, the payment of security deposits for new apartments), help in finding alternative housing, and the payment of moving expenses. In addition, the developer and the ombudsman worked directly with the county's tenant landlord commission to provide special handling for foreign speaking, low-income, disabled, and elderly tenants.

In Hartford, Connecticut, the developer of three conversion projects contracted with a private firm to establish and implement a relocation assistance program for those tenants who were displaced. The assistance program for these conversions included the following:

- Tenants were not given specific dates to vacate.
- Tenants were given assistance in finding new units.
- All moving expenses were paid.
- Security deposits for new apartments were paid by the developer and the old security deposits for vacated units were returned to tenants.

[9] HUD Report, p. IX-17.

Table 4—Status of Tenants: Before and After Conversion

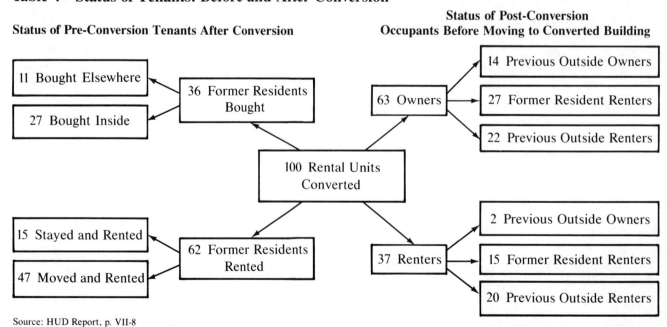

Status of Pre-Conversion Tenants After Conversion

Status of Post-Conversion Occupants Before Moving to Converted Building

11 Bought Elsewhere

27 Bought Inside

36 Former Residents Bought

100 Rental Units Converted

63 Owners

14 Previous Outside Owners

27 Former Resident Renters

22 Previous Outside Renters

15 Stayed and Rented

47 Moved and Rented

62 Former Residents Rented

37 Renters

2 Previous Outside Owners

15 Former Resident Renters

20 Previous Outside Renters

Source: HUD Report, p. VII-8

- Tenants relocating had to find comparable units.
- No harassment of tenants was allowed and no work could be done in the units while they were still occupied by tenants.

It is estimated that the cost to the developer for this relocation assistance program was approximately $1,000 per unit ($700 for moving expenses and $300 for new security deposits).[10]

Impact on the Rental Housing Market

The true impact of conversions on the rental housing market has been intensely debated. It has been stated by some that conversions have so severely depleted the rental supply that few rental options are available to those who cannot afford to or do not wish to purchase units. However, the overall reduction of the nation's rental supply due to conversions has not been nearly as extensive as many have stated. The 366,000 units converted during the 1970s represented only 1.3 percent of the total number of rental apartments in the nation. In fact, far more of the nation's rental housing stock is lost to abandonment and demolition than to conversions. Further, the dwindling number of unsubsidized rental housing starts is not related to conversions, but rather to the declining profitability of owning and operating rental housing. Although there is no doubt that in some instances conversions have exacerbated already tight rental markets, their impact on the supply of rental housing at the national level has been negligible.

The effect of conversions on the rental supply and on rental demand is not a one-to-one relationship for several reasons. First, the impact on rental supply is modified since a significant percentage of the units in converted buildings are often purchased by investors and then rented, or are rented by the converter. Nationally, for every 100 rental units converted, 63 are occupied by owners and 37 are occupied by renters. Second, the impact on rental demand is modified since those renters who buy contribute to a reduction of overall rental demand and since some tenants who move out when their unit is converted purchase a unit elsewhere.

According to the U.S. Housing and Urban Development report, *The Conversion of Rental Housing to Condominiums and Cooperatives,* of every 100 rental units in the nation which are converted, 63 units are lost to the rental supply because they are occupied by purchasers. Out of these 63 purchasers, 49 were previously renters. In addition, 58 tenants move out for every 100 units converted, with 47 of these continuing to rent elsewhere and 11 buying units elsewhere. Therefore, for every 100 units converted, renter demand is reduced by 58 households—the 49 former renters who purchased converted units, the 11 former tenants who bought units elsewhere, and two previous homeowners who moved to converted units as renters (thus increasing the renter demand by two households).

---

[10] HUD Report, pp. IX-3 and IX-4.

Table 5—Percent of Rental Housing Converted

	1970–75	1976	1977	1978	1979 Three Quarters	Total 1970–79	Total 1977–79
Occupied Rental Housing[1]	25,656,000	26,101,000	26,515,000	26,515,000	26,515,000	26,515,000	26,515,000
Total Conversion[2]	85,746	19,976	45,527	80,334	114,893	346,476	240,754
Percent Converted	.32	.08	.17	.30	.43	1.31	.91
Loss of Units to Rental Supply[3]	54,020	12,585	28,682	50,610	72,383	218,280	151,675
Drop in Renter Demand[4]	49,733	11,586	26,406	46,594	66,638	200,956	139,637
Net Shortfall of Rental Supply[5]	4,287	999	2,276	4,017	5,745	17,324	12,038
Net Shortfall of Rental Supply as Percent of Rental Supply	.017	.004	.009	.016	.022	.065	.045

[1] Annual Housing Survey, Series H-150-75,-76,-77, Bureau of the Census, Washington, D.C., 1976-77-78. The 1977 figure is used for 1978 and 1979.

[2] Department of Housing and Urban Development, field interviews in 37 SMSAs conducted by HUD staff, September and November 1979.

[3] Sixty-three percent of the converted units were owner-occupied after conversion. The remaining 37 percent were rented out by their owners.

[4] Forty-nine percent of those who bought converted units had previously rented, and 11 percent of the renters who moved from the converted building bought housing elsewhere. However, two percent of those who moved into the converted building as renters were former homeowners; hence, renter demand has dropped by 58 percent of the total units converted.

[5] Forty-two percent of the current residents had rented units elsewhere; 27 percent are now owners and 15 percent are renters in the converted building. However, 47 percent of all former residents now rent outside of the converted building, resulting in a net shortfall of rental supply equal to five percent of all converted units.

Source: HUD Report, p. VII-11

The conversion of every 100 units in the nation creates a demand for 47 additional vacant rental units (made up of the 47 out of 100 tenants who move out upon conversion and continue to rent elsewhere). However, with the conversion of each 100 units only 42 vacant rented units are created (made up of 27 former renters living outside the conversion, who move to the converted building or complex and buy units, and 15 former renters from outside the conversion, who move to the converted building or complex and continue to rent). Therefore, for every 100 units converted, there are only five previously vacant units in the rental housing market which become occupied.[11]

The conversion of 366,000 units in the United States between 1970 and 1979 resulted in the following:

- A reduction in the nation's rental housing supply of 231,000 units out of approximately 26.5 million rental units
- A reduction in renter demand by 212,000 households
- A net total of 18,000 previously vacant rental units being occupied by former tenants of converted buildings.

Impact on Tax Revenues

While it is apparent that the reassessment of property following conversion leads to increased revenue from local property taxes, the extent of this increased revenue varies significantly from one local jurisdiction to the next. The degree of impact depends on the extent of conversions within the jurisdiction as well as on the particular jurisdiction's tax rates for various classes of property, its assessment practices, and tax relief provisions for special classes of property owners, such as the elderly and the disabled.

1-8   Park City West, a 334-unit high-rise conversion in Philadelphia.

1-9   The Cairo, a deteriorating, turn-of-the-century hotel in Washington, D.C., was converted to 178 condominium units.

Typically, a rental building or complex prior to conversion is assessed as a single entity, with the assessment based on the property's income producing capacity or on the recent sales prices of comparable properties. However, following conversion, each unit is usually assessed individually. This individual assessment of each unit, together with the renovation and improvements undertaken during conversion, generally will result in a significant increase in the assessed value of the property.

While increases in assessed value on a project by project basis as a result of conversion have been significant, the total impact of conversions, to date, on local property tax revenues has been small. In only 11 percent of all jurisdictions with conversions do local officials believe that increased assessments following conversion have had a major impact on the local tax base. Thus, although most jurisdictions experience an increase in real estate assessments as a result of conversions, this increase is minor compared to the total existing assessments within the jurisdiction. However, conversions can be expected to have a more significant cumulative impact on municipal tax revenue (with additional tax revenues collected year-after-year).

Impact on Neighborhoods

In general, it may be stated that most conversions undertaken to date have not had a major impact on the revitalization of declining neighborhoods. A majority of the conversions have been located in desirable, economically viable neighborhoods which have experienced continuous private investment. And, in most cases, those conversions undertaken in neighborhoods which are revitalizing have generally lagged behind the revitalization efforts rather than acting as catalysts for the revitalization.

---

[11] HUD Report, p. VII-5 to VII-10.

Table 6—Estimated Assessment Increases Due to Conversion

SMSA	1978 SMSA Real Property Assessed Values (In Billions)	Conversions in 1978	Largest Per Unit Increase in Assessed Value[1]	Total Increase as Percent of Total Assessment[2]	Per Unit Average Increase[3]	Average Increase as Percent of Total Assessment
Baltimore	$11.74	762	$1,604	.0001	—	—
Boston	19.32	2,224	486	.0001	310	.00004
Chicago	30.54	11,355	474	.0002	422	.00016
Denver	4.95	6,743	94	.0001	33	.00004
Houston	12.60	5,615	83	*	25	**
Los Angeles	25.87	4,506	1,235	.0002	1,205	.00019
Miami	20.03	1,970	401	*	208	.00003
Minneapolis-St. Paul	7.89	1,703	146	*	−340	−.00008
San Francisco-Oakland	15.78	2,639	6,141	.0010	2,004	.00032
Seattle	21.32	2.828	446	*	427	.00005
Washington, D.C.	10.69	3,761	356	.0001	—	—

* = Less than one one-hundredth of one percent
** = Less than .00001

[1] Of two buildings sampled; one building in Baltimore.
[2] Using the largest per unit increase as the basis for calculation.
[3] Average of two buildings sampled.

Source: HUD Report, p. VIII-10

However, this does not mean that conversions have played no role whatsoever in revitalizing and stabilizing neighborhoods which had been declining. The physical repair and renovation of the buildings, together with the replacement of renters with homeowners (who tend to be less transient and to participate more actively in neighborhood activities), definitely has a stabilizing and revitalizing effect on previously declining neighborhoods. Generally, however, a conversion undertaken in a declining neighborhood which is not undergoing concurrent revitalization activity will not be a sufficient force for revitalization and may not be successful.

There are exceptions to this rule, particularly with large-scale conversion projects. For example, the conversion of The Arlington (518 units located five miles from downtown Washington, D.C.) definitely acted as a catalyst for neighborhood revitalization. The project's progressive deterioration prior to conversion was having a negative impact on the surrounding neighborhood. The project and the neighborhood were becoming high crime areas, placing a financial burden on the county. However, with the conversion this trend has been reversed completely and the conversion has made a significant contribution to the county's tax base.

It can be expected that as conversions continue in the future they will gradually play a larger role in the revitalization of declining neighborhoods. As conversions continue, most of the rental apartments in the most desirable, economically viable neighborhoods will already have been converted. Thus, it is likely that an increasing number of conversions will take place in less desirable neighborhoods which have been deteriorating or are just in the initial stages of revitalization.

Impact on Housing Quality

There is no doubt that conversions are playing a role in preserving and renovating multifamily housing which might be subject to decay and abandonment if left as rental apartments. As mentioned earlier, the declining profitability of owning rental property due to rapidly rising operating costs has left most owners of rental apartments with little or no economic incentive to undertake necessary renovation and repair work. Conversions, however, offer the financial motivation to renovate rental apartment structures.

1-10 The Arlington, a 518-unit conversion in the Washington, D.C., metropolitan area, has been a catalyst for neighborhood revitalization.

Although conversions are already playing a role in the renovation and upgrading of multifamily housing, it is expected that in the future the positive impact of conversions on housing quality will become more pronounced. During the 1970s, more than half of the nation's conversions took place in relatively new buildings (the average age of buildings was generally between 11 and 20 years in central cities and between five and 10 years in the suburbs) which were in relatively good condition and did not require major repairs. Therefore, a considerable number of conversions during this period involved only minor or cosmetic renovation. However, during the last decade conversions were also undertaken involving major renovation to buildings in substandard condition, including the repair or replacement of heating or air conditioning systems, plumbing, wiring, the roof, and the elevators. Some conversions even involved the "gut rehabilitation" of buildings. This has been especially true of conversions involving the renovation of formerly nonresidential buildings, such as warehouses, factories, hotels, and schools. It is expected that during the remainder of the 1980s a far greater number of substandard and deteriorating rental buildings presently considered unsuitable for conversion will be converted due to the increasing scarcity of choice buildings, thereby exerting an even greater impact on the improvement of housing quality.

Regulation of Conversions

In response to the conversion phenomenon a variety of legislation has been enacted, primarily at the state and local levels, designed to protect tenants as well as the buyers of converted units. Legislation protecting tenants has received the most attention, particularly among the development community, because it has sometimes resulted in the restriction or temporary prohibition of conversions.

Following is a discussion of some of the existing conversion legislation at the state and local levels. It should be noted that this legislation is not static. As conversions become more prevalent, existing legislation is frequently amended and new legislation is enacted.

Existing State Legislation

Presently, approximately one-half of the states have legislation which is designed to protect tenants of apartments which are being converted. A majority of this tenant protection legislation at the state level is related to tenant notification of the conversion; tenant notification of an intent to evict; a minimum percent of tenants in the project who must approve the conversion or agree to purchase units; the right of first refusal to tenants; and relocation assistance. Special tenant protections for the elderly, the handicapped, or for families with minor children are required by only three states—New York, Connecticut, and Minnesota.

Eighteen states presently require that tenants be notified of the intent to convert. Most states requiring conversion notification to tenants specify a minimum period of tenancy following the notification. The tenant may continue to occupy the unit throughout the period or until the termination of the lease, whichever is longer. The time required for the notification period varies among the 18 states from 60 days to 270 days, with 120 days being the most common length. Some states also require extended notification periods based upon the tenant's age, physical disability, family status, the tenant's length of residence, or the existence of a local housing emergency. Three states (Colorado, Florida, and Tennessee) have legislation that permits a converter to shorten the notification period if reasonable moving expenses of the tenant will be paid.

A number of states require notice to tenants of the intent to evict as well as of the intent to convert. Such legislation often prohibits eviction of tenants for long periods of time. For example, New Jersey requires that tenants receive 60 days notice of intent to convert which is then followed by a three-year notice of intent to institute eviction proceedings. New Jersey law also provides for a court ordered stay of evictions after the minimum three-year period.

New York State has the most extensive legislation regarding a minimum tenant purchase or approval before a conversion can take place. Two separate bills have been enacted by the New York State legislature, one of which applies to all conversions in New York City and the other to conversions in three counties in the New York metropolitan area (Nassau, Westchester, and Rockland). The legislation pertaining to New York City requires that 35 percent of the tenants in occupancy on the date a plan to convert is filed must consent to buy their units before conversion can occur. If less than 35 percent of the tenants agree to the conversion, the conversion can still take place but tenants who choose to remain as renters cannot be evicted. In addition, tenants over 62 years of age who have lived in the project for two years or more and whose annual income is less than $30,000 cannot be evicted. The legislation pertaining to the three counties authorizes local governments to require that a minimum of 35 percent of the sales be to tenants if there is a plan to evict and that 15 percent of sales be to tenants if there is a noneviction plan.

Fourteen states presently require the developer to give tenants the right of first refusal—that is, tenants must be given an exclusive option to purchase their units. However, the tenant must decide whether or not to purchase the unit within a specific period of time, which ranges in the various states from 30 to 120 days.

Five states require the converter to pay moving expenses of those tenants who relocate or to establish a relocation assistance program.[12] New Jersey requires the developer to provide moving expense compensation equal to one month's rent to all tenants who are evicted or move because of the conversion. In addition, the legislation provides that tenants in occupancy prior to the recording of the master deed have a right for 18 months to demand that the developer offer them a reasonable opportunity to examine and rent comparable housing. The developer must prove that these requirements have been met before eviction proceedings can begin.

Connecticut requires that low-income tenants receive moving and relocation expenses equal to one month's rent or up to $500. In addition, the Connecticut legislation stipulates that the converter provide nonpurchasing tenants with relocation assistance, including information on the availability of alternative housing financing programs and federal, state, and municipal housing assistance.

---

[12] These states include California, Colorado, Connecticut, New Jersey, and Tennessee.

Table 7—Notification of Intent to Convert*

Notification Required	States
60 days	New Jersey and Tennessee
90 days	Colorado, New Hampshire, Oregon, and Virginia
120 days	Arizona, California, Illinois, Michigan, Minnesota, Ohio, West Virginia, and Wisconsin
180 days	Connecticut and Maryland
270 days	Florida**

*Notice in New York varies for rent control and rent stabilization housing.
**In Florida, a tenant who has been a resident of a project undergoing conversion for six months or more prior to the notice of the conversion may extend the lease 180 days. In both cases, the tenant must notify the developer of the decision to extend the lease within 45 days of the notice of conversion.

Source: HUD Report, p. XI-5

Three states allow the developer to terminate or shorten the required notification period if they pay the tenant's moving expenses or other agreed upon compensation. Colorado legislation enables the developer to terminate the tenancy in less than the required 90-day period if the developer pays all moving expenses or other agreed upon compensation. Florida legislation permits developers to offer tenants entitled to 270 days notice the option of accepting 120 days notice plus one month's rent to cover the cost of moving. Tennessee legislation stipulates that if the developer fails to give two month's notice, the tenant may choose to vacate immediately upon receiving a belated notice and the developer must then pay all reasonable moving expenses. However, if a tenant is in a position to make this choice and does not vacate the premises immediately, the developer is not required to pay moving expenses.

The Uniform Condominium Act

Adopted by the National Conference of Commissioners on Uniform State Laws in 1977 and approved by the American Bar Association in 1978, the Uniform Condominium Act (UCA) is intended to unify and modernize the "first generation" of condominium legislation passed in the 1960s. The UCA, which was drafted by the National Conference of Commissioners on Uniform State Laws, is expected to serve as the basis for future revisions of condominium legislation in many states. As of February 1981, the act had been adopted by Minnesota, Pennsylvania, and West Virginia. During 1981, the UCA is being considered by a dozen state legislatures including Maine, Vermont, Massachusetts, Rhode Island, North Carolina, Michigan, Illinois, Tennessee, Missouri, Arizona, Colorado, and Wyoming.

The UCA provides two basic protections to tenants living in apartments which are being converted. First, tenants must be given at least 120 days notice of the conversion. This notice may also constitute the statutory notice to vacate if it specifies a date by which the unit must be vacated. No tenant with a valid lease can be evicted until the lease has expired, except for nonpayment of rent, destruction of property, or creating a disturbance for neighbors.

Second, tenants must be given the right of first refusal; that is, the right to purchase the unit on terms equal to those offered to the public. The act recommends that this right of first refusal be available for 60 days after the notice of the conversion. In addition, it recommends that if the tenant does not exercise the right to purchase, the unit should not be sold at a lower price or on more favorable terms for at least 180 days, thereby discouraging unreasonable developer offers to tenants.

Existing Local Ordinances

Some municipalities, particularly the larger cities with high conversion volumes, have adopted ordinances regulating conversions. These ordinances may be placed in the following categories: moratoria, protection of the rental stock, protection of tenants, and preservation of low- and moderate-income housing.

Moratoria. Upon experiencing conversions for the first time, some local jurisdictions have adopted a moratorium on all conversions. These moratoria are intended to be short-term, emergency measures (generally, they vary in length from 30 days to 12 months) to allow the local jurisdiction to study conversions and their impacts within the jurisdiction and to prepare and enact any permanent conversion regulations which might be necessary. Local moratoria have occasionally been de-

clared invalid by the courts. Generally, a moratorium may be ruled invalid if it is preempted by state legislation or if the local governing body does not have adequate findings to justify the moratorium's existence. For example, following the expiration of its original conversions moratorium, Washington, D.C., adopted a series of short-term moratoria. On about the third round of them the Washington, D.C., Superior Court struck down one of these emergency enactments on the grounds that there were no independent legislative findings to support each of the successive moratoria.

Protection of the rental stock. A number of municipalities have adopted ordinances intended to prevent conversions from severely depleting the rental housing supply in tight rental markets. These ordinances usually take one of three forms. First, conversions may be limited based on the vacancy rate. That is, conversions are prohibited once the vacancy rate within the jurisdiction falls below a certain percentage, usually between three and six percent. Many jurisdictions, however, provide exceptions to the vacancy rate limitation on conversions. For example, in Washington, D.C., the vacancy rate restriction (three percent or lower) does not apply if a majority of tenants in the building or complex agree to the conversion or if the units being converted are luxury or high rent units. In Palo Alto, California, conversions are prohibited whenever the vacancy rate, measured twice each year, falls below three percent, unless 67 percent of the tenants in a building or complex agree to exempt it from the vacancy rate provision.

Second, conversions may be limited by the adoption of conversion quota ordinances. These quotas generally limit conversions to an annual percentage of the rental

1-11 Landscaped courtyards distinguish Mira Vista, a 140-unit conversion in Southern California.

Table 8—Local Condominium and Cooperative Conversion Regulations in the Nation's Largest Metropolitan Areas

Standard Metropolitan Statistical Areas	Conversion Moratorium (1970-1980) Date	Length	Conversion Ordinance or Policy	Standard Metropolitan Statistical Areas	Conversion Moratorium (1970-1980) Date	Length	Conversion Ordinance or Policy
Anaheim, Santa Ana, Garden Grove, CA				**Kansas City, MO-KS**			
Anaheim City			†	Kansas City			
Santa Ana City			A B	**Los Angeles-Long Beach**			
Garden Grove City			A B	Long Beach City			A B
Costa Mesa City			B C	Los Angeles City			A B C D
Newport Beach City			A B C D	Duane City	10/79-4/80	6 mo	A B C
Orange County*			A B C D	Gardena City			B C
Atlanta, GA				Los Angeles County*			A C D
Atlanta City			A B	**Miami, FL**			
Baltimore, MD				Miami City			
Baltimore City			A C	Miami Beach	2/80-3/80	1 mo	A
Boston, MA				**Milwaukee, WI**			
Boston City			A	Milwaukee City			
Brookline City			A	**Minneapolis-St. Paul, MN-WI**			
Cambridge City			C	Minneapolis City			A B
Buffalo, NY				St. Paul City			
Buffalo City				Little Canada	12/79		†
Chicago, IL				Wayzata			A B
Chicago City	3/79-4/79		A B	**Nassau-Suffolk, NY¹**			
Arlington Hts	6/78-8/78	2 mo	A B	No Central City			
Evanston City	7/78-3/79	9 mo	A B	*			
Skokie City*	11/77-7/78	8 mo	A B	**New Orleans, LA**			
Cincinnati OH-KY-IN				New Orleans City			
Cincinnati City				**New York, NY-NJ²**			
Cleveland, OH				New York City			§
Cleveland City				Fort Lee City	11/79-12/79	2 mo	
Beachwood City	8/79-11/79	3 mo	A B C	*			§
Lakewood City	2/79-5/79	3 mo	A B C	**Newark, NJ**			
Lyndhurst City*			A B C	Newark City			
Columbus, OH				Verona City	8/79-12/79	4 mo	
Columbus City				**Philadelphia, PA**			
Dallas-Ft. Worth, TX				Philadelphia City	9/79-3/80	6 mo	A B
Dallas City				Cheltenham Twp			A
Ft. Worth City				Lower Marion Twp			A B
Denver-Boulder, CO				**Phoenix, AZ**			
Denver City			A	Phoenix City			
Boulder City			A	Mesa City			B
Detroit, MI				**Pittsburgh, PA**			
Detroit City				Pittsburgh City			
Hartford, CT				**Portland, OR-WA**			
Hartford City				Portland City			
Glastonbury	12/79-11/80	1 mo	A C	**St. Louis, MO-IL**			
Houston, TX				St. Louis City			
Houston City				University City			A B
Indianapolis, IN				Webster Grove City	8/79-2/80	6 mo	A B
Indianapolis City			A B	**San Antonio, TX**			
				San Antonio City			

Standard Metropolitan Statistical Areas	Conversion Moratorium (1970-1980) Date	Length	Conversion Ordinance or Policy
San Bernardino-Riverside-Ontario, CA			
San Bernardino City			C
Riverside City	2/79		†
Ontario City			
Montclair City			A B C
Placentia City	10/79-11/80	11 mo	†
Upland City*	11/79		†
San Diego, CA			
San Diego City			A C
Chula Vista City			A B
La Mesa City			B C
Oceanside City*	3/79-11/79	8 mo	A B C D
San Francisco-Oakland, CA			
San Francisco City	4/74-5/75	13 mo	A B C D
	5/79-8/79	3 mo	A B C D
Oakland City	10/78-12/78	2 mo	A B C
Concord City			A B C
Marin County			A B C
Walnut Creek*			A B C D

Standard Metropolitan Statistical Areas	Conversion Moratorium (1970-1980) Date	Length	Conversion Ordinance or Policy
San Jose, CA			
San Jose City	11/73-8/75		A B
Cupertino City			A B C
Mountain View	3/74-9/75	18 mo	A B C
	3/76-3/77	12 mo	A B C
	4/77-4/78	12 mo	A B C
Palo Alto City*	12/73-11/74	11 mo	A B C
Seattle-Everett, WA			
Seattle City	7/78-11/78		A B
Everett City			A B
Lynnwood City	6/78-10/78		A B C
King County			A B
Mercer Island*			A B
Tampa-St. Petersburg, FL			
Tampa City			
St. Petersburg City			
Washington, DC-MD-VA			
Washington City	2/76-2/80	6 mo	A B C D
	2/80-8/80	6 mo	A B C D
Montgomery County	7/79-11/79	4 mo	A B C D

† Ordinance Pending
* Additional outside central city jurisdictions in the SMSA having ordinances.
A. Tenant Protection
B. Buyer Protection
C. Rental Stock Protection
D. Preservation of Low- and Moderate-Income Housing
[1] Local jurisdictions in Nassau, Rockland, and Westchester Counties may also be covered by state law protections for the elderly by passing a local option ordinance.
[2] New York City has special state statutory authority covering elderly persons in conversions.

Source: HUD Report, p. XII-4

stock within the jurisdiction or to an annual number of rental units within the jurisdiction. For example, in Walnut Creek, California, (located in the San Francisco-Oakland SMSA) conversions are limited each year to five percent of the city's rental stock. Palo Alto, California, and other cities with vacancy rate limitations have also adopted a quota approach when the vacancy rate threshold is exceeded. Palo Alto defines the number of vacant units in excess of three percent as a vacancy surplus and permits applications for conversions which do not exceed the vacancy surplus plus 40 percent. In San Francisco, no more than 1,000 rental units each year may be converted within the city.

Third, conversions may be limited by requiring the converter to construct rental housing to replace those units which are being converted, or by relating the number of conversions permitted to the construction of new rental housing within the jurisdiction. For example, La Mesa, California's (San Diego SMSA) conversion ordinance stipulates that the maximum number of units which may be converted within La Mesa each year shall be equal to 50 percent of the yearly average of apartment units constructed in the previous two fiscal years.

In Oakland, California, conversions of buildings with five or more units are permitted only when each unit converted is replaced by a rental unit added to the city's housing stock. Thus, in order for developers to undertake conversions they must earn ''conversion rights'' equal to the number of units they plan to convert. Conversion rights may be earned by a developer by building new rental structures, converting nonresidential buildings to residential rentals, renovating buildings that have been vacated for at least a year, or building a new condominium or cooperative and agreeing to keep all the units rental for at least seven years.[13]

Protection of tenants. The most common aspect of local ordinances regulating conversions is the protection of tenants. Tenant protections often involve notification of the conversion; minimum tenant purchase or tenant approval; the right of first refusal; relocation assistance; special protections for the poor, the handicapped, and elderly; and tenant group right of first purchase. Three-fourths of local conversion ordinances require that tenants be given a minimum notification period, which commonly lasts anywhere from 90 to 180 days. This period is intended to give tenants adequate time to decide whether to purchase their unit or to relocate. Notice to tenants usually must be in writing. In some municipalities, such as Chicago, Boston, and Philadelphia, the notice regulations specify that the tenant may continue to occupy the unit either for the specified notification period or for the duration of the lease, whichever is longer. Some ordinances indicate at what point during the conversion process notice must be given to tenants. Most ordinances requiring tenant notification stipulate that during the notification period any prospective tenants must be advised of the conversion before signing a lease.

The requirement of some municipalities that a conversion cannot take place until a minimum percentage of tenants either has approved the conversion or agreed to purchase units has probably limited conversion volumes more than any of the other tenant protection measures. In San Francisco, at least 40 percent of the tenants in every proposed conversion must sign an intent-to-purchase agreement. In New York City, 35 percent of the tenants must agree to purchase their units before the conversion can take place. The city of Newport Beach, California, requires that at least 30 percent of the tenants express written interest in exercising their option to purchase their unit.

Most local conversion regulations require that tenants be given the right to purchase the unit which they are occupying. Generally, most ordinances require that a tenant be given the right of first refusal for a period lasting anywhere from 30 to 180 days. For example, Washington, D.C., Atlanta, and Minneapolis require that tenants be given a 60-day right of first refusal after being notified of the conversion.

About one-fourth of the local jurisdictions with conversion ordinances require that relocation assistance be provided for nonpurchasing tenants. Such relocation assistance regulations typically require that the developer pay relocation expenses or devise a comprehensive relocation assistance plan. In those jurisdictions requiring the payment of relocation expenses, the amount of compensation is usually either the actual moving costs (with a maximum amount specified) or an amount set by the ordinance. In Duarte, California, the tenant is entitled to one and one-half times the monthly rent to cover moving expenses. In Los Angeles, the converter must pay up to $500 for moving expenses, with the amount of relocation assistance depending on the increase in the tenant's rent (with special provisions for low-income tenants). In Washington, D.C., the developer must pay moving expenses of $125 a room. Seattle requires that $350 per unit be paid by the developer to vacating tenants. In those jurisdictions where the developer is required to prepare a relocation assistance plan, the plan often consists of a list of comparable rental housing available in the immediate area, the payment of moving expenses, and the payment of security deposits. In San Francisco, the developer must contract with the city's Central Relocation Services to provide permanent relocation services to tenants.

A number of local jurisdictions provide special protections for poor, handicapped, or elderly tenants. In at least 15 municipalities, the elderly, the poor, and the handicapped receive the benefit of longer tenancies or a longer period of notice before their units may be converted. For example, the usual one-year notification period required in Boston is extended to two years for elderly and handicapped tenants with incomes below a certain limit. Skokie, Illinois, grants a six-month lease extension to persons over 65, the disabled, and households with two or more minor children. Conversion ordinances in Oakland, San Francisco, and Walnut Creek, California, and in New York grant life tenancies to elderly tenants.

A handful of cities permit a tenant group to be formed (once notice has been given of intent to convert) and to be given the first right to purchase the building or complex. The Washington, D.C., ordinance mandates that the landlord may not sell a building containing more than four units unless the landlord first offers the building to a tenant organization at a bona fide price. Such an organization has 90 days to contract with the landlord for purchase of the building (120 days if the tenants need to form an organization legally capable of owning real estate). The Montgomery County, Maryland, ordinance requires that the contract purchaser of a rental project must give written notice of the proposed purchase to each tenant. Tenants are then given 30 days to execute a contract with the owner to purchase the property.

---

[13] *Planning* (February 1981), pp. 20–21.

Preservation of low- and moderate-income housing.
Several municipalities have adopted ordinances which are intended to preserve the supply of low- and moderate-income rental housing within the jurisdiction. These ordinances usually require either that a certain percentage of units in a converted project be set aside by the developer for low- and moderate-income households or that the developer assist with the replacement of low- and moderate-income housing.

For example, Marin County, California, has an ordinance which states that its planning commission may require a reasonable percentage of converted units to be reserved for persons of moderate income. In San Francisco, converters of buildings that contain low- or moderate-income units can either continue to rent these units (under special rent limitations) or they can sell them at a price that is no more than two and a half times the upper income limit of low- to moderate-income households. In addition, converters of all projects of five or more units must reserve 10 percent of the units for these categories. If more than 10 percent of the units were low- or moderate-income prior to the conversion, then the same amount must be reserved for low- and moderate-income housing.

Those jurisdictions requiring converters to assist with the replacement of low- and moderate-income housing have done so by requiring converters to allocate a portion of newly constructed units for low- and moderate-income households, to pay a tax, or to contribute to a public fund used for furthering low- and moderate-income housing opportunities. As an alternative to the requirements just mentioned, San Francisco allows a converter to construct an equal number of low- or moderate-income units or to contribute a certain amount (determined by formula) to the city's Housing Development Fund. Los Angeles requires that the converter pay $500 per unit to the city for the development of low- and moderate-income rental housing.

Federal, State, and Local Conversion Programs

The various conversion regulations discussed in the previous section are intended to lessen the impact of conversions on tenants who do not purchase units and on the rental housing supply. Although such regulations have no doubt been necessary in many cases, they have the drawback of being primarily restrictive in nature. That is, they have helped to control conversion volumes, thereby minimizing the impact on tenants and the rental supply, but they have not helped low- and moderate-income tenants to take advantage of the expanded home ownership opportunities presented by conversions. Fortunately, in addition to these regulations restricting conversions, there are many programs in existence at the federal, state, and local levels which are making it possible for low- and moderate-income households to purchase converted units and to enjoy the advantages of owning rather than renting. In addition to these existing programs, several programs are presently being considered for future implementation.

Federal Programs

Among the federal government housing programs which may be used to assist individuals in purchasing converted units are:

- The Section 245 Graduated Payment Mortgage (GPM) program, which is available to eligible condominium purchasers using a mortgage insured under the Department of Housing and Urban Development's Section 234(c) program.
- The Section 235 program, which is intended to help low- and moderate-income families to become homeowners. This program was extended by Congress in 1979 to include eligible households who have moved from a rental building that was converted.
- The Government National Mortgage Association's Targeted Tandem Programs, under which individuals holding Section 234(d) or Section 234(c) mortgages may be eligible for financing at the Federal Housing Administration rate.[14]

State and Local Programs

At the state and local levels, programs have been developed to provide financial and technical assistance to tenant groups converting their buildings and to subsidize low- and moderate-income persons in the purchase of converted units.

Assistance to Tenant Groups. Assistance by state and local governments to tenant groups who wish to convert their buildings comes in several forms including loan insurance, loans, education, and direct technical assistance. California has several programs to assist low- and moderate-income households in purchasing and converting. The home ownership coinvestment concept program provides assistance through public or private coinvestment and by deferring the repayment or servicing of coinvestment funds. Funding sources for this program include Community Development Block Grants as well as contributions from state grant programs, HUD's Innovative Grants Program, and from the private sector.

California's home ownership loan program authorizes the state Housing Finance Agency to assist low- and moderate-income households to obtain loans for the purchase of condominium or cooperative units. In addition, this agency administers a program which insures loans to finance limited equity cooperatives.

---

[14] To qualify for the program, the units must be located in cities eligible for HUD's Urban Development Action Grant program or in designated neighborhood strategy areas under HUD's Community Development Block Grant Program.

In Washington, D.C., a program has been established which offers professional technical assistance to help tenant associations determine the feasibility of their cooperative conversion proposals. Under the program, tenant groups are able to hire consultants, engineers, and architects to assist them in planning a cooperative conversion.

Subsidies for the Purchase of Converted Units. A variety of state and local programs either provide or plan to provide loans or grants to assist individuals, particularly the elderly or low- and moderate-income persons, in purchasing converted units. The California Department of Housing and Community Development and the California Housing Finance Agency have been granted authority to assist low- and moderate-income households to purchase converted units. The purchaser must make a downpayment of at least three percent and loan amounts may not exceed 45 percent of the sales price.

The city of Baltimore intends to use grant funds to establish a nonprofit real estate corporation which will provide home ownership and cooperative housing opportunities to low- and moderate-income households. The corporation will identify, acquire, repair, and sell residential properties. The city's home ownership programs and Section 8 subsidies will be made available to participants in the program.

The city of Brookline, Massachusetts, plans to use grant funds to provide equity assistance to low-income households for the purchase of converted units. The equity assistance will be secured by a lien on the unit which will be recovered when the unit is resold. The balance of the financing is expected to be provided by the state Home Mortgage Finance Agency, which provides financing to low-income households at interest rates of 1.5 to 2 percent below conventional market rates.

Future Trends

Based on the dramatic increase in conversion volumes during the second half of the 1970s (increasing from an annual nationwide total of 20,000 units in 1976 to 135,000 units in 1979), it appears likely that annual conversion volumes will continue to increase during the remainder of the 1980 to 1985 period. A simple projection based on conversion trends from 1977 through 1979 indicates that approximately 1,457,000 additional rental units in the United States will have been converted between 1980 and 1985. While it is likely that the number of conversions during this period will increase each year, the annual increases may be at successively smaller rates.

It is also probable that the simple projection (based on past volumes) of 1,457,000 additional units converted during the 1980 to 1985 period will be affected by several factors, particularly factors such as limits in the supply of convertible units and changes in financial conditions. For example, in some of the mature conversion markets, the existing supply of rental units which are most suitable for conversion may be depleted, thus contributing to a smaller growth in conversion volume. In addition, conversion volume during the 1980 to 1985 period may be affected by short-term fluctuations in the economy and in the housing market. High interest rates may result in a reduction in volume, although conversions appear to be less influenced by high financing costs than other segments of the housing market. When these two factors are considered, it appears likely that conversion volume during the 1980 through 1985 period will be less than that projected based solely on past trends.

Thus, when considering supply limits for convertible units and the effect of high interest rates, together with past trends, it is projected that approximately 1,140,000 units will have been converted in the United States during the 1980 through 1985 period. This projection is 317,000 units lower than that based solely on figures for 1977 through 1979.

It is expected that future conversion rates will also be affected by a number of other factors, although it is difficult to accurately determine their quantitative impact. These additional factors which could influence future conversion activity include household demand, regulatory actions, tax code changes, new construction, and the advent of planned conversions.

It is expected that household demand will continue to increase during the 1980 through 1985 period, with a demand of nearly eight million households projected (including both newly formed households and those shifting from renter to owner status). This continuing increase in household demand would appear to indicate that there will be a concomitant demand for converted units. The increasing prevalence of planned conversions (that is, the design and construction of rental apartments specifically for future conversion) would also seem to indicate that conversion volume will continue to remain high in the near future, as new rental apartments in the form of planned conversions are added to the supply of convertible units. Planned conversions can be expected to become more popular because they offer a significant economic incentive to the developer; since the units are specifically designed for future conversion, the renovation costs upon conversion are usually minimal, offering a significant profit potential for the converter.

Table 9—Projection of Conversion Activity, 1980–85

Projection Year	12 High Activity SMSAs	25 Other Large SMSAs	Balance of U.S.	Total U.S.
1980	52,767	21,569	27,047	101,383
1981	67,150	26,227	37,573	130,950
1982	77,982	35,548	55,188	168,718
1983	74,794	44,869	72,803	192,466
1984	107,853	54,190	90,418	252,461
1985	121,942	63,779	108,033	293,754
Total 1980-85	**502,488**	**246,182**	**391,062**	**1,139,732**

Source: HUD Report, p. VII-37

Although increasing household demand and the increasing number of planned conversions point toward a continuation of a relatively high level of conversion activity, factors such as regulatory actions, tax code changes, and new construction could result in a future decline in conversion volumes. Regulatory actions such as local moratoria and other conversion restrictions no doubt can exert a major impact on future national conversion volumes. Any changes in the federal tax code which would reduce the advantages of home ownership over renting could result in a decrease in the demand for converted units. Finally, newly built condominiums and other housing types may in the future be priced more competitively with conversions, as building acquisition costs and other conversion costs keep rising.

As discussed earlier, conversion trends during the latter part of the 1970s indicate a gradual dispersal of conversion activity outside of the nation's largest metropolitan areas. Thus, conversions taking place outside the nation's 37 largest SMSAs increased from 20 percent of the nation's total during the 1970 to 1976 period to 25 percent of the nation's total during the 1977 to 1979 period, and nearly half of all conversions undertaken outside of the 37 largest SMSAs took place in 1979. This increasing movement of conversion activity to smaller metropolitan areas can be expected to continue in the future as the supply of rental apartments in large metropolitan areas which are most suitable for conversion is gradually depleted. However, while there will be a continuing dispersal of conversions to smaller metropolitan areas, it is unlikely that conversions will ever spread to nonmetropolitan areas since the rental supply in such areas consists primarily of single-family detached homes.

Within metropolitan areas, it can be expected that conversions will spread in greater numbers to less desirable neighborhoods which are presently deteriorating or are in the initial stages of revitalization. This will be particularly true in the mature conversion markets, where most of the rental apartments in the desirable and/or economically viable neighborhoods will already have been converted. Thus, in the future it is likely that conversions will exert a greater impact on the improvement of housing quality and on neighborhood revitalization.

The Conversion Process

2-1   As illustrated by the framed promotional posters, location is the most important consideration in selecting a project for conversion.

At first glance, the conversion of a rental structure or complex to condominiums may appear to be a relatively simple and straightforward process which offers the potential for a significant profit in a short period of time. However, in reality, it is often complex. When undertaken by the inexperienced converter without adequate research and preparation, a conversion can often be unsuccessful and unprofitable. As many have stated, undertaking a condominium conversion is not for amateurs. The successful converter is one who has a thorough understanding of the various steps involved in the conversion process and has done his homework. The purpose of this chapter, therefore, is to review the basic steps which are required to undertake and complete a successful conversion. It is intended to provide the relatively inexperienced converter with a practical, nuts-and-bolts description of the conversion process.

While each conversion undertaken has its unique problems and opportunities, there are basic stages in the conversion process which are essential to the success of any conversion. These stages can be defined as:

- Identifying general conversion feasibility
- Identifying economic feasibility
- Determining and obtaining the necessary financing
- Reviewing the various legal aspects
- Undertaking the necessary renovation work
- Developing a marketing and tenant relations program
- Providing for project management.

Identifying General Conversion Feasibility ■

The general feasibility of a project for conversion is determined by examining the project's location, the suitability of the structure or complex, the project's rental history, and the market potential. The most important of these, as with other forms of real estate development, is the project's location. A superior location is nearly always imperative for a conversion to be successful. Thus, it has been found that although a project may have all of the physical attributes necessary for success, it may not be successful if it is poorly located. On the other hand, buildings or complexes that do not completely meet the physical criteria for a successful conversion have indeed been successful because of an outstanding location. As a general guide, it should be remembered that the complexities of conversion and renovation are large enough without adding the problem of overcoming a poor location.

What makes a location superior? First, it should be convenient—close to major employment centers, shopping centers, local convenience stores, cultural facilities, recreational areas or facilities, and easily accessible via major transportation arteries and mass transit. Second, the location and surrounding area should generally be known as a good residential neighborhood. Home values in the area should preferably be increasing or at least be stable. Typically, conversions have been most successful in mature, established neighborhoods in which existing homes are appreciating in value and in which new residential construction is limited. In areas where new construction is limited, conversions may provide one of the only sources of available ownership housing. Third, the project should be located within a tight rental market characterized by low vacancy rates and high rents. In addition, the area should be growing and should have a strong home ownership demand and high construction costs for new homes and new condominiums. Fourth, the project should not be located in a jurisdiction in which there are conversion moratoria or excessive restrictions on conversions, or in which there is an unfavorable attitude toward conversions.

Suitability of the Structure or Complex

A determination of the suitability of the structure or complex for conversion should be based on factors such as the age and condition of the building or buildings, the size of the project, the unit size and mix, and the available amenities. The actual age of the building or complex is often not a critical factor; many projects of greater than 50 years old have been successfully converted. Older, well-maintained structures often offer the advantage of extremely high quality construction. However, at the same time, older buildings or complexes sometimes have limitations, such as a lack of amenities, lack of parking, and poor window views and interior room layout, which may be difficult and expensive to correct. Such limitations should be considered when evaluating the feasibility of converting an older structure.

While the project's age is not necessarily a critical factor, the project's condition is one of the most important factors in determining its suitability for conversion and, therefore, should be carefully examined. The building or buildings should be structurally sound and of high quality construction so that extensive renovation and rehabilitation work will not be necessary. As a general rule, a building which will require significant rehabilitation is not recommended, particularly for the first-time converter. The need for extensive renovation will not only increase the actual renovation costs but also will increase the carrying costs of the project as a result of the extra renovation time required. In addition, as a general rule the extra money required for structural restoration does not significantly enhance the marketability of the individual units. Thus, it is best if the building is well built, has good sound control between the units, and gives the potential buyer the appearance of durability and strength.

2-3 Convenience to Capitol Hill was one of the significant factors in the success of this Washington, D.C., conversion.

2-2 Parkfairfax (outlined in white) in Northern Virginia enjoys convenient access to an interstate highway and to downtown Washington, D.C.

In determining the building's physical condition, it is advisable to prepare a checklist of the various physical aspects which should be evaluated. The checklist will typically include the following items: structural components (the foundation, roof, exterior siding, floors, interior walls, insulation, ceilings, windows, doors, stairs, elevators, and balconies); utilities (electrical, plumbing, heating, and air conditioning); and kitchen and bathroom equipment (cabinets, counter tops, sinks, appliances, bathtubs and showers, and toilets). Listing the various items will minimize the possibility of omitting any major items which should be examined, thus assuring that the necessary renovation work will be undertaken and that the estimate of renovation costs will be as accurate as possible. A comprehensive architectural and engineering inspection of all structural and engineering systems should then be undertaken to determine the condition of all items on the checklist.

While there is no ideal size for a conversion project, it is often advisable for the converter to select a building or complex of relatively small size. This will allow the conversion process to proceed much more quickly, thereby reducing the carrying changes, which can be a substantial portion of the total cost. Also, smaller projects are generally more manageable and are often more attractive to buyers.

The optimum unit size and unit mix will vary according to the market. However, there are a number of general guidelines with regard to unit size and mix which should be kept in mind. Good convertible units range in size from as small as 500 square feet for a studio, 800 square feet for a one-bedroom, 1,100 to 1,200 square feet for a two-bedroom, and 1,300 square feet for a three-bedroom unit. In addition to overall unit size, the existence of adequate storage space will be an important factor. With regard to unit mix, most buyers typically will be interested in one- and two-bedroom units. As a general rule, the more urbanized the area, the greater the demand for smaller studio and one-bedroom units. Thus, in major urban areas an ideal unit mix probably would be about 40 percent studios and one-bedroom units, 50 percent two-bedroom units, and 10 percent three-bedroom units. In less urbanized areas the optimum mix probably would be about 60 percent two-bedroom, 25 percent studio and one-bedroom, and 15 percent three-bedroom.

Southglenn Commons. An exceptional combination of location and value in an established South Suburban Denver neighborhood.

Your exciting condominium at Southglenn Commons provides a full complement of spare-time conveniences, including a private pool, hot tub, championship volleyball court, basketball and child play areas as well as a professionally decorated and functional clubhouse with party room, fireplace, recreation room and complete kitchen facility.

SHOPPING
Southglenn Commons residents have just a short walk or drive to Southglenn Mall and fine stores like Sears, May D&F, The Denver, Fashion Bar, Triple Cinemas and a Post Office. Local shopping includes the Cherry Knolls Center with Safeway, Skaggs and Twin Cinemas; Cherrywood Square with King Soopers; and University Towne Center with LaBelle's.

BANKING
Within a few blocks of Southglenn Commons are an extraordinary number of financial institutions for banking and savings convenience. They are 1st National Bank of Southglenn, Arapahoe Colorado National Bank, Columbia Savings, Empire Savings, Western Federal Savings, Colorado Federal Savings, Majestic Savings, and World Savings.

SCHOOLS
Children living at Southglenn Commons will attend schools close to their homes in the Littleton School District, which include Arapahoe High School, Euclid Junior High and Mark Twain Elementary. You may also want to take advantage of higher education opportunities at Arapahoe Community College or The University of Denver, both just a short commute from your Southglenn Commons home.

RECREATION
In addition to the spare-time facilities within Southglenn Commons the area abounds in a full spectrum of sport and leisure facilities. The most prominent is DeKoevend Park which includes the South Suburban Recreation Center, 6 lighted tennis courts, 4 hand/racquet ball courts, gymnasium, sauna, arts and craft shop, babysitting facilities, weight lifting gym, softball field, picnic areas and South Suburban Ice Rink. If that isn't enough, Arapahoe High School has an indoor olympic pool and Holly Tennis-Swim Center is just a short jaunt away. For golfers, the South Suburban golf course is just 5 minutes from your doorstep.

ENTERTAINMENT
Eating out, celebrating an event or just catching the latest flick, you've got lots of choices right around the corner or along the Interstate 25 corridor. Some of the finest restaurants in Denver are just minutes away ...along with hotel discos and live entertainment.

TRANSPORTATION
Conveniently located, Southglenn Commons allows easy access to Interstate 25 and 225, and State Highway 85. RTD provides local bus service to downtown and nearby employment centers plus Express Routes to downtown Denver.

EMPLOYMENT
A short commute makes sense. Southglenn Commons is located near many fine employment centers such as The Denver Tech Center, Greenwood Plaza, Inverness, the Ken-Caryl Ranch, and downtown Englewood and Littleton. Major employers in the area include Hospal Medical Corporation, Storage Technology, Honeywell, and Johns-Manville.

2-4   This promotional material for Southglen Commons stresses the importance of location. The project should be convenient and the surrounding area should be known as a good residential neighborhood.

2-5 Buildings which are structurally sound and of high quality construction make the best candidates for conversion.

Finally, the project's amenities should be comparable in type and number with those of competitive projects in the area and should not require significant renovation. Thus, if other conversions and new condominiums in the area have amenities (such as swimming pools, tennis courts, saunas, exercise facilities, and community recreation rooms), the project should have similar amenities in existence. Most experienced converters consider the cost of adding a major package of amenities to be prohibitive and, therefore, will usually not consider a project for conversion if a significant number of additional amenities are considered necessary for a successful sell-out.

History as a Rental Project

A project's rental history is often a good indication of its potential as a successful conversion. Generally, a project with an unsuccessful rental history will not be a successful conversion. This is particularly true of projects undertaken by the inexperienced converter. Often it can be extremely difficult to reverse the negative image which has been acquired by an unsuccessful rental project. Factors such as the project's turnover, vacancy rates, and the status of existing leases generally are good indicators of the project's potential success as a conversion. A successful rental project will have low turnover and low vacancy rates. A high turnover and high vacancy rates could indicate a problem with the project, such as improper maintenance or inadequate facilities, or with the area in which it is located, such as an extremely transient population which is not given to home ownership. With regard to the status of leases, it

is important to have enough leases about to expire to allow the conversion to be started. However, at the same time, having too many leases expire at the outset of the project can severely deplete the rent roll, which is an important cash flow component during the initial stages of the project.

The Market Potential

In assessing the market potential of a proposed conversion there are two markets which must be considered: the existing tenants and the outside buyers. Existing tenants represent an extremely valuable, ready-made market for the converter. A high percentage of sales to existing tenants has the advantages of allowing the conversion to be completed rapidly, thus minimizing carrying costs, maintaining the maximum possible cash flow through rents, and minimizing marketing and advertising costs. A high percentage of sales to existing tenants means fewer vacant units and less likelihood of tenant opposition to the conversion. Therefore, it is to the converter's advantage to select a project in which a high percentage of tenant sales is feasible and then to encourage tenants to purchase their units through various incentives. Such incentives might include tenant discounts or offering tenants the option of buying units

29

in "as is" condition. Prior to selecting and purchasing a project for conversion, the converter should have some idea of how many tenants will purchase units. This can be done by preparing a research questionnaire and distributing it to tenants. In a typical conversion at least 30 percent of tenants will purchase units, provided that they are properly notified by the developer (the tenant notification process will be discussed later in this chapter). Also, as indicated previously in the first chapter, there have been conversions where a majority of tenants have purchased units.

In order to determine the marketability of a project to outside buyers a standard feasibility analysis will be required. This will involve an analysis of factors such as demographic characteristics, economic conditions, existing competition, housing demand, and buyer profiles.[1]

Economic Feasibility of Conversion

Having determined the general feasibility of a conversion, the next step is to determine whether the conversion is economically feasible. Will the sale of units following the purchase and conversion of the project result in a reasonable profit? As a general rule, a conversion should not be undertaken unless the price that can be obtained from converting the project and selling it as condominiums is at least 20 percent greater than the price that can be obtained by selling the project to a single investor.[2]

Identification of Potential Revenue

The first step in determining the economic feasibility of a conversion is the identification of anticipated revenue. Revenue will be derived primarily from two sources: the sale of units and rental income during the early stages of the conversion. The projection of revenue from unit sales will require that realistic unit prices be established.

While the unit prices established should be low enough so that the project is readily marketable and a significant percentage of existing tenants will be encouraged to purchase their units, they should not be so low that potential profits are sacrificed. As a general rule, when conversions are competing with newly constructed condominiums in the same area, they will need to be priced 20 to 30 percent below comparable new units in order to sell in the local market.

Keeping these general guidelines in mind, there are several methods which may be used to establish average unit prices, thus determining the project's potential sales revenue. The first method of establishing rough unit prices is the rental multiplier approach. With this method the units are priced by multiplying their monthly rent by a multiple. A multiple of 125 is usually used, although the multiple can be as high as 140 depending on factors such as the project's location, the amenities, and the condition of the local housing market. When using the rental multiplier method, it is important that the rent figures used represent the current market rent plus the next planned increase. Thus, a unit with a current market rent of $280 plus a planned increase of $20 would have a price range of $37,500 to $42,000 ($300 multiplied by 125 and $300 multiplied by 140).[3]

A second technique for establishing rough unit prices is the cost approach. With the cost approach, average unit prices are determined based on the cost of acquiring and converting the project. Using this approach, unit prices are established by dividing the total estimated costs of the conversion by the total number of units and then dividing again by 70 percent. This ensures that the established unit prices will exceed the total conversion costs by 30 percent. Since the cost

[1] For further discussion of the steps involved in a feasibility analysis see Chapter 2 of *Residential Development Handbook* (Washington: ULI–the Urban Land Institute, 1978).

[2] Keith Romney, *Condominium Development Guide* (Boston: Warren, Gorham & Lamont, 1974), p. 10-7.

[3] "A New Strategy for Condo Conversions," *Housing*, (May 1981), p. 74.

2-6 The project's amenities should be comparable in type and number with those of competitive projects in the area.

approach to determining unit prices does not consider marketability, when using this approach it is imperative to remember that the established unit prices should be 20 to 30 percent below the sales prices of comparable new units in the area. If the sales prices required to cover conversion costs must be greater than this level, it is an indication that the project's conversion costs will not allow it to be economically feasible.[4]

A third way to establish rough unit prices is the fair rental value approach. This approach establishes unit prices based on the general rule that the unit's monthly carrying cost to the purchaser (that is, mortgage charges, taxes, insurance, and condominium association fees) should not exceed the monthly rental cost of a comparable apartment by more than 10 to 15 percent. The rationale for this approach is that the project's marketability to existing tenants will be severely impaired if the monthly costs of owning greatly exceed the monthly costs of renting.

It is important to remember that while the establishment of average unit prices using any of these methods is a necessary step in determining the economic feasibility of a proposed conversion, it is not a substitute for the final pricing of individual units. The final pricing of units is a highly specialized process which is based on criteria such as a unit's size, location, and amenities. The final pricing of units should reflect the various differences between units.

As mentioned earlier, continued rental income will also be an important source of revenue, particularly during the early stages of the conversion process, and, therefore, must also be considered in determining the project's economic feasibility. While an adequate inventory of vacant units will be necessary in order to allow the conversion process to continue uninterrupted, it is important that a majority of the remaining units which are not needed for this inventory be occupied by tenants. The inability to keep a significant number of units occupied prior to conversion, with the exception of the required inventory of vacant units, can sometimes jeopardize the economic feasibility of a conversion. In order to ensure a continuous rental income, it may be necessary to re-lease on a short-term basis those units which are immediately vacated by existing tenants. Re-leasing units to short-term renters will generally require an advertising program and the use of a rental agent.

Finally, in addition to revenue from unit sales and rental income, miscellaneous revenue sources should be considered. This might include revenue from the sale of model furnishings or from the sale of appliances or other items which are replaced during renovation.

Identification of Conversion Costs

Typically, significant conversion costs consist of the following items:

- *Acquisition cost.* The major cost for most converters will be that of acquiring the project, except in those instances where the converter is also the owner of the project prior to the conversion.
- *Renovation costs.* A determination of renovation costs will be based on a detailed architectural and engineering survey of the project which will indicate essential renovation and repair work. In addition to essential renovation work as determined by this survey, certain renovation of a cosmetic nature may be required to enhance the project's marketability. Such cosmetic renovation must be included in calculating the total cost of renovation. As a rule-of-thumb, it is recommended that renovation costs be approximately three to five percent of the total costs of conversion.
- *Financing costs.* Normally, interim financing is required to pay off any existing mortgages on the property and to take care of any prepayment penalties, as well as to cover renovation costs and other expenses incurred during the conversion. The interest costs for this financing will be high, since the loan is similar to a construction loan.[5]
- *Consultant fees.* These include legal fees (which can be substantial because of the documentation required and the need to comply with local statutes), engineering and architectural fees (since the building or complex must be thoroughly examined and each unit must be identified and described), and fees for marketing and feasibility studies.
- *Management costs.* These include the costs incurred for the continued operation of the property during the conversion period, such as costs incurred in the maintenance of units prior to their renovation and sale, and costs incurred for maintenance personnel.
- *Marketing costs.* These include the costs for sales personnel, advertising, the establishment of a sales office and model units, and related items.

In addition to determining the major conversion costs discussed above, the successful converter must be aware of various "hidden costs" which do not normally appear on the conversion budget. Significant hidden costs can include the reduction in cash flow as non-buying tenants move out after notification of the conversion or upon the expiration of their leases. Other hidden costs may include those accrued because of delays in renovation due to the need to renovate units while they are occupied, slow sales, and the payment of various fees which the inexperienced converter may not consider. It is imperative that the potential for such hidden costs be accounted for in determining the economic feasibility of a conversion.

---

[4] *Housing* (May 1981), p. 74.

[5] A detailed discussion of financing is provided later in this chapter.

Table 1—Pro Forma Profit and Loss Statement*

Gross Sales		**$3,100,000**
Less Expenses of Purchase		
1% Origination Fee—Interim	$ 21,700	
1% Permanent End Loan Commitment	15,000	
Legal Fees	2,500	
Ground Survey, Condo Survey, Appraisal	4,200	
Miscellaneous Closing Costs	7,000	
		$ 50,400
Less Monies Reserved for Exterior Improvements		
Painting of Exterior of Property	$ 10,000	
Ground Clean-up & Sprinkler System Overhaul	6,500	
Swimming Pool Rehabilitation	500	
		$ 17,000
Less Monies Reserved for Interior Improvement		
Model Homes	$ 10,000	
Interior Refurbishment	42,000	
		$ 52,000
Conversion Expenses Due at First Closing		
Legal Fees	$ 15,000	
Real Estate Taxes	34,000	
Hazard Insurance & Liability	8,500	
		$ 57,500
Conversion Expenses Due at Individual Closings		
Closing Costs	$ 37,000	
Real Estate Commissions	124,000	
Advertising	7,000	
	168,000	
Total Expenses of Conversion		**344,900**
Gross Before Debt Service		$2,755,100
Debt Service		2,170,000
Net Profit Before Depreciation and Income Tax Reserve		585,100

*This profit and loss statement is for a garden apartment conversion, undertaken in 1978–79, of approximately 75 units.

Table 2—Cash Flow Statement*

	1st Month	2nd Month	3rd Month	4th Month	5th Month	6th Month	7th Month	8th Month	9th Month
Inflow									
Funding	$2,170,000	$ 0	$ 0	$ 0	$ 0	$ 0	$ 0	$ 0	$ 0
Rental Income	29,910	29,910	29,910	29,910	27,600	25,330	23,040	20,760	18,470
Closed Sales	0	0	0	0	0	240,000	232,000	234,000	233,000
Cash In	$2,199,910	$ 29,910	$ 29,910	$ 29,910	$ 27,600	$ 265,330	$ 255,040	$ 254,760	$ 251,470
Outflow									
Acquisition Cost	$2,090,000	$ 0	$ 0	$ 0	$ 0	$ 0	$ 0	$ 0	$ 0
Operational Expense	9,589	9,589	9,589	9,589	9,589	9,589	8,843	8,121	7,406
Exterior Refurbishment	0	0	0	0	0	5,000	3,000	3,000	3,000
Interior Refurbishment	0	0	0	0	3,000	3,000	3,000	3,000	3,000
Model Homes	0	0	0	0	10,000	0	0	0	0
Repayment of Interim	0	0	0	0	0	210,000	203,000	204,750	203,875
Interim Interest	18,083	18,083	18,083	18,083	18,083	18,083	16,333	14,642	12,935
Tax and Ins. Reserve	3,625	3,625	3,625	3,625	3,625	3,625	3,345	3,065	2,785
Closing @ $500 p/u	0	0	0	0	0	3,000	3,000	3,000	3,000
Retail Sale Commission	0	0	0	0	0	9,600	9,280	9,360	9,320
Promotional Expense	0	0	0	0	500	500	500	500	500
Cash Out	$2,121,297	$ 31,297	$ 31,297	$ 31,297	$ 44,797	$ 262,397	$ 250,301	$ 249,438	$ 245,821
Cash Flow	$ 78,613	($ 1,387)	($ 1,387)	($ 1,387)	($ 17,197)	2,933	$ 4,739	$ 5,322	$ 5,649
Cumulative Cash Flow	$ 78,613	$ 77,226	$ 75,839	$ 74,452	$ 57,255	$ 60,188	$ 64,927	$ 70,249	$ 75,898
Balance of Interim	$2,170,000	$2,170,000	$2,170,000	$2,170,000	$2,170,000	$1,960,000	$1,757,000	$1,552,250	$1,348,375

*This cash flow statement is for a garden apartment conversion, undertaken in 1978–79, of approximately 75 units.

The Profit and Loss and Cash Flow Statements

Once the revenue and costs of the conversion have been determined, they are combined in a profit and loss statement in order to arrive at the "bottom line," that is, the potential profit as a result of the conversion. The items listed in Table 1 are intended to act as guides and not as absolute rules.

Although the profit and loss statement indicates the "bottom line" or profit and is essential in determining the economic feasibility of a conversion, it does not present the entire picture of a conversion's economic feasibility. Since the profit and loss statement ignores timing (except insofar as the financing costs are predetermined by timed events), it has only limited use during the course of a conversion. Therefore, a cash flow statement must also be prepared in order to identify the sequence of events and the cost of financing. In addition to its role in determining the timing of the conversion and the amount of borrowing, the cash flow statement is a valuable aid in ordering priorities, determining critical path, and identifying potential delays.

The cash flow statement allows all quantifiable data to be listed in relation to time. It shows all revenues and all costs in the period in which they will be received and expended. Table 2 is an example of a cash flow statement for a condominium conversion. As the cash flow statement indicates, rental income will be an important cash flow component during the initial stages of the conversion process. In addition, due to the high carrying costs today, the absorption rate (that is, how fast the units are sold) will be a critical factor in determining the project's economic viability.

The Go/No-Go Decision

Once the profit and loss and cash flow statements have been prepared an initial decision can be made whether to proceed with the project or not. At this time, it is advisable to compare the potential profit from the conversion with the potential profit which could be obtained from selling the project as a rental complex to a single investor. As stated earlier, most experienced convertors recommend that a project not be converted unless the profit from the conversion is at least 20 percent greater than the profit which could be obtained by selling the project as a rental apartment complex.

If an initial go decision is made based on the pro forma statements and a comparison of the project's profit potential as a conversion and a rental, this decision does not mean that an absolute commitment has been made to undertake the conversion process; rather, it means that the developer can begin to seek financing for the project and begin or continue to negotiate for the purchase of the project (if it is not already owned by the developer).

Once the actual financing and acquisition costs of the project are known, a second go/no-go decision must be made. In order to make this decision, it will probably be necessary to prepare revised cash flow and profit and loss statements to reflect changes from the projected financing and acquisition costs. If a go decision is made at this time, a commitment has now been made to proceed with the conversion.

10th Month	11th Month	12th Month	13th Month	14th Month	15th Month	16th Month	17th Month	18th Month	Total
$ 0	$ 0	$ 0	$ 0	$ 0	$ 0	$ 0	$ 0	$ 0	$2,170,000
16,160	13,870	11,560	9,280	6,950	4,630	2,320	0	0	299,610
238,000	232,000	234,000	232,000	241,000	249,500	245,500	243,000	246,000	3,100,000
$ 254,160	$245,870	$245,560	$241,280	$247,950	$254,130	$247,820	$243,000	$246,000	$5,569,610
$ 0	$ 0	$ 0	$ 0	$ 0	$ 0	$ 0	$ 0	$ 0	$2,090,000
6,686	5,952	5,230	4,508	3,792	3,048	2,268	1,514	762	115,664
3,000	0	0	0	0	0	0	0	0	17,000
3,000	3,000	3,000	3,000	3,000	3,000	3,000	3,000	3,000	42,000
0	0	0	0	0	0	0	0	0	10,000
208,250	203,000	204,750	203,000	210,875	218,313	100,187	0	0	2,170,000
11,236	9,501	7,809	6,103	4,411	2,654	835	0	0	194,957
2,505	2,225	1,945	1,665	1,385	1,105	825	545	265	43,410
3,000	3,000	3,000	3,000	3,000	3,000	3,000	3,000	3,000	39,000
9,520	9,280	9,360	9,280	9,640	9,980	9,820	9,720	9,840	124,000
500	500	500	500	500	500	500	500	500	7,000
$ 247,697	$236,458	$235,594	$231,056	$236,603	$241,600	$120,435	$ 18,279	$ 17,367	$4,853,031
$ 6,463	$ 9,412	$ 9,966	$ 10,224	$ 11,347	$ 12,530	$127,385	$224,721	$228,633	$ 716,579
$ 82,361	$ 91,773	$101,739	$111,963	$123,310	$135,840	$263,225	$487,946	$716,579	
$1,140,125	$937,125	$732,375	$529,375	$318,500	$100,187	$ 0	$ 0	$ 0	

Financing

Obtaining the required financing is crucial to the success of a conversion project. Financing for conversions, as for other real estate development, is usually provided by a combination of equity and debt. Two forms of debt financing, interim and permanent, are required.

Interim Financing. With a condominium conversion, interim financing is generally used to cover the "hard costs" of the conversion, such as acquisition of the project and renovation, as well as the "soft costs," such as fees paid to attorneys, architects, engineers, real estate firms and government agencies; costs of paying off any existing mortgages on the conversion property; and costs for any prepayment penalties, taxes, interest, and all other expenses incurred in the course of the conversion.

Interest rates for interim loans are high, with rates for interim loans tending to be in the ballpark of the prime interest rate, plus two to five points, with a loan fee of one to two points.[6] Because the interest rates are high, the profit resulting from the conversion will be directly related to how quickly the converted units are sold and the interim loan can be repaid. Therefore, it is often advantageous to the converter to expedite the sale of units by offering discounts to tenants (thereby encouraging a greater percentage of tenant purchasers) and to offer buyers the option of purchasing units in "as is" condition or with minimal renovation.

Permanent Financing. Permanent financing involves a commitment by the lender to provide individual permanent mortgage loans for the condominium unit buyers. In order to ensure a successful conversion during a period of high interest rates, it is essential that the converter secure a permanent financing commitment. In this regard, the availability of attractive, below-market financing for buyers can have as much of an impact on the absorption rate as the sales prices of the units. In some instances, the converter may find that it is necessary to buy-down interest rates to assure the success of the conversion. The availability of attractive below-market financing is even more crucial if the converter is seeking a high percentage of sales to existing tenants, since existing tenants will generally be seeking mortgage payments which are comparable to their net annual cost of renting.

Permanent financing is critical not only because of its impact on sales, but also because of its impact on the ability of the converter to secure the interim financing required to undertake the conversion. This is because a lender of interim financing normally requires that a permanent financing commitment be secured by the developer before he will be willing to underwrite the cost of the conversion. The interim lender does not want to risk committing money for the purpose of creating condominium units which may remain unsold due to the inability of the developer to find permanent financing for buyers.

In obtaining a permanent financing commitment, it is important that the converter obtain a commitment from the lender which stipulates the various terms and conditions of the financing in detail. The lender must not merely promise to make permanent loans available, but also must commit to a certain amount of dollars for loans to unit buyers, to an agreed-upon loan-to-value ratio, and to an appraisal figure for the condominium units themselves. The converter who does not obtain binding commitments on any of these items may find that there are insufficient marketable loans available for purchasers at the time the units are ready to sell.

The appraisal of the buildings and the property to be converted is often a critical factor in obtaining the necessary permanent financing. Frequently, appraisers who have not had experience with conversions will appraise the project at its current "wholesale" value as a rental apartment complex, rather than at its "retail" value as a condominium complex. This ignores the fact that the project's value based on the sales prices of all of the units if sold separately as condominiums is generally considerably greater than its value based on the sale to a single investor as a rental apartment complex. Therefore, it is imperative that the project be correctly appraised in order to enable the converter to obtain sufficient permanent financing. In some instances, it may be necessary for the converter to go to nonlocal appraisers in order to receive a fair assessment of the value of a conversion project.

Obtaining Financing

Since the various contractual requirements of the permanent lender may be unacceptable to the interim lender, it is advisable for the converter to negotiate with both the permanent and the interim lender before contracting with either. If such negotiations are carefully timed, it may be possible for the converter to obtain concessions that will make it easier to secure the necessary financing commitments.

The presentation to the lender is an important factor in securing the necessary financing. Therefore, it is essential that the converter understand what the lender is looking for and prepare the presentation accordingly. The converter's presentation should incorporate the various feasibility studies and analyses which were prepared in advance by the converter in order to make the initial go/no-go decision. It is imperative that the presentation reveal the converter to be a competent, experienced professional who is fully capable of under-

---

[6] A "point" is a payment made to the lender at the time the loan is made and which is equal to one percent of the loan amount. Points are usually charged by the lender to increase the lender's return and to make the loan competitive with other types of loans the lender could make.

taking the conversion in an efficient and successful manner. Since the presentation will create an image of the converter for the lender, it must be organized, thorough, and professional. It must reflect the lender's concerns, such as the developer's track record and financial strength, and the market potential and profit potential of the conversion. As with other real estate development, if the converter is favorably known to the lender, it will usually be considerably easier to obtain both interim and permanent financing.

Sources of Financing

Most interim financing for conversions is provided by commercial banks. As stated previously, the interest rates for interim financing are high and the loans are repaid by the converter with funds from the sale of the individual condominium units.

Permanent financing for conversions is most often provided by savings and loan associations, mortgage banks, and mutual savings banks. Most financial institutions making permanent mortgage loans require the converter to meet certain "presale" requirements. That is, the converter must have nonbinding agreements from a certain percentage of people indicating that they want to buy units in the conversion project before a permanent financing commitment can be secured.

In addition to financial institutions, the converter may look to joint ventures or limited partnerships to finance the conversion. A joint venture not only has the advantage of providing needed equity capital for the converter, but also allows the converter to leverage his funds and, therefore, to undertake more projects at a faster rate. It allows the conversion to be undertaken without the converter having to supply extensive capital. However, a joint venture has the disadvantage of cutting the converter's usable profits significantly since most joint venture partners will expect a 50 percent return on net income. A limited partnership will have the same advantages for the converter as a joint venture as well as the advantage of a limited partner expecting a lower return on net income (usually 25 percent) than would a joint venture partner. However, with a limited partnership it can be more difficult for the converter to obtain any additional capital which might be needed later on in the conversion process.

Finally, it is important to remember that while outside financing is needed for a conversion, the developer's own financial resources can often mean the difference between a successful conversion and a failure. The converter must have adequate financial resources to be able to pay unexpected expenses and to withstand economic downturns.

Legal Aspects

There are several legal factors which must be considered when undertaking a conversion. These include government regulation of conversions, the lease agreements at the time of conversion, the tax implications of converting, and the legal creation of a condominium.

As noted briefly in the discussion on determining the general feasibility of a conversion, it is imperative that the converter be aware of various government regulations affecting conversions. A variety of legislation has been enacted at the state and local levels which is intended primarily to protect tenants from the impacts of conversions (see p. 14 for further discussion of state legislation and local ordinances). While protecting tenants, such legislation has also resulted at times in the restriction or temporary prohibition of conversions. Therefore, in order to assure a smooth conversion process and to avoid time consuming and costly litigation, the converter must be familiar with existing regulations in the jurisdiction.

In addition to being familiar with existing regulations, the converter should be sensitive to local attitudes toward his project and to conversions in general. A negative public or official attitude toward conversions, even if there are no existing ordinances restricting conversions, must be considered by the converter in evaluating the feasibility of the proposed project.

As a rule, there is no need for the converter to obtain approval of the project from the local zoning board or planning board. In most local jurisdictions, if the existing apartment complex that is being converted conformed to the local zoning ordinance, then the condominium that succeeds it also complies. The conversion is merely a change of ownership, with the same buildings existing on the same location devoted to the same use. Therefore, the converter need not become involved with the local zoning board unless the zoning ordinance states that the conversion is a change of use which requires its approval.

The Lease Agreement

Since every residential rental agreement provides the tenant with a warranty of habitability, it is important that the converter make certain that the disruption to tenants during the renovation is kept to a minimum so that tenants do not hold the developer liable for breaking the warranty of habitability. In a recent court case, tenants sued the converter for breach of habitability due to the extreme disruption of common areas during the conversion of a garden apartment complex. The court concluded that there were conditions in the common areas of the complex (as a result of the renovation work during the conversion) which were detrimental to the tenants' life, health, or safety, which frustrated the uses which the tenants reasonably intended to make of their premises, and which constituted a breach of the implied warranty of habitability. The tenants recovered for damages to the common areas during the conversion.[7]

Tax Implications

An important tax question to consider when undertaking a conversion is whether the profits from the conversion can be treated as ordinary income (and taxed at a relatively high rate) or as capital gains (and taxed at a much lower rate than ordinary income). This is an especially important issue for owners of rental apartment projects who are trying to decide whether to undertake the conversion of the project themselves or to sell the project to someone else for conversion.

The availability of capital gains tax treatment depends on the owner's status at the time of the conversion. That is, if the owner sells the project to someone else for conversion, his profits from the sale will be considered a capital gain. However, if the owner undertakes the conversion himself and sells the individual condominium units, he will be considered a dealer in real estate and the profits will be treated as ordinary income.

It is recommended that the owner of a rental apartment project who would like to convert the project himself and is seeking tax advantages obtain qualified legal counsel. However, it is worth noting one possibility for mitigating the tax consequences if the owner undertakes the conversion: the owner of the property to be converted could sell, at arm's length, his interest in the property to a newly created corporation in which he would hold a 79 percent interest and outsiders would have a 21 percent interest. The new corporation could then go through the actual conversion process and would pick up a reasonable profit, which would be taxed as ordinary income. The owner of the property would have created a situation in which he could get capital gains treatment on a significant portion of this sale and ordinary income treatment on another smaller portion. In order to use such a plan, the original owner must hold less than 80 percent of the corporation's stock after the sale of the property to the corporation.

Despite possibilities such as this, the simplest route for an owner of rental property who wishes to convert and to have the profit treated as capital gains is to sell the property to someone else for conversion. In many instances, the capital gains treatment of the profit can, in fact, result in a greater after tax profit than if the owner undertakes the conversion himself and thus has the profit treated as ordinary income. For example, if a rental project has a gross sales value of $2,400,000 when the owner sells it directly to a converter, he could conceivably end up, after paying capital gains only, with a net profit of $2,040,000. On the other hand, if the owner undertakes the conversion himself, he would

make a greater gross profit but this profit would be taxed as ordinary income. Using the same numbers, the after-tax profit would be $1,800,000, a considerably lower figure than the profit from the sale of the property to someone else for conversion.

In addition to being familiar with the tax treatment of conversions under existing legislation, the converter must be aware of possible changes in federal tax laws. In the last two years, two bills were introduced in Congress which would change the Internal Revenue Service (IRS) treatment of profits from conversions. The first bill, which was introduced in September 1979 by Representative Benjamin Rosenthal, would change the Internal Revenue Code (that is, it would codify the present IRS interpretation) to provide that all profit on a condominium conversion would be taxed as ordinary income. This bill, which also proposed a nationwide condominium and cooperative conversion moratorium, is currently dormant. However, the Rosenthal bill would not prevent the original owner of a rental apartment project who sold the property to another party for conversion from taking most of the profit as long-term capital gains.

The second bill was introduced in July 1980 by Senator Harrison Williams. Unlike Rosenthal's bill, this bill would adopt an approach under which the original owner of a rental project could get long-term capital gains treatment on all of the conversion profits. In addition, the converter could exclude up to half of his profits from taxable income if the conversion proceeds were reinvested in the construction of residential rental property. However, for this favorable tax treatment, the converter would have to obtain agreement to the terms and conditions of the sale of the converted units in advance from an authorized representative negotiating on behalf of at least 51 percent of the tenants.[8]

The Legal Creation of a Condominium

The legal establishment of a condominium requires the preparation and recording of a condominium declaration. The declaration dedicates the property to a condominium form of ownership and must be in compliance with state and local legislation. It usually includes the following:[9]

- The name of the condominium.
- A description of the property and buildings, including a legal description of the units. This generally requires the preparation of a plot plan or a survey map.
- A description of each unit including its location, size, number of rooms, and its proportionate ownership of the common areas. This will require the preparation of floor plans.

---

[7] *Forest Hill No. 1 Co. v. Schimmel,* February 4, 1981, Queens County, New York Housing Court.

[8] *Real Estate Newsletter* (September 1980).

[9] Peter J. Arnold, *Condominium Conversion Guidelines* (Chicago: U.S. Investors Resources, Inc.), pp. 1–2.

- A description of the common areas.
- A statement submitting the property for a condominium form of ownership.
- A provision for possible amendment of the declaration.
- The formation of a condominium association and bylaws to govern the association.[10]
- Any additional provisions regulating the use and maintenance of the individual units and the common areas.

Once the declaration has been prepared it usually must be examined at the state level by the Real Estate Commission or the Attorney General's office and then must be recorded with the registrar's office of the county in which the project is located. Prior to the preparation of the declaration, the converter or his attorney should review pertinent state and local legislation in order to assure that the declaration will be in accordance with all governmental requirements.

Renovation

In nearly all conversions, renovation will be an important component of the conversion process. However, the extent of renovation which is undertaken will obviously vary significantly from one conversion project to the next. The extent of the renovation which is required will be based on the physical condition of the project as well as the market which the converter has targeted. In addition to determining the amount of renovation which should be undertaken, it is important for the developer to devise a strategy related to the logistics of the renovation.

2-7 The condition of bathrooms and kitchens will be an important selling feature to most buyers.

The Extent of the Renovation

Two basic types of renovation will often be required: structural and systems renovation and cosmetic renovation. A decision as to the structural and systems renovation which is necessary will be based upon the thorough architectural and engineering inspection which was undertaken in determining the project's feasibility for conversion. Since it is essential that all structural and systems defects be remedied, the decision as to this first aspect of the renovation is relatively straightforward.

On the other hand, deciding on the cosmetic renovation which is necessary is a more complex process which is directly tied to the project's marketing program. That is, the converter must know what market he is shooting for and then determine how much cosmetic renovation will be necessary to attract this market. Making this decision correctly will require full knowledge of the competition. The converter must determine whether the

---

[10] The preparation of the condominium bylaws will be discussed in detail later in this chapter.

2-8 and 2-9 Interior and exterior common areas were extensively refurbished at Gateway Towers in Pittsburgh, Pennsylvania.

units will be more marketable if sold in "as is" condition or with only minor cosmetic renovation at a bargain price or if they are extensively renovated and sold at higher prices. Such a decision should be reached in the early stages of the project when the converter is preparing the pro forma statements and determining the economic feasibility of the conversion.

While the extent of cosmetic renovation will, therefore, vary according to the converter's targeted market and the competition, there are a number of general guidelines with regard to cosmetic renovation which are followed by many successful converters. These are:

- The converter should start exterior renovation such as painting and landscaping improvements before the conversion is announced to tenants. This will sell the tenants on the idea of the conversion and will encourage them to purchase their unit.
- All exterior and interior common areas should be refurbished if they are in poor condition. Walls should be painted; parking lots should be repaved and relined; landscaping should be spruced up and new landscaping added where necessary; and lobbies, corridors, and elevators should be provided with new carpet and new light fixtures.
- The emphasis on renovation to unit interiors should be on the refurbishing of kitchens and bathrooms, since the condition of kitchens and bathrooms will be an important selling feature to most buyers. If kitchen appliances such as the range, oven, dishwasher, disposal, and refrigerator are old and outdated, they should be replaced with new appliances. If not outdated and in good condition, they should be thoroughly cleaned. Parts which cannot be cleaned thoroughly, such as broiler pans and other oven hardware, can be easily replaced at minimal cost. Kitchen flooring in older buildings should be replaced even if in acceptable condition since old styles and colors will be unattractive to most buyers. Worn and shabby bathroom fixtures should be thoroughly cleaned or replaced and, if necessary, tile work in the bathrooms should be grouted and caulked.
- In living rooms, dining rooms, and bedrooms, new carpeting and padding should be installed in almost every instance. The one exception might be in those situations where new carpeting and padding were installed recently.
- All rooms should be painted, preferably in a standard off-white color. Interior design options with regard to paint colors, carpet selection, and appliances should generally be limited, except when dealing with the upper end of the market. This will help to expedite the renovation process.
- If possible, washer and drier connections should be provided in all units. This will be an important selling feature to renters who have been using laundry rooms for some time.

2-10   As part of the renovation, new carpeting and padding should be installed in bedrooms, living rooms, and dining rooms.

- It is generally advisable to give both tenants and outside buyers the option of purchasing units in "as is" condition at a discount. This can not only reduce cosmetic renovation costs but also make a more rapid sell-out possible, thereby reducing the carrying costs of the project.

Renovation Logistics

There are a number of factors which the converter must consider with regard to the logistics of the renovation. First, the converter must decide how to go about renovating units which have been purchased by tenants and are occupied. Generally, when renovating occupied units it is best to work around the occupants, even though this will be a bit more time consuming and expensive. Requiring tenants who have purchased units to relocate temporarily during the renovation will be extremely unpopular with occupants, particularly if the developer does not provide alternative accommodations for them. However, one possibility is for the converter to provide several furnished units which can be used during the renovation by occupants who have health problems which would be aggravated as a result of the renovation work.

Second, the converter must make sure to minimize the disruption to common areas and amenities during the renovation so that tenants are not totally prevented from using them. As noted earlier, if this is not done, the converter could possibly be sued by tenants for breaching the warranty of habitability which is stipulated in the lease. If the significant disruption of common areas is unavoidable, then the converter should at least make sure that appropriate measures are taken to ensure the safety of tenants during the renovation.

Third, the converter must carefully consider the phasing of the renovation. While it is important that there always be an adequate inventory of vacant units in order to allow the renovation process to continue uninterrupted, creating too large an inventory of vacant units will result in a significant loss of rental income, thereby hurting the cash flow during the initial stages of the conversion.

Tenant Relations and Marketing

The marketing program for a conversion involves two components: marketing to tenants and marketing to outside buyers. Since the existing tenants in a project generally represent a ready-made market for the converter, the skillful handling of tenants is an important factor when undertaking a conversion. Smooth tenant relations can often lead to a high percentage of sales to tenants which, in turn, will result in a more rapid sell-out and reduced marketing and carrying costs. Therefore, the establishment of good tenant relations is an integral part of the entire conversion process as well as of the marketing program.

The first step in establishing good tenant relations is to properly notify individual tenants of the conversion. Tenants should be notified as soon as possible since inaccurate rumors can spread rapidly and can have a negative impact on any sales program to tenants before such a program is even initiated. Further, the spread of rumors can also result in a mass moveout and a considerable reduction in the rent roll, thereby creating cash flow problems. Informing tenants of the conversion at the outset of the project will increase the converter's credibility with tenants.

How should the converter notify tenants? It is usually recommended that tenants receive their initial notification of the conversion in writing. The letter should be mailed to all tenants and should do the following:

- Inform tenants of the conversion
- Attempt to alleviate the anxiety of tenants by assuring them that all leases will be honored
- Indicate to tenants that they will receive a substantial discount in the purchase price (compared to prices for the general public) if they decide to purchase
- Inform them that they will have the right of first refusal and indicate how long this will be in effect
- Outline the investment and tax advantages of owning over renting.

It is recommended that this initial notification be kept relatively brief and not discuss details with regard to sales prices, renovation, financing, tenant discounts, and so forth. However, it should inform tenants that they will be contacted shortly with further details.

A second letter should then be mailed to tenants which outlines the various options to them. This letter should serve as a marketing package and should include the following:

- A list of sales prices for all units
- A list of discounts in sales prices which are available to tenants, including any additional discounts which are offered to elderly, handicapped, and long-term tenants or to tenants who purchase units within a short period of time
- A list of the renovation work which will be undertaken
- A list of options to tenants such as buying the unit at an additional discount in "as is" condition or requesting upgrading of the standard renovation work
- Floor plans of all units
- A discussion of financing plans available
- An analysis of the monthly costs when buying a unit versus the monthly costs when renting
- A copy of the condominium association budget and monthly dues
- A discussion of any options available to tenants who wish to continue renting in the complex
- A review of any relocation assistance which will be provided to any tenants who decide to relocate.

2-11 An older structure undergoing significant renovation as part of the conversion process. When undertaking such renovation, the converter must be aware of the impact on tenants and on the surrounding neighborhood.

2-12 The sales office should be separate and isolated from the rental management office.

This second letter should be mailed to tenants only several days after the initial notification. It should also inform tenants of the opportunity to meet personally with the converter and his sales staff to discuss the conversion and the possible purchase of a unit.

The initial personal contact with tenants can either be made through a group meeting or by contacting each tenant individually. There is disagreement among experienced converters as to which method of personal contact is more effective. While a group meeting allows the converter to answer tenants' questions at one time, assembling a majority of tenants in the same place at the same time sets up the possibility for the establishment of organized tenant resistance to the conversion. Further, the converter who holds a group meeting will have to be able to answer questions quickly and intelligently while under pressure. On the other hand, holding individual meetings with tenants will lessen the possibility of an organized tenant protest. However, individual meetings will usually require a large sales staff.

Regardless of which method of personal contact is selected, the meeting should focus on alleviating tenant fears. While a sales pitch to tenants will obviously be required, high pressure sales tactics are not recommended. Such tactics will not be appreciated by tenants and can often backfire, resulting in a low percentage of tenant purchases. In addition, if the converter does not eliminate unnecessary tenant fears by demonstrating his sincere concern for tenants, he can expect a significant amount of tenant hostility, considerable adverse publicity, and a low number of sales to tenants.

Obviously, achieving a high percentage of tenant purchases will be related to more than just having smooth relations with tenants. The sales prices of the units will have to be affordable to tenants. That is, tenants will have to be given the opportunity to purchase their units for approximately the same net annual cost as renting. This will require the availability of attractive financing plans, as well as discounts on sales prices to tenants and the opportunity to purchase units in "as is" condition.

Despite the affordability of the sales prices to tenants and the establishment of smooth tenant relations, in any conversion there will, of course, be tenants who do not purchase and will have to relocate. Therefore, the converter should consider providing some form of relocation assistance for nonpurchasing tenants. Providing special assistance for tenants who relocate, particularly the elderly and the handicapped, can be an important public relations tool. When undertaking the conversion of a large project, the converter should consider providing a full-time, on-site relocation director to meet with tenants and to assist them with relocation. Relocation allowances may be provided as well as assistance in selecting a comparable apartment in the area and in selecting a moving firm.

Finally, the converter should remember that the percentage of tenant purchases can vary significantly from project to project and from market to market. In projects which require significant renovation, the sales prices needed to recoup the renovation costs will probably make the units unaffordable to most tenants. Similarly, projects containing primarily tenants with occupations which require frequent relocation will not have a high percentage of tenant purchasers. Markets which are highly transient or in which rental apartment vacancy rates are high will also be less likely to have a high rate of tenant purchases.

2-13 The theme or image of the project should be part of the sales office signage.

Marketing to Outside Buyers

The marketing program for outside buyers should be prepared simultaneously with the marketing program for tenants. Marketing to outside buyers should begin shortly after the initial notification of tenants, and prospects should be placed on a waiting list and given the first chance to purchase units as soon as sales are opened to the public. In this regard, the exclusive tenant purchase period should be long enough to comply with state and local legislation and to encourage tenant purchases, yet short enough so that the opening of sales to the general public is not unduly delayed.

A sales office should be established, with one or several of the vacant units used for this purpose (thus minimizing the expense of creating a separate sales office). It should be well-designed and relate to the theme or image of the project.[11] In addition, it is imperative that the sales office be separate and isolated from the rental management office (which will be needed throughout most of the conversion process). This will avoid contact between potential purchasers and tenants who are visiting the rental office to discuss management problems. The sales office should have marketing brochures with current pricing and product information (including unit features, floor plans, a description of the renovation to be undertaken as well as any options, financing plans, and a copy of the condominium association budget and monthly dues). If purchasers have the option of upgrading appliances, carpeting, paint selection, and so forth, then a décor center should be provided at the sales office. However, it is generally recommended that options be kept to a minimum in order to expedite the conversion process.

If the project being converted is relatively large and the conversion process will continue for some time, then model units should be provided. If possible, models should be clustered adjacent to the sales office or in a location which is visible from the sales office. Ideally, each plan which is offered for sale should be shown as a model that the buyer can physically inspect. If the project is not large enough to justify the expense of providing a model for each unit type, then models should be provided for several units which typify the unit mix. Decoration and furnishing of models can be important to the success of the sales program and, therefore, should be done by a professional. All models should be furnished in a manner consistent with the tastes and lifestyles of the anticipated buyer profile.

An on-site signage program can also be an important aspect of the marketing effort. This is particularly true when the project is large and when the models and the sales office are separated. In addition to directional and identification signing, a large on-site sign at the entrance should be an essential part of the sales effort.

2-14 Models should be furnished in a manner consistent with the tastes and lifestyles of the anticipated buyer.

Advertising in local newspapers is also used by most converters. The copy used in these advertisements should focus on the units' affordability (with regard to both sales prices and financing) as well as the project's other features which tend to distinguish it from newly constructed condominiums (such as its quality of construction, mature landscaping, and location in an established neighborhood with proximity to employment, shopping, and various community facilities).

The Sales Staff

It is essential that the converter have an expert sales staff. The additional cost of acquiring expert salespeople will be more than recouped as a result of a more rapid sell-out (and lower carrying costs). The salespeople should be able to deal effectively with all types of people and be totally familiar with the project and with the various facets of condominium ownership. They should be able to tailor their sales pitch to the particular needs of each buyer, ranging from the first-time buyer to the investor. The method of compensation to salespeople should provide maximum incentive. Generally, the most effective form of compensation will be a salary plus a bonus with each sale or after a certain quota of sales has been met. Sales on a straight commission basis usually will not provide sufficient motivation to keep top flight personnel unless the sales volume is quite large.

---

[11] *Housing* (May 1981), pp. 72–78.

41

2-15 In the Southern California market, amenities are usually necessary to be competitive with other conversions.

Project Management

Project management is an extremely important aspect of the conversion process which is likely to receive inadequate attention from the inexperienced converter. When undertaking a conversion, there are two facets of project management which must be considered—management of the project as a rental property and as a condominium.

During the initial stages of the conversion process when most of the units are still occupied by tenants, it will be essential for the converter to establish an effective rental management program. The fact that the project is being converted does not mean that there will no longer be tenant related matters which must be addressed. Good rental management will be important both in encouraging a higher percentage of tenant purchases and in encouraging smooth tenant relations. In addition, proper rental management will help to avoid rapid tenant move-outs and thereby help to maintain adequate rental income during the early stages of the conversion.

As indicated previously, a separate rental management office with its own staff must be provided apart from the sales office. If the converter does not have the expertise and staff to effectively manage the rental units, then he should engage a professional property management firm.

Management of the project as a condominium is a complex process which is critical to the success of a conversion. In this regard, it is imperative that the converter devote considerable time and effort to the establishment of a condominium association and to the smooth transition of association control from the converter to the condominium owners. The converter who fails to establish an effective association and to provide for a smooth transition can expect to encounter considerable problems.

In order to assure the establishment of an association which will function smoothly and effectively, it is advisable for the converter or his staff to be involved in the formation of the association from the outset. The converter must make certain that the various legal documents which establish the condominium and the association are drafted properly by the attorney and are workable. The converter must know and understand the concepts that must be established in the legal documents in order to properly and fairly protect his and the owners' interests and to provide for the long-term operation of the association. For the documents to be truly workable they must not follow a rigid format from one project to the next but must be modified to meet the requirements of the individual project.

The condominium declaration, the articles of incorporation, and the bylaws will be required to establish the condominium and the condominium association.[12] These documents will not only create the condominium and the association but also guide the association in its operations.

The Condominium Declaration

As noted earlier in the discussion of the legal aspects of conversions, the condominium declaration contains the basic covenants that create the condominium, define the ownership interests, create the association, and indicate the process of transition from developer control to control by the homeowners. The declaration also defines the precise physical limits of each unit and of the common areas. For this reason, the condominium plat is often included in the declaration. The percentage of ownership interest held by each individual unit owner is the basis for determining the owner's share of the assessments and his share of the votes. In essence, the declaration grants certain broad authority to the association but does not place specific constraints or parameters on that authority. Rather, the bylaws are used to carry out the mandate from the declaration by establishing specific implementation procedures and rules which are consistent with the declaration.[13]

---

[12] The required legal documents will vary according to state enabling legislation. For example, in most states the Articles of Incorporation will not be required.

[13] See Appendix A for an example of a condominium declaration.

42

The Articles of Incorporation

The articles of incorporation for a condominium association are generally not required because most state laws recognize it as an unincorporated association. However, because of increasing concern over the liability of association leaders and members, more and more state legislation and some attorneys are recommending incorporation as a means of partially limiting liability. In those cases where articles of incorporation are required, they should include the following:

- A legal description of the property
- Provisions for association membership
- The allocation of votes
- A description of the powers of the association
- The establishment of the board of directors.

These provisions establish the administrative basis for the association.[14]

The Bylaws

The bylaws, which are necessary whether or not the condominium association is incorporated, designate the specific procedures for the administration and operation of the association. The bylaws for an association which is not incorporated typically include the following provisions:[15]

- *A legal description of the property.* This establishes the various areas of ownership including the common areas and the units. Language and provisions from the condominium declaration can be used for this purpose.
- *Provisions for association membership.* The membership definition must provide that each owner of a unit is a member of the association.
- *Voting rights.* The condominium declaration establishes the percentage of interest for each unit owner and the bylaws assign votes to the owner in the same proportion as this interest. All association decisions are based on whether the required percentage for passage has been met.
- *Powers of the association.* The powers of the association will be based on the state enabling legislation. These powers typically include maintaining and caring for common areas and facilities and delivering common services; making and enforcing the established covenants, restrictions, and rules; and establishing and collecting assessments.
- *The board of directors.* The bylaws specify the number of directors, the term of office of the directors, and the names of the initial directors. The initial members of the board are generally appointed by the developer and need not be members of the association. They generally remain in office until they are either replaced by the developer or the first annual membership meeting is held to elect new directors.
- *Powers and duties of the board.* The bylaws should stipulate the general powers and duties of the board of directors. These include enforcing the provisions of the bylaws; contracting for insurance for the association, the board, and the common elements; contracting or providing for maintenance and services relating to the common areas; paying taxes or special use assessments; delegating powers to appropriate committees, agents, or personnel; and maintaining and providing security for the common areas and facilities. Other duties include preparing the annual operating budget; establishing the assessment fee levels; collecting assessments; maintaining necessary ledgers and accounting records to reflect receipts, disbursements, capital reserves, and other financial transactions of the association; and performing other duties and tasks that may be necessary to assure the proper functioning of the association.
- *Membership meetings.* The bylaws specify the time and place of the membership meetings. These meetings are held at least once a year for the purpose of election and other business. Provisions regarding appropriate notice of the meetings must be included in the bylaws. The date of the first annual membership meeting is fixed by either a percentage of units having been sold or by a date on which the conversion is expected to be completed, whichever comes first.
- *Management and maintenance.* The bylaws should carefully define the responsibilities for management and maintenance. Usually, they indicate that the association should operate and maintain the common areas of the project and pay these costs out of the common assessments. The bylaws should also include a list of those specific operational and maintenance services for which the association is responsible and those for which the homeowner is responsible.
- *Assessments and expenses.* Assessments are determined by assigning each unit owner the responsibility for the same percentage of interest. Since the association is responsible for maintenance, repair, and replacement of the common elements, including most of the capital equipment and structures, it is advisable to require that a capital reserve fund be established and financed as a common expense.
- *Insurance.* Specific insurance coverage requirements should be set forth in the bylaws, although the general requirement to obtain insurance to protect the assets of the members should be set forth in the declaration.[16]

---

[14] See Appendix E for an example of the Articles of Incorporation for a condominium association.

[15] The exact provisions included in the bylaws will be based on the state enabling legislation. If incorporation is required, then a number of the provisions normally included in the bylaws will instead be included in the Articles of Incorporation.

[16] See Appendix B for an example of condominium association bylaws.

The Association Budget

As mentioned previously, the board of directors of the association is responsible for the preparation and adoption of an annual budget for the association which is then used to determine the amount of the annual assessments. However, it is the converter's responsibility to prepare the initial budget for the association and to establish fee levels before the first units are sold. This initial budget should be carefully prepared by the converter and should be verified by an experienced property manager. The converter must make certain that the budget is adequate to cover association expenses, since the financial stability of the association is extremely important to the project's success. The association budget must be fine tuned based on the market for the project and the association dues should be clearly stated to all purchasers.[17]

The Transition Process

The process of transferring control of the condominium association from the converter to the owners of the individual condominium units can often be a problem area for the converter if it is not handled carefully. In order to achieve a smooth and effective transition of control, the converter must be concerned not only with the actual legal transfer of control but also with the education and training of the homeowners so that they will be capable of administering the association. While an effective transition program requires considerable skill and patience on the part of the converter, it is in the converter's best interest.

The process of transition for the condominium association must be clearly stated in the condominium declaration. The inexperienced converter who is unfamiliar with the transition process will want to know when the transition process should be completed and how to provide for a successful transition. There is no rule-of-thumb as to when the transition process should be completed with the legal transfer of actual control of the association to the homeowners. However, it is generally recommended that the transition be scheduled according to a certain percentage of closings (usually ranging from 25 to 75 percent).

In order for the homeowners to be fully prepared to assume control of the association on the scheduled transition date, it will be necessary for the converter to begin to prepare the homeowners from the early stages of the conversion. Thus, the converter must remember that while a date should be scheduled for the actual legal transfer of control based on a certain percentage of closings, the training of homeowners for the transition is a gradual process.

What steps are involved in gradually preparing homeowners to assume total control of the association? First, the developer must make certain that the project's marketing program and buyer orientation provide buyers with an understanding of the association process and the owners' role and responsibilities. Second, the developer should take the responsibility of seeking out and identifying potential homeowner leaders who would be good candidates for the board of directors and begin to train them by involving them in various association activities. Third, the developer should begin to involve various homeowners in association management activities by creating various functional owner committees, each of which recommends or carries out activities or policies approved by the board of directors. Finally, during the gradual process of transition a series of meetings should be held between the developer and the homeowners. At these meetings, all of the essential functions and duties to be performed by the board of directors should be reviewed as well as the following key documents and records:

- The budget, the accounting system, assessments, dues, delinquencies, escrow reserves, and taxes.
- The management of the physical plant and the maintenance program. The converter should recommend a professional management organization which can be used by the association to carry out the essential day-to-day management activities.[18]
- The service contracts for maintenance of open space and amenities, trash removal, extermination, and so forth.
- The insurance coverage on the association and the association's leaders.
- The committee structure of the association—how each will function, its duties and powers.
- The governance of the association by the homeowners, the residual interest of the developer, and how the developer will function during the transition phase.
- The legal basis of the condominium declaration which empowers the board.
- All corporate records or documents pertaining to the statutes, structure, or policies of the association.

---

[17] See Appendix C for an example of a condominium association budget.

[18] See Appendix D for an example of a management agreement between a condominium association and a management company.

The meetings which are held to review the above items should be convened by the developer-controlled board of directors. These meetings should act as informational meetings and orientation sessions for the homeowners on the association. In addition to reviewing the various documents at these meetings, the developer must be prepared to answer questions about the role of the association.

Following these initial meetings to increase homeowner understanding of and involvement in the association, the first annual meeting of the association membership will be held (in accordance with the scheduled transition date as specified in the condominium declaration) for the purpose of electing a new homeowner-controlled board of directors. At the time the new homeowner-controlled board is elected, all completed legal documentation for the project is transferred from the old developer-controlled board to the new board. This is the final step in the transition process and control of the association is now in the hands of the homeowners.[19] This also completes the conversion process.

---

[19] For further information on establishing a condominium association see *Creating a Community Association: The Developer's Role in Condominium and Homeowner Associations* (Washington: ULI–the Urban Land Institute and CAI–the Community Associations Institute, 1976). Other helpful ULI/CAI publications are: *Community Associations: A Guide for Public Officials* (1980); *Condominium and Homeowner Associations That Work: On Paper and In Action* (1978); *Financial Management of Condominium and Homeowner Associations* (1975); and *Managing a Successful Community Association* (1976).

Case Studies

The case studies which follow are intended to provide a project-by-project analysis of the requirements for a successful conversion. They include basic economic information on the project, an in-depth discussion of the experience gained by the developer as a result of undertaking the project, and a discussion of various aspects of the conversion process, such as the identification of conversion feasibility, renovation, marketing, tenant relations, management, and financing.

The projects covered by the case studies are located throughout the United States and vary as to size, age, condition, building types, unit sizes, price ranges, and densities. The mixture of project types is intended to provide an understanding of some of the variations which are possible in conversion strategy, as well as an understanding of the factors which are fundamental to all successful conversions. For convenient reference, the chart provides a brief summary of the projects included in the case studies which follow.

Case Studies

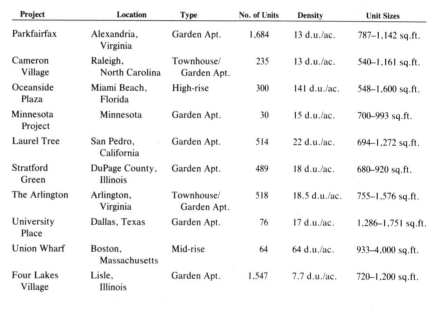

Project	Location	Type	No. of Units	Density	Unit Sizes
Parkfairfax	Alexandria, Virginia	Garden Apt.	1,684	13 d.u./ac.	787–1,142 sq.ft.
Cameron Village	Raleigh, North Carolina	Townhouse/ Garden Apt.	235	13 d.u./ac.	540–1,161 sq.ft.
Oceanside Plaza	Miami Beach, Florida	High-rise	300	141 d.u./ac.	548–1,600 sq.ft.
Minnesota Project	Minnesota	Garden Apt.	30	15 d.u./ac.	700–993 sq.ft.
Laurel Tree	San Pedro, California	Garden Apt.	514	22 d.u./ac.	694–1,272 sq.ft.
Stratford Green	DuPage County, Illinois	Garden Apt.	489	18 d.u./ac.	680–920 sq.ft.
The Arlington	Arlington, Virginia	Townhouse/ Garden Apt.	518	18.5 d.u./ac.	755–1,576 sq.ft.
University Place	Dallas, Texas	Garden Apt.	76	17 d.u./ac.	1,286–1,751 sq.ft.
Union Wharf	Boston, Massachusetts	Mid-rise	64	64 d.u./ac.	933–4,000 sq.ft.
Four Lakes Village	Lisle, Illinois	Garden Apt.	1,547	7.7 d.u./ac.	720–1,200 sq.ft.

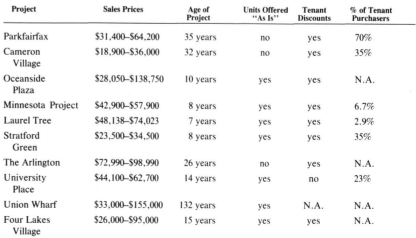

Project	Sales Prices	Age of Project	Units Offered "As Is"	Tenant Discounts	% of Tenant Purchasers
Parkfairfax	$31,400–$64,200	35 years	no	yes	70%
Cameron Village	$18,900–$36,000	32 years	no	yes	35%
Oceanside Plaza	$28,050–$138,750	10 years	yes	yes	N.A.
Minnesota Project	$42,900–$57,900	8 years	yes	yes	6.7%
Laurel Tree	$48,138–$74,023	7 years	yes	yes	2.9%
Stratford Green	$23,500–$34,500	8 years	yes	yes	35%
The Arlington	$72,990–$98,990	26 years	no	yes	N.A.
University Place	$44,100–$62,700	14 years	yes	no	23%
Union Wharf	$33,000–$155,000	132 years	yes	N.A.	N.A.
Four Lakes Village	$26,000–$95,000	15 years	yes	yes	N.A.

Parkfairfax

3-1 A 1,684-unit conversion in which approximately 70 percent of tenants purchased units.

Parkfairfax in Alexandria, Virginia, has probably received more nationwide publicity than any other conversion. And, indeed, this attention is well justified. The project is extremely noteworthy, not only as a very successful and profitable conversion (the return on investment during the conversion was approximately 35 percent a year) but also as an example of a conversion which demonstrated that:

- Conversion does not necessarily mean eviction and relocation for most tenants, even when converting low- and moderate-income projects. Approximately 70 percent of the tenants purchased their units and another 10 percent remained as renters with fixed-rent, long-term leases.
- Conversions can play an important role in meeting the demand for affordable ownership housing. Prices in the project's fourth and final phase, which opened early in 1979, ranged from $35,000 to $56,000.
- Units need not be vacated during renovation. The renovation of occupied units is a practical alternative which is often preferred by residents.
- Sensitivity and responsiveness to tenants' needs and concerns is an important part of the conversion process.

3-2 The site features rolling, wooded terrain, large open spaces, and curving streets.

50

Parkfairfax was built by the Metropolitan Life Insurance Company in the 1940s and was one of the nation's first garden apartment projects. It contains 1,684 units in 285 buildings located on a 132-acre site. The buildings are of a traditional colonial style. Units are one, two, and three bedrooms and range in size from 787 to 1,142 square feet. The project was purchased for conversion in February 1977 and was sold out by May 1979.

Conversion Feasibility

Several factors made the project ideal for conversion. First, it was conveniently located. It was only a short commute from downtown Washington, D.C., and was served by excellent highways and public transportation. It also enjoyed a strong identity with historic "Old Town" Alexandria (which is only a short drive from the site). Second, the project's natural setting, combined with skillful planning and design, presented an attractive appearance. The site features rolling, wooded terrain, large open spaces, and curving streets. Density is only 13 dwelling units per acre despite a zoning ordinance which permits a maximum density of 27 units per acre. Third, the traditional, colonial style brick buildings were structurally sound and were carefully sited. An individual identity was provided for each unit through the use of private entrances with no common hallways. This individuality was further enhanced by a variety of facades and setbacks, changing elevations, and differing architectural treatments. Fourth, the project's size was suited to conversion. It was large enough to justify the cost of a major organization set-up, yet the density was low enough to promote a sense of privacy.

Finally, the project's social character prior to the conversion was sound. That is, the overall view of Parkfairfax by its residents was quite positive, vacancies were low (only seven percent), and the "rent roll" was stable. However, the project's cash flow prior to conversion was poor.

Conversion Strategy

The conversion of Parkfairfax was designed to achieve the following two goals: (1) to offer a privately financed solution to the need for moderately priced ownership housing; and (2) to offer middle-income tenants the opportunity to become homeowners at a cost equivalent to the net annual cost of renting.

Sales prices affordable for most tenants were assured without jeopardizing the project's profitability to the developer by minimizing renovation (and thus renovation costs) and by maintaining rental income (cash flow) from units prior to their sale. By keeping sales prices at moderate levels and allowing a high percentage of tenants to purchase units, it was possible to maintain the same social and economic character which the project had had as a rental complex.

The renovation work was not intended to change the existing character of the project, but rather to preserve and restore it to its original quality. Since the buildings at Parkfairfax were soundly constructed and had been modernized periodically, it was possible to limit the renovation of unit interiors and to avoid cosmetic renovation. Thus, the focus of the renovation was on the restoration of the building exteriors, the complete renovation of the basic utility systems, and the revitalization of the community through a unique complex of recreational facilities.

The basic conversion strategy of the developer was to substantially improve the quality (and consequently, the real estate value) of the project by performing the work which the homeowner could never perform himself while leaving other interior improvements to the homeowner's discretion. This basic conversion plan not only allowed the developer to offer the basic dwelling units at exceptionally low prices, but also offered purchasers the opportunity to achieve considerably higher unit values by undertaking interior improvements according to their own personal tastes and financial plans.

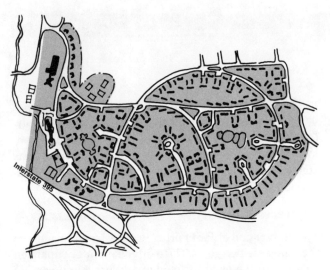

3-3   Site plan.

3-4   The existing landscaping was refurbished and some new landscaping was provided.

Sales prices were kept down by minimizing interior and cosmetic renovation and also by maintaining the maximum possible rental income from units prior to their sale. The maximum possible rental income was maintained by performing all renovation work while units were occupied, thus eliminating the need for tenants to relocate temporarily or to be evicted. Although conducting the interior repair work without occupants would have been a much more desirable approach technically and would have been less expensive, it would have resulted in a sustained loss of rent receipts. These losses in rental income would then have had to be compensated for in the form of higher sales prices which would have been unaffordable to many tenants.

3-5   The traditional, colonial style brick buildings are structurally sound.

Renovation Program

Although the project was for the most part in good condition and was structurally sound prior to conversion, it had been undergoing increasing problems in the operations of its physical systems. There had been major power outages in the private electrical system and interruptions in the supply of heat and hot water. The need to repair and upgrade the physical systems, together with the fact that occupied units were being renovated, made it necessary to prepare the renovation program in detail.

The renovation program began with the selection of a typical building to serve as an experimental center. At the experimental center, materials, techniques, procedures, work sequences, and time requirements for the various renovation tasks were tested. Following this testing, a project control center was established to ensure the central coordination of renovation activities. Its primary functions were: (1) scheduling, (2) communications with tenants, and (3) receiving and investigating inquiries and complaints.

Ten building coordinators were used to assure timely and adequate communications with tenants and the least disruption to tenant comfort. The coordinators were specially trained to meet with tenants and explain in detail how, when, and where the interior renovation in their unit would be done. Special scripts and checklists were prepared for the building coordinators to make sure that they covered all aspects including tips to avoid damage, security problems, and general discomfort. The developer gave tenants a rental credit equal to one-half the monthly cost of a tenant's personal property insurance policy to further reduce damage and security claims. Upon request, residents were provided with boxes and furniture covering materials.

Recognizing that some residents might have medical problems which could be aggravated by the interior renovation work within their unit, four fully furnished hospitality suites were established for use during the eight- to 10-day renovation period (the number of hospitality units was later increased to seven). In addition to the overnight hospitality suites, a furnished day lounge was established with reading materials, television, games, and kitchen facilities. Transportation to and from both facilities was provided.

Tenants were first notified of upcoming renovation work through the general progress reports included in the project's monthly newsletter. Approximately 30 days prior to the start of the renovation work a notice was mailed to tenants indicating when their unit would be renovated. Approximately two weeks before the renovation work actually began, a building coordinator was assigned to the specific building and met with residents.

The building coordinator accompanied the workmen to each unit throughout the renovation and was the only person holding a key to the apartment. Rules regarding smoking, radios, and eating were imposed on the work crews, and the building coordinator made periodic rounds, checking on performance and solving day-to-day problems. Originally, the general contractor assigned clean-up crews to remove debris at the end of each day. However, following complaints from residents, a professional cleaning contractor was hired to perform this function. Quality control checks were made throughout the renovation of each unit, and upon completion of work a final inspection was made by the general contractor. Following the inspection, an appointment was made with the resident to arrange for any work needing correction or completion. The final step in the renovation process for each unit was the inspection of the unit by the purchaser and the signing of a work completed form by the purchaser.

As mentioned earlier, the project's physical systems were deteriorating and required major renovation work. This included replacing the obsolete oil boilers with new individual electric heating systems; providing new individual electric meters and a new underground electric distribution system; providing new plumbing (hot and cold water) for each building and new central electric hot water boilers; and replacing and reconditioning air conditioning units. Energy conservation features provided included new interior-mounted storm windows and additional attic insulation for all buildings.

The exterior renovation of the project involved the refurbishing of existing landscaping and the installation of new landscaping; the repair of sidewalks, stoops, and curbs; grading along building perimeters to improve drainage; the repair of gutters and downspouts; the repair of damaged masonry; the repair and painting of wood trim; and the installation of shutters in selected locations. In addition to this exterior refurbishing, a variety of recreational amenities were provided, including eight tennis courts (four lit), two new additional outdoor swimming pools, renovation of the existing pool and bath house, volleyball courts, jogging trails, and play areas. Nontraditional amenities, such as workshops, hobby rooms, and meeting rooms, were provided as well.

In keeping with the overall strategy of minimizing renovation costs to assure affordability, the renovation of unit interiors was limited. All units sold to the public were painted, and doors, hardware, windows, and flooring were reconditioned where necessary. Kitchens were provided with new stainless steel sinks and faucets, garbage disposals, and reconditioned appliances and cabinets. Bathrooms were provided with new faucets on sinks and new shower assemblies. Units purchased by tenants received similar reconditioning but were not repainted, and other cosmetic work was deleted.

3-6 A variety of recreational amenities were provided as part of the conversion.

Tenant Relations

One of the primary concerns in the conversion of Park-fairfax was the establishment of a good working relationship with tenants. This included performing the necessary renovation work in a manner which would be as sensitive to the tenant's comfort and general interest as possible, and would be consistent with the economic and market goals set for the project. The tenant relations program was specifically designed to anticipate tenants' problems and needs prior to the actual conversion rather than to develop policy solely as a matter of reaction to tenant complaints and dissatisfaction during the conversion.

As a first step in assuring smooth tenant relations, the developer announced his conversion plans directly to tenants prior to taking title. This was done by inviting residents to a general meeting held several weeks before the closing and by preparing a fact package outlining the conversion program which was distributed to all residents.

The initial meeting with tenants prior to the closing was designed to achieve the following four objectives:

- *Reduce tension.* It was recognized by the developer that rumors regarding conversion or uncertainty as to the effect of the conversion can deeply unsettle the lives of tenants, particularly if tenants are elderly and have been living in the complex for a long time. Therefore, the developer's first objective was to put tenants at ease as much as possible by fully explaining the conversion process.

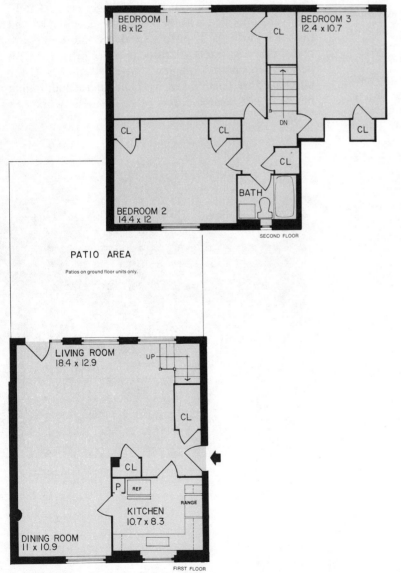

3-7 Three-bedroom unit.

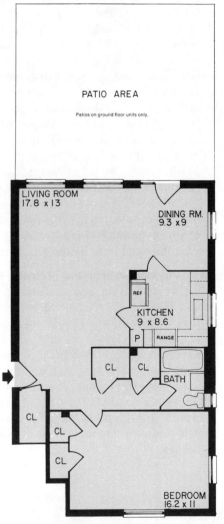

3-8 One-bedroom unit.

- *Establish the developer's credibility.* The fact that the developer was willing to go on record at the outset regarding his plans helped to avoid the suspicion, mistrust, and cynicism which can often arise between the developer and tenants during a conversion. The early briefing to tenants also allowed them to express their opinions early enough for the developer to react prior to the initiation of the conversion and to make changes where appropriate.
- *Inhibit the establishment of an anti-conversion coalition.* The developer felt that by being completely open with tenants and by encouraging active communications, it would be possible for the developer and residents to work together on a continuing basis in a positive frame of mind characterized by trust. This would lessen the likelihood of any anti-conversion action.
- *Establish a basis for continuing communications.* Through the briefing session and the distribution of the fact package, the developer sought to demonstrate his desire for continuing communications with tenants.

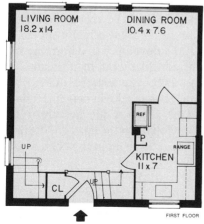

3-9 Two-bedroom unit.

Following the initial meeting, these four objectives were furthered in a variety of ways. First, a community relations office was established to provide tenants with an ombudsman. A community relations director was given complete authority to meet with tenants who were confused or dissatisfied, to investigate problems, and to report to top management on behalf of tenants. Second, a monthly newsletter was established to keep residents informed of the conversion's progress as well as other concerns. In addition, the developer attempted to promote a good understanding in the public sector of the conversion's objectives and programs through meetings and the dissemination of newsletters to public officials and through a concerted publicity campaign in the news media. Third, the attitudes and questions of tenants were sought and a study was conducted to evaluate how the developer might more closely reflect residents' desires. Finally, meetings were held between the development team, representatives of the Parkfairfax Citizens Association, and representatives of the project's management agent to develop priorities for handling the huge backlog of uncompleted work requests present as a result of deferred maintenance of the project prior to its purchase for conversion. Priority was first given to the repair of health related items (such as major problems in heating, cooling, plumbing, and electrical systems), then to the repair of general comfort items (such as minor problems in the various systems), and, finally, to the repair of cosmetic items (such as carpentry work, painting, repair of the grounds, etc.).

An extremely important factor in the project's smooth tenant relations was the affordability of the units to most tenants, offering them the opportunity to purchase their units for approximately the same monthly cost as renting. This affordability was increased further by establishing special discounts for certain tenants. Two discount programs were provided, designed to enable elderly and long-time residents to purchase their units or to continue renting.

The "Founders" program offered residents of 30 years or more a $2,000 discount on the sales price in addition to the discounts of $3,000 to $5,000 (based on unit size) that all qualified buyers (tenants when the project was purchased for conversion) were offered. These original discounts, offered in 1977 during the project's first phase, had been increased to $6,000 to $10,000 per unit by the final phase, reflecting increases in sales prices and interest rates. Those tenants eligible for the "Founders" program who wished to remain renters were given a $50 reduction in their monthly rent for the duration of their lease.

The "70–10" discount program was designed for those elderly tenants who had not resided in Parkfairfax for 30 years or more. This program entitled tenants 70 years of age or older with continuous residency of 10 or more years to receive the same discounts as did members of the "Founders" program.

In addition to the sales discount programs, those tenants who could not afford to buy or did not want to had the option of getting three- to five-year fixed-rent leases. The leased apartments were then sold to investors. However, under constraints imposed by the secondary mortgage market agencies, no more than 20 percent of the units could be purchased by investors. Approximately 10 percent of the tenants chose the leasing option.

Parkfairfax was the first condominium conversion to receive approval from the Federal National Mortgage Association (Fannie Mae), the Federal Home Loan Mortgage Corporation (Freddie Mac), the Veterans Administration (VA), and the Federal Housing Administration (FHA).

Experience Gained

- While there are higher costs associated with renovating occupied units than unoccupied units, the uninterrupted rent flow provides a significant additional income benefit to the developer which can be passed on to the buyer in the form of lower sales prices.
- The eviction of tenants as part of the conversion not only would have prevented the developer from achieving the goal of lower cost housing, but also would have substantially changed the social and economic characteristics of the project. Also, in terms of community relations, it makes sense to have a large number of tenants purchase units.
- The success of Parkfairfax has demonstrated to public officials how the benefits of home ownership can be extended to broad numbers of moderate-income people and has demonstrated to the development industry that such a project can be profitable without the involvement of public funds.
- When renovating occupied units, careful clean-up at the end of each day will be essential in order to avoid resident complaints. This clean-up can best be handled by a professional cleaning contractor rather than by the clean-up crews of the general contractor.
- The original project budget called for $80,000 in clean-up costs for occupied apartments. However, based upon the actual costs of hiring a professional cleaning contractor, the cleaning budget was increased to $256,000.

- The conversion of a project the size of Parkfairfax would normally require a supervisory staff of four people and a $600,000 budget for supervising and administering general conditions. However, due to the decision to renovate occupied units at Parkfairfax, a supervisory staff of 23 was required and supervisory costs were approximately $1,650,000.
- The conversion approach taken with Parkfairfax works best with large projects (more than 700 to 800 units) due to the additional supervision requirements, set-up costs, and related items.
- Since elderly and long-term residents can be greatly handicapped by relocation, either emotionally or financially, they should be given special consideration with regard to purchasing their units.
- Restoration and renovation must be planned and tested in extreme detail prior to being implemented. This is particularly true when renovating occupied units.
- The decision not to put in completely new kitchens worked very well. It was an important factor in the units' affordability to tenants and gave buyers the option of investing in a new kitchen at a later date.
- It is better to spend conversion money on "the guts of the buildings," that is, the plumbing and electrical systems, instead of spending it on cosmetic renovation.
- It is important for the developer's staff to be properly trained so that they can communicate effectively with tenants and outside buyers on a one-to-one basis. The staff must be able to explain the entire conversion program, what is being done and why.
- Constant communication with tenants during the conversion will minimize the number of problems which arise. The developer and his staff must be fully aware of tenants' concerns and should not assume that tenants have fully understood any written material which has been presented to them. Constant communication between the developer and tenants not only ensures that the developer is aware of tenants' concerns, but also that tenants are aware of the developer's constraints.
- The developer should be very selective when selling units to investors. Some attempt should be made on the part of the developer to determine which investors will be considerate of their tenants.
- In order to undertake a successful conversion, it is essential that the developer establish credibility with tenants. This requires the developer to establish goals and objectives at the outset of the project and to adhere to them throughout the conversion.

Parkfairfax Summary

Acquisition of Project:	Village I	Village II	Village III	Village IV
2/28/77				
Date Leasing Went to Six Months	3/1/77	5/1/77	3/20/78	7/19/78
Date Leasing Stopped	7/18/77	1/21/78	5/19/78	10/31/78
Date Application Filed with Virginia Real Estate Commission	7/21/77	3/22/78	8/3/78	8/3/78
Date Approved by Virginia Real Estate Commission	9/6/77	4/19/78	9/14/78	9/15/78
Date Interior Renovation Began	10/11/77	1/30/78	5/19/78	10/10/78
Date Exterior Renovation Began	8/1/77	3/13/78	6/30/78	10/2/78
Date Notice of Conversion Sent	9/6/77	4/21/78	9/18/78	1/8/79
Date Sales to General Public	11/22/77	7/15/78	12/6/78	3/24/79
Date Sold Out	1/31/78	10/18/78	12/6/78	4/12/79
Date of First Settlement	2/18/78	9/9/78	1/19/79	5/16/79

PROJECT DATA

Land Use Information:

Site Area: 132 acres (53.46 hectares)
Gross Density: 13 d.u. per acre
Total Dwelling Units: 1,684

Land Use Plan:

	Acres	Percent
Open Space[1]	105.6	80.0
Buildings	26.4	20.0
Total	132.0	100.0

Economic Information:

Site Acquisition Cost: $30.5 million (1977)
Construction Cost: $15,000 per unit[3]
Total Conversion Cost: $55.5 million
Initial Condominium Association Assessments: $59–90 per month

Unit Information:

Unit Type	D.U. Size	Bathrooms	Sales Price[2]
One bedroom	787 sq.ft.	1	$31,400–43,600
Two bedroom	924 sq.ft.	1	$44,500–53,400
Three bedroom	1,142 sq.ft.	1	$59,900–64,200

Notes:
[1] Includes parking and streets.
[2] Sales prices during the final phase (1979). Sales prices during the first phase (1977) were as follows: one-bedroom—$27,500 to $31,000; two-bedroom—$34,000 to $38,000; three-bedroom—$43,000 to $46,000. Standard tenant discounts were $3,000 to 5,000 in the first phase and $6,000 to $10,000 in the final phase. This does not include the additional discounts given to elderly and long-term tenants.
[3] Includes hard and soft costs.

Developer:

Parkfairfax Improvement Associates
(an affiliate of International Developers, Inc.)
1700 North Moore Street
Suite 1900
Rosslyn, Virginia 22209
(703) 558-7300

Project Manager:

R. Leon McFillen
Vice President
International Developers, Inc.

Planning and Design:

Smith and Williams
1414 Fair Oaks Avenue
Pasadena, California 91030
(213) 799-9188

Brown and Page
1320 Prince Street
Alexandria, Virginia
(703) 549-7474

Mechanical and Electrical Engineering:

Shefferman and Bigelson
1111 Spring Street
Silver Spring, Maryland 20910
(301) 587-4433

Civil Engineering:

Dewberry, Nealon, and Davis
8400 Arlington Boulevard
Fairfax, Virginia 22030
(703) 560-1100

Delashmutt Associates
1327 North Courthouse Road
Arlington, Virginia 22201
(703) 527-5588

Construction Management:

Majestic Builders
5530 Wisconsin Avenue
Suite 900
Chevy Chase, Maryland 20015
(301) 951-0900

Interim Financing:

Dominion National Bank
8150 Leesburg Pike
Vienna, Virginia 22180
(703) 442-3500

Permanent Financing:

Metropolitan Mortgage Fund, Inc.
500 Montgomery Street
Alexandria, Virgina 22314
(703) 836-6400

Washington and Lee Savings and Loan Association
8200 Greensboro Drive
McLean, Virginia 22101
(703) 442-7000

Legal Assistance:

Thomas & Sewell, P.C.
510 King Street
Suite 200
Alexandria, Virginia 22314
(703) 836-8400

Cameron Village

3-10 A majority of the units are two-story townhouses.

Cameron Village is a 235-unit condominium conversion located in Raleigh, North Carolina. It is part of a 551-unit community of two-story townhouses and one-story garden apartments built in 1948. The conversion is being undertaken by the project's original developer and owner and is the first conversion in the city of Raleigh marketed to individual homeowners rather than investors. The first phase of the conversion, consisting of 54 units, was completed in May 1980 and it is expected that the entire conversion will be completed in approximately two years.

In order to maximize the affordability of units to tenants, the focus during the renovation work has been on performing essential repairs rather than on cosmetic renovation. In addition, a five percent discount was provided to tenants who purchased their own units. This discount, by encouraging a greater percentage of tenants to purchase their units, not only minimized the rent loss to the developer during the conversion, but also helped to minimize advertising costs and to maintain good public relations. Approximately 35 percent of the tenants purchased units in phase one. Prices for the 540- to 1,161-square-foot units in phase one ranged from $18,900 to $36,000. The project was virtually vacancy-free prior to the conversion with rents ranging from $130 to $230 per month.

3-11 The small number of units per building and the use of a variety of exterior finishes enhances the project's townhouse appearance.

Several factors made the project ideal for conversion. First, the project was extremely marketable as condominiums. Since there had been no prior conversions directed at homeowners in the city of Raleigh and there was no ownership housing available in the projected price range, the project had absolutely no competition. In addition, the project enjoys an excellent location and several tenants had requested conversion. Second, the project was relatively easy to convert. The solid, townhouse construction of the buildings and the small number of units per building not only made the units suitable for conversion, but also made them easy to convert physically. The developer's existing management staff also was capable of overseeing the renovation work and of maintaining the project's rental status during the conversion process. Further, there were no government restrictions or regulations relating to conversions, although units did have to conform to existing building codes. Third, the developer was able to personally finance the units at a below-market rate (12 to 12.5 percent), thus increasing their affordability to tenants. These mortgages were processed by a local savings and loan and were subsequently packaged and sold to an out-of-state banking group.

Tenants were notified by letter of the owner's intent to convert to condominiums. They were given 60 days to decide whether to purchase (with the five percent discount being given to those tenants who decided within 30 days to purchase their units). Those tenants who did not purchase were given an additional 60 days to relocate. Nonpurchasing tenants were placed on a priority list for relocation to another Cameron Village apartment (if they desired), and all relocating tenants were given $100 to assist with relocation.

The Site

The project is strategically located and is very close to the geographic center of the city of Raleigh. It is approximately two miles from the central business district and one mile from North Carolina State University. Raleigh, the state capital, has a population of 150,000 and is comprised primarily of white-collar government employees and those associated with the surrounding universities and the Research Triangle Park.

The 4.16-acre site (phase one) is located at the northeast corner of the project at the intersection of Wade Avenue, a major east-west thoroughfare, and St. Mary's Street, a primary residential neighborhood connector. The project is adjacent to the Cameron Village

3-12 All units contain private front and rear entrances.

Shopping Center, a 650,000-square-foot regional center developed at the same time as the apartments; the Cameron Village Offices, nine buildings containing approximately 250,000 square feet; and 120 single-family detached homes that were a part of the original Cameron Village development.

The site is an irregular "L" shape with rolling terrain, mature trees, and open space. It has over 3,400 feet of road frontage and unlimited access. Bus transportation to downtown is available and phase one contains on-site parking for 60 cars. All public utilities are also available.

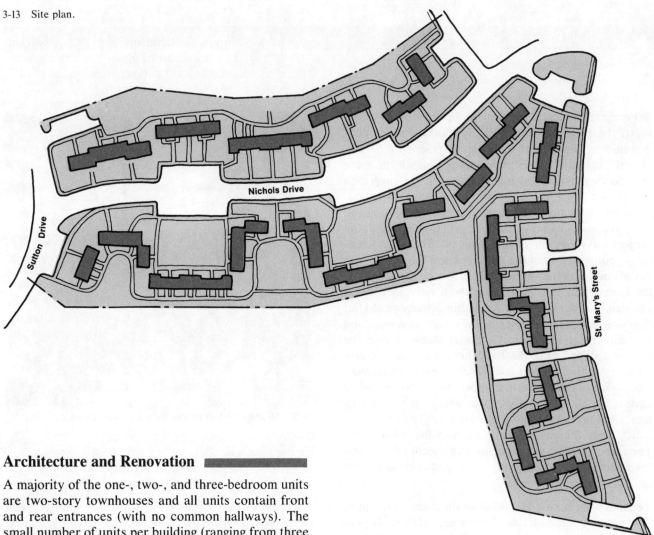

Nichols Drive

Sutton Drive

St. Mary's Street

Architecture and Renovation

A majority of the one-, two-, and three-bedroom units are two-story townhouses and all units contain front and rear entrances (with no common hallways). The small number of units per building (ranging from three to eight units) and the use of a variety of exterior finishes enhances the project's townhouse appearance. Buildings are of wood frame construction with concrete block foundation walls. Exteriors are either red brick veneer, clapboard, cut stone, cedar shakes, or board and batten. The siding on the rear of all buildings is asbestos shingles. Roofs are of ''A'' framed or hipped construction and have asphalt shingles.

Although the 32-year-old buildings were structurally sound, renovation and upgrading were required to offset damage resulting from moisture, wear, exposure, and abuse. Undertaking this renovation work with the project remaining as a rental complex would have required substantial rent increases in order to recoup the cost of renovation, thereby making the units unaffordable to a majority of the existing tenants. Conversion to condominiums represented an alternative which enabled the developer to profitably complete the necessary renovation and upgrading, while at the same time providing ownership housing which would be affordable to many tenants.

In order to determine the exact renovation work which was required, the buildings were carefully inspected by an independent architect who prepared a punch list for the renovation of the exterior and interior of each building and each dwelling unit. A vacant unit was then completely remodeled by an outside contractor to determine the cost of renovation and conversion and to identify problems which might be encountered. The cost to convert and renovate this unit was $10,000 (this unit later served as the project's model unit). The contractor was then asked to bid on the total renovation based on the architect's punch list and the knowledge gained from the work done on the model unit. At this time, it was determined that it would be more economical (both in terms of installation costs and future operating costs) to provide gas-fired forced air furnaces and electric air conditioning units instead of the through-the-wall heat pump which was installed in the model unit. Also, it was decided at this time to use thermopane windows (both for superior energy conservation and architectural appeal) instead of the storm windows installed on the model unit. Units which were purchased by tenants were renovated while occupied.

Exterior renovation of the buildings included the repair or replacement of all deteriorating siding, soffits, and fascias, and the painting of all exteriors. The existing steel casement windows were replaced with double hung wood thermopane windows (with the exception of kitchen and bathroom windows which were not replaced due to their irregular size and the cost of replacement) and six-panel thermopane storm doors were provided for each unit. Finally, a number of minor structural defects were repaired.

The punch list prepared for each unit determined the exact interior renovation. However, as a minimum, the renovation to each unit included new insulation, the repair and painting of all interior walls, the replacement of sliding closet doors with new bifold doors, the replacement of kitchen counter tops, the installation of washer and dryer connections, the refinishing of the existing hardwood floors, and the installation of individually metered heating and cooling systems. Options provided in phase one include a half-bath on the ground floor of the townhouse units; carpeting in the living room/dining room area and the bedrooms; a new refrigerator, range, and dishwasher; a garbage disposal; and a dryer vent. In order to simplify and expedite future phases of the conversion, several of the options have been eliminated (the carpeting, the refrigerator, and the range) and several options (the half-bath, the dishwasher, and the disposal) have been made standard to all buyers except tenants who purchase their own units.

Renovation of common areas was limited. It included the resurfacing of parking areas and the addition of some new landscaping in phase one. Privacy fences were installed in phase one at the rear doors of some units. However, due to the proximity of some units to walkways, the privacy fences have been discontinued in subsequent phases.

Condominium Association

The condominium association was created upon approval of the conversion by Raleigh's city council. The approval was given in two separate sessions, first for phase one and then for the balance of the units. The bylaws required that upon the sale of 10 units an organizational meeting for the election of the governing board would be held. Because unit sales were being processed so quickly, the organizational meeting was actually held after some 12 to 14 units had been closed. The vice president of the managing firm presided at the meeting and held the developer's proxy for all unsold units.

The association's board of directors contains three members, with each member elected for a one-year term. It is responsible for the operation, maintenance, and care of common areas; the determination and collection of dues for the operation and maintenance of common areas; the employment and dismissal of maintenance personnel; the purchase and sale of units acquired through foreclosure; and any maintenance or repair work to any unit which is necessary to protect common areas.

Monthly association dues are $42.50 per unit. This is based on a budget that includes grounds maintenance, utility charges for hot and cold water (which is provided to each unit by a central system), outside lighting, repair and maintenance, insurance, management, and reserves for roof repairs and exterior painting.

Market Considerations

The project's marketing program has been limited due to the extremely high market demand. For example, although no advertising was used in phase one, there were over 500 applicants for the 54 units available. These included tenants from the phase one units as well as from other units within the complex, employees of

3-14 and 3-15 Although the buildings were structurally sound, both exterior and interior renovation and upgrading were required to offset damage resulting from moisture, wear, exposure, and abuse.

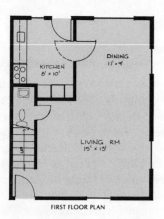

FIRST FLOOR PLAN

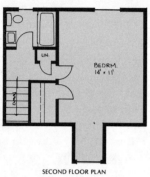

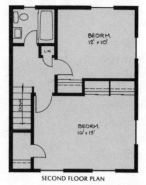

SECOND FLOOR PLAN

3-16 One-bedroom townhouse. 3-17 Two-bedroom townhouse. 3-18 Three-bedroom townhouse.

the developer, and the general public. A sales office and model unit were established from the outset of phase one. A marketing brochure with floor plans has been used during the project's second phase. However, there has been no media advertising in the second phase and none is planned for the project's remaining phases, unless it becomes necessary. An independent outside sales agent is being used in the marketing of the units. Most buyers in phase one have been either young singles or older retirees with moderate incomes.

Experience Gained

- There were a number of complaints from tenants who purchased their units about the inconvenience resulting from the renovation of units while they were occupied. Many tenants who purchased their units expected to receive some additional compensation (beyond the five percent discount in sales price) for this inconvenience, such as a reduction in rent during the renovation period. In order to alleviate this problem in future phases, it will be stressed that units will be renovated while occupied and that the five percent discount to tenant purchasers is intended to compensate for any inconvenience resulting from the renovation of units while they are occupied.

- The five percent discount in sales price should have been stated more clearly. It was intended to apply only to tenants who purchased the units which they were occupying, thereby encouraging tenants to purchase their units and reducing rent loss during the conversion. However, tenants who bought units other than their own also expected the discount.

- It is important for the project to be inspected by an outside source both prior to the conversion to determine the project's condition and the renovation work required, and after the renovation to make sure that the work has been completed satisfactorily. Inspection by an outside source prior to the conversion will enhance the substance and credibility of the conversion when it is presented for the various governmental approvals. This will be particularly important when undertaking the initial conversion in a market. Inspection following the completion of the renovation work will increase the confidence of potential buyers and, therefore, will be important from a marketing standpoint.

- The sale of units to investors should not be permitted, provided sales are going well. This will avoid problems resulting from having both buyers and renters living in the project. All sales contracts for Cameron Village have specified that buyers must live in their units.

- The discount to tenants purchasing their units has benefited the developer because it has reduced the rent loss during the conversion process by encouraging tenants to purchase, has allowed advertising costs to be minimized, and has improved public relations.

- A rule-of-thumb for conversions is that renovation costs per unit should not exceed approximately 20 percent of the sales price.

- When undertaking the first conversion in a market, it is critical to proceed slowly and to maintain good tenant relations. Undertaking the conversion in small increments will make it possible to assist those tenants who relocate and to minimize any adverse publicity.

- In order to succeed with a conversion in a tight money market, it is imperative that the developer have a financing commitment for qualified buyers. Local savings and loans are the most likely source of financing. Obtaining this commitment prior to notifying tenants of the conversion will also increase the likelihood that a greater percentage of tenants will purchase units.

- The simultaneous conversion of 54 units during phase one created management problems, particularly in the areas of construction scheduling, rent loss, and the relocation of tenants. In future phases, the conversion will be limited to 20 units per phase.

- The appraised prices for the units in phase one were used as the sales prices, resulting in the sales prices being considerably below the market value. Sales prices for subsequent phases are being determined by the market and appraisals are being ordered only after a sales contract has been executed.

- In order to simplify the renovation process, many of the options offered in phase one are being provided as standard conversion items in future phases or have been eliminated completely. Options are now being provided only to those tenants who buy the same unit which they were renting.

- Surprisingly, those tenants who were the most vocal in their opposition to the conversion often purchased their units.

- The construction of privacy fences in phase one created problems due to the fact that some of the units were located as close as three feet to the sidewalks. Some buyers wanted a privacy fence but the unit location would not allow it. Others did not want a fence and expected a price abatement.

- Although the project was the first conversion in Raleigh, it is important to note that newly constructed condominiums had been in existence in the market for some time, thus assuring that the concept of condominium ownership was firmly established in the market. If this had not been the case, gaining acceptance and credibility for the conversion probably would have been a more difficult and time-consuming process.

- The project has demonstrated that conversions not only can play an important role in meeting the demand for affordable ownership housing for the lower end of the market, but also can provide a means to profitably upgrade and renovate older rental housing which might otherwise become substandard or be demolished.

- The three factors most important to the project's success were its strategic location, the availability of below market rate financing to buyers, and the extremely affordable sales prices.

- The conversion must be carefully phased in order to allow the conversion process to continue uninterrupted, while at the same time allowing the maximum possible cash flow from rental income to be maintained. The conversion of Cameron Village has been scheduled to allow the conversion/renovation process to be continuous from one phase to the next.

PROJECT DATA[1]

Land Use Information:

Site Area: 4.16 acres (1.68 hectares)
Total Dwelling Units: 54
Gross Density: 12.98 d.u. per acre
Net Density: 44.63 d.u. per acre
Parking: 60 spaces

Land Use Plan:

	Acres	Percent
Buildings	1.21	29.08
Parking	.35	8.42
Open Space/Walkways	2.60	62.50
Total	4.16	100.00

Economic Information:

Site Cost: N.A.[2]
Construction Cost: $602,300
Marketing Costs: $84,000
Finance Costs: $29,800
Total Conversion Costs: $716,000[3]

Total Sales: $1,683,000
Total Rental Income: $39,000[4]

Unit Information:

Unit Type	D.U. Size (sq. ft.)	Number	Bedrooms	Bathrooms	Sales Price	Preconversion Rent
Efficiency	540	2	1	1	$18,900	$130
Townhouse	708	6	1	1	$22,800	$170
Townhouse	850	3	1	1	$27,200	$170
Flat	928	2	2	1	$29,700	$195
Townhouse	1,027	38	2	1	$32,900	$195
Townhouse	1,161	3	3	1	$36,000	$230

Notes:
[1] All data is for phase one only.
[2] The project was owned by the developer prior to conversion.
[3] Total costs for the conversion of the 54 units in phase one. Projected costs for the total conversion (235 units) are $2.85 million.
[4] During conversion.

Developer/Financing/Management:

J. W. York & Company, Inc.
1900 Cameron Street
Raleigh, North Carolina 27605
(919) 821-1350

Architecture:

Dale Blosser & Associates
2008 Hillsborough Street
Raleigh, North Carolina 27607
(919) 833-6439

Engineering:

John A. Edwards & Company
333 Wade Avenue
Raleigh, North Carolina
(919) 828-4428

Sales:

Bacon & Company Realtors
4460 Six Forks Road
Raleigh, North Carolina
(919) 787-8101

Oceanside Plaza

3-19 and 3-20 A heavily landscaped entrance (right) creates a luxurious ambiance for the 17-story, 300-unit high-rise conversion in Miami Beach (above).

Oceanside Plaza is a 17-story, 300-unit oceanfront conversion located in Miami Beach, Florida. The project was acquired by the developer for conversion in May 1978, and by April 1979 all of the units had been sold. The project was the quickest conversion sell-out in the Miami Beach market and one of the quickest sell-outs ever (both conversion and new construction) in the market. Its success is due to its excellent location, amenities, and sales prices.

The building was constructed in 1968–1969 and was originally conceived to be a condominium. However, it became, and remained, a rental until it was acquired by the current developer in 1978. The building's architecture can best be described as above average ''Miami Beach'' design. The undulation and curvatures of the corners of the building created an attractive design feature. Units range from 1,600-square-foot penthouses to 548-square-foot studio apartments, with an average unit size of approximately 1,030 square feet. All of the units are well laid out, highly functional, and afford above average closet space, livability, and lifestyle.

The project also features a full complement of amenities including a heated outdoor swimming pool, a 22,300-square-foot pool deck which overlooks the beach, a billiard room, women's and men's card rooms, a meeting room, a party room, a kitchen, shuffleboard courts, and a putting green. In addition, an existing exercise facility at the penthouse level was expanded and totally redone to provide separate men's and women's exercise facilities (with each facility consisting of a fully equipped exercise room, a steam room, locker and toilet facilities, and an individual sun deck area). A redwood deck area was installed at the south end of the roof to be used as an entertainment, sunning, and observation area. Two enclosed air conditioned racquetball courts were installed on the pool deck, and an elevated hot tub (with a reduced deck) was installed adjacent to the pool. The swimming pool and its equipment were totally refurbished.

3-21 Amenities include an outdoor swimming pool and deck, racquetball courts, a billiard room, card rooms, exercise rooms, a party room, shuffleboard courts, and a putting green.

The Site

The project is located at 55th Street and Collins Avenue in Miami Beach and has approximately 400 feet of frontage on the Atlantic Ocean. This area is considered to be the most luxurious portion of Miami Beach. The Doral-on-the-Ocean, Eden Roc, and Fountain Bleau hotels are located south of the project. North of the site (on the ocean side) and across Collins Avenue (on the intracoastal waterway) there are luxury condominiums and rental apartments. Collins Avenue is a divided roadway in this 30-block area, with a heavily landscaped median which creates a ''boulevard'' atmosphere.

A landscaped driveway leads to the building's entrance and main lobby. The driveway is straddled by two landscaped pools with fountains which create a luxurious ambiance. The building's location on the site offers water views from all units, with units fronting on either the Atlantic Ocean or the intracoastal waterway and Biscayne Bay. The site's 230-foot depth and 400-foot width allows optimum use of the pool deck, the covered parking (with 282 underground parking spaces), and the building.

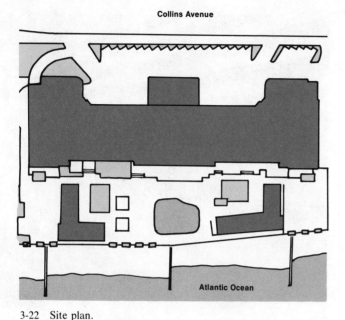

Collins Avenue

Atlantic Ocean

3-22   Site plan.

Conversion Feasibility

The developer has had considerable experience in the Miami/Fort Lauderdale market. Using this experience in both new condominium developments and conversions of existing rental projects, the developer was able to identify a market demand for the project. However, the fact that there had not been a conversion on Miami Beach itself in four years made it difficult to determine sales prices for the units. Using his collective experience, the developer was able to establish sales prices which were appropriate for the market. The combination of these established sales prices with the acquisition cost and the construction, renovation, and marketing costs indicated that the project was economically viable.

Financing

Interim financing was arranged with Continental Illinois National Bank and Trust Company of Chicago. This included financing for site and building acquisition, marketing (including models), construction (including renovation of existing common areas and the units), normal soft costs, and closing costs. The loan was based on an 18-month pro forma statement.

Permanent mortgages for the condominium purchasers were arranged through a $15 million commitment which was negotiated and obtained through First Federal Savings and Loan Association of Miami, now known as Amerifirst. The normal commitment fee was paid for this loan and an excellent relationship between the developer and the lender resulted. A unique feature of the agreement with Amerifirst was that for the intensive sell-out period the lender provided loan officers at the project for approximately four weeks to take loan applications, thereby expediting this phase of the marketing process.

Renovation of Exterior and Common Areas

The building's exterior, the lobbies, and the other common areas were all in above average condition. Since the building had been completely painted the year before it was acquired for conversion, renovation of the building proper was limited to repair work on the balconies, some exterior caulking, and the installation of a new roof (except for the roof over the penthouses, which was in good condition). In addition, artificial grass carpeting was installed on all the balconies and a kiosk was added in front of the building for use by the front doorman and the valet parking service.

Renovation of the common areas included the installation of new carpeting, new wall covering, and new lighting in the corridors on floors three through 17; the installation of new air conditioning and new ceilings in the card rooms, billiard room, and club room; the installation of new wall covering, new floor covering, new lighting, new air conditioning, and new ceilings in the meeting room; and the refurbishing of existing amenities and the addition of a number of new amenities (as discussed earlier). Finally, the interiors and exteriors of the cabanas on the pool deck level were refurbished, and the cabanas were then sold to purchasers of units in the building.

3-23   A front doorman and valet parking service are provided.

Interior Renovation

A standard interior renovation package was provided for both tenant purchasers and outside buyers. In addition, tenants were offered the option of purchasing their unit in "as is" condition. However, only about 10 percent of the tenant purchasers exercised this option. This renovation package included painting of units, new carpeting, new appliances, new kitchen flooring, and the completion of necessary patch work and repairs. Buyers were also given the option of selecting upgraded appliances and carpeting, and a décor center was provided for this purpose. Approximately 40 percent of the purchasers selected upgraded carpeting. Relatively few buyers exercised the option of upgrading appliances.

Intensive investigation prior to the acquisition of the project by the developer had indicated the need to replace all of the hot water piping in the building. This involved the replacement of 44 risers, all main supply runs, and associated valves and pumps. The replacement of the hot water piping took about 90 days to complete and was the most disruptive aspect of the renovation work since it required cutting into risers in all of the units for each bathroom and each kitchen and subsequent dry wall and ceramic tile replacement and repainting. However, since many tenants who purchased units and requested renovation occupied the units seasonally, there were some opportunities to undertake this most disruptive portion of the renovation work while units were vacant.

Marketing

A total marketing program was prepared to cover the period from the initial notification of tenants through the initial public opening. The marketing program was essentially a three-tier price program targeted to derive the maximum percentage of tenant purchasers and to stimulate initial upfront sales.

The first phase of the marketing program was to tenants only. In July 1978 a meeting was held by the developer during which tenants were notified of the intent to convert. At this meeting a booklet was given to tenants examining the various options to them. All tenants were given three weeks notice by mail of this meeting. A 45-day period was established from the date of this meeting during which tenants had the option of purchasing

their unit in "as is" condition at a discount or renovated at a somewhat lower discount. Tenants who did not wish to purchase had the opportunity to take advantage of the developer's "lease breaker" program, which provided a $500 relocation allowance to those tenants who moved within 120 days from the date of the conversion notification meeting.

3-24 The project features 400 feet of frontage on the Atlantic Ocean.

The second phase of the marketing program was the coupon period, which was initiated 45 days after the notification of the tenants. Full page display ads were run in the *Miami Herald* offering those wishing to purchase a unit the opportunity to buy a $500 coupon which would place them on a waiting list to purchase a unit at a discount (before the units were offered to "off the street" buyers). The coupon period was extremely successful. In fact, it was so successful that the project was sold out before the third phase of the marketing program (that is, sales to the general public at higher prices) could be implemented.

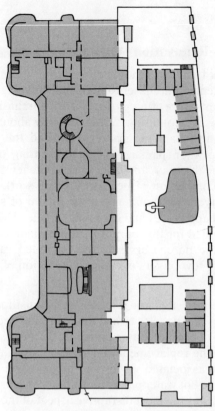

3-27 Mezzanine and pool deck.

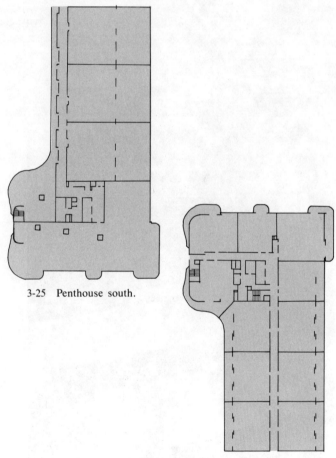

3-25 Penthouse south.

3-26 Typical floor plan north.

Experience Gained

- Since Oceanside Plaza was the first conversion to take place on Miami Beach in approximately four years, the lack of comparable conversion units in the market made it difficult to establish sales prices. Using his experience in the south Florida market, the developer established the initial sales prices based on new condominium unit sales prices. However, the extremely rapid sell-out (within approximately eight weeks) indicated that the units might have been priced higher.

- The acquisition cost is critical to the success of a conversion. Several months after the project was acquired for conversion there was a dramatic increase in acquisition costs (20 to 50 percent) in the Miami Beach area. Thus, any delay by the developer in purchasing the project would have had a significant impact on the profitability of the conversion. Extremely high acquisition costs in the Miami Beach area today are a severe impediment to a successful conversion.

- The coupon period of the marketing program was much more successful than anticipated. As mentioned earlier, sales rates during the coupon period resulted in the project being sold out before the third phase of the marketing program could be implemented. Therefore, it would have been desirable to limit the number of coupons available.

- As a result of today's excessive carrying costs, a short-term sell-out is an important factor in the success of a conversion. In this regard, it is essential that renovation work be completed as quickly as possible.

- The developer must be aware of the deadlines for the filing of the various condominium documents and should have the documents prepared prior to the notification of tenants. The early preparation of the various documents will avoid any problems further on in the conversion process.
- The developer should not seek the input of tenants when deciding what cosmetic renovation to undertake since tenants frequently do not really know what renovation they want. Decisions on cosmetic renovation should be based on a thorough market analysis.
- "Human engineering" is an important aspect of conversions. That is, the developer should be concerned not only with profit, but also with respecting the rights of tenants and buyers. Sensitivity to the needs of human beings is essential for a converter's long-term success.
- Most buyers of condominiums which are located in a resort area rent their units seasonally. Therefore, they generally prefer to purchase a renovated unit since a renovated unit will have greater appeal to potential renters. Long-term tenants who buy their units, however, usually will prefer to buy the unit in "as is" condition. After living in the same unit for a considerable time, they probably will have added a lot of personal touches which they will not want changed.

PROJECT DATA

Land Use Information:

Site Area: 2.12 acres (.86 hectares)
Total Dwelling Units: 300
Gross Density: 141 d.u. per acre
Parking Spaces:

Underground 282
Surface 22
        Total 304

Economic Information:

Acquisition Cost: $13,228,980
Construction Cost: $2,257,200[1]
Marketing Cost: $1,150,000
Finance Cost: $1,130,000
Total Conversion Costs: $17,766,180
Total Sales: $21,000,000
Total Rental Income: $361,500[2]

Unit Information:

D.U. Size	Bedrooms	Bathrooms	Sales Price	Preconversion Rents
1,043 sq.ft.	1	1	$60,000–$78,000	$435 (median)
1,025 sq.ft.	1	2	$62,000–$70,300	$450
862 sq.ft.	1	1½	$50,000–$53,000	$375
1,315 sq.ft.	2	2	$90,500–$100,300	$565
951 sq.ft.	1	1½	$64,750–$70,300	$405
1,065 sq.ft.	1	2	$62,750–$81,400	$400–$500
548 sq.ft.	Studio	1	$28,050–$28,523	$300
1,321 sq.ft.	2	2	$79,550–$85,100	$610
1,600 sq.ft.	2	3	$127,500–$138,750	$800–$1,000

Notes:
[1] Includes approximately $350,000 for refurbishing of amenities and other common areas.
[2] During conversion.

Developer:

Oceanside Capital, Inc. (wholly-owned subsidiary of Union Capital Corporation)
Suite 213
66 Luckie Street
Atlanta, Georgia 30303
(404) 523-7629

Interim Financing:

Continental Illinois National Bank & Trust Company of Chicago
231 S. LaSalle Street
Chicago, Illinois 60693
(312) 828-2900

Permanent Financing:

Amerifirst
900 N.E. 125th Street
North Miami, Florida 33161

Management:

Keyes Management Company
100 N. Biscayne Boulevard
Miami, Florida 33132
(305) 371-3592

Engineering:

Florida Engineering Services
352 N.E. 167th Street
Suite D
North Miami Beach, Florida 33162
(305) 945-4743

Clement Di Fillipo
1301 Dade Boulevard, 2nd Floor
Miami Beach, Florida 33139
(305) 672-6312

Landscape Architecture:

Walter Taft Bradshaw & Associates
Fort Lauderdale, Florida
(305) 772-0724

Minnesota Project

Located in suburban Minneapolis, this project is an example of a relatively small conversion—a single building with 30 one- and two-bedroom units which range in size from 700 to 993 square feet—with limited amenities. Due to the project's small size, the developer has requested that the name of the project not be included in order to assure the residents' privacy.

The building is two stories in height and is of wood frame construction on a masonry foundation with a brick and shingle exterior. Amenities are limited to a sauna with toilet and shower facilities, an exercise room, a small party/guest room, and open space with a picnic area. The east half of the building's basement contains walkout garden apartments, while the west half of the basement contains 42 underground parking stalls. The building also contains one elevator, three storage rooms, and three laundry rooms (one on each level). All units have patios or balconies.

3-28, 3-29, 3-30, and 3-31 Features of this converted two-story, 30-unit building include patios or balconies, a heated underground garage, and large open spaces to the rear of the building.

The project is the smallest of a considerable number of conversions and new condominium projects undertaken by Lanvesco Corporation in the Minneapolis area and in other areas of the country. It is an atypical project for the developer, whose projects generally include between 125 and 300 units.

The building was originally constructed in 1971 and was purchased by the developer in 1979. The conversion process was initiated in September 1979 and was completed with the final sale in October 1980. Both tenants and outside buyers had the option of purchasing units "as is" or "decorated" units. Only two units were purchased by tenants; relocation assistance was provided for the other tenants. All existing tenants were offered discounts and those tenants who agreed to purchase before a specified date were also offered redecorating allowances and rent refunds. Sales prices ranged from $42,900 for a one-bedroom unit in "as is" condition to $57,900 for a two-bedroom "decorated" unit. The project was planned for adults only and occupancy has been limited to persons 17 years of age or older.

The Site

The approximately two-acre site is ideally located. It is close to major freeways which provide direct access to downtown Minneapolis and to the Minneapolis-St. Paul International Airport. The site lies within a quiet residential area and is surrounded by single-family detached housing to the east, undeveloped land to the west (which is projected to be developed with multi-family housing), apartments to the north, and a church to the south. While adjacent to residential development, the site is also close to a major financial center, office buildings, a hotel, major restaurants, and a major shopping center.

The project sits on top of a hill which helps to provide a sense of separation from the nearby commercial areas. The site slopes sharply from west to east (that is, from the front property line to the rear property line). To the rear of the building there is a large open area containing mature trees and picnic facilities. The entire site is nicely landscaped and the grounds were well maintained prior to the conversion.

3-32 On the grounds to the rear of the building are picnic facilities and mature trees.

Conversion Feasibility

A number of factors made the conversion feasible. First, as already indicated, the project enjoys an excellent location with its quiet residential setting as well as its easy access and proximity to major commercial development. Second, the building was structurally sound and did not require extensive renovation. This made it possible for renovation costs to be kept low, and thereby allowed the developer to keep sales prices low while making a reasonable profit. Third, the size of the units also helped to make them affordable to young singles, young couples, and empty-nesters of moderate incomes. Fourth, the availability of heated underground parking was an extremely important selling feature due to the harsh winter climate in Minnesota. Fifth, while the project contains relatively few amenities, the upkeep of those amenities which are available could be supported by the rather limited income (due to size) of the condominium association. In a small, moderate-income project, the ability of the condominium association to support amenities is an extremely important consideration. Finally, interim financing was not required and the developer was able to secure a permanent financing commitment from a local savings and loan. These financing arrangements assured the project's economic feasibility in the market.

Conversion and Renovation Process

The first step in the conversion and renovation process was to undertake a preliminary inspection of the property. The building and the grounds were inspected by the developer's staff from a structural, mechanical, and cosmetic standpoint to determine what renovation work would be required. Following this initial inspection, a preliminary list of the necessary renovation work was prepared together with a preliminary capital improvement budget; preliminary financing and condominium association budgets were prepared at the same time. The units were then priced based on the conversion costs and a decision was made as to their marketability. Once a decision was made to proceed with the conversion, structural and mechanical engineers were hired to undertake a complete inspection of the property and a final capital improvement budget was prepared based on this inspection.

Major common area renovation included restaining the building's wood siding and balconies, upgrading the landscaping, restriping the underground parking stalls, waterproofing the garage, recaulking the outside of the windows, repainting the wrought iron railings, repairing the driveway, redecorating the entrance lobby with wallpaper, carpet, and drapes, installing new hallway light fixtures, repainting hallways, redecorating the guest/party room and the three laundry rooms, and shampooing the hallway carpeting.

As mentioned previously, buyers had the option of purchasing units either "as is" or "decorated." Renovation of "as is" units was limited to the painting of all walls and ceilings, the shampooing of existing carpeting, and the inspection of existing appliances and the repair or replacement of any defective parts, with a 90-day warranty provided on the appliances from the date of the closing. "Decorated" units were painted and provided with new carpeting and new kitchen appliances. A number of options as to paint and carpet colors were offered by the developer.

Handling of Tenants

At the time the conversion was undertaken, the local jurisdiction had no restrictions on conversions or requirements for the number of days notice tenants were required to be given. However, all tenants were given 120 days notice, a policy later adopted by the Minnesota legislature in its 1980 Uniform Condominium Act. The original notice was in writing and was mailed to all tenants. This letter also outlined the purchase discount to tenants who purchased a unit within 90 days (a $2,000 discount for a one-bedroom unit and a $2,500 discount for a two-bedroom unit). Tenants purchasing within 30 days received a redecorating allowance ($1,000 for a one-bedroom unit and $1,250 for a two-bedroom unit) and a rent refund ($1,000 for a one-bedroom unit and $1,250 for a two-bedroom unit). After the written notice was given, individual sales sessions were held with tenants.

Twenty-eight of the 30 tenants did, in fact, relocate. The Minneapolis market has a relatively high vacancy rate and, therefore, many tenants who did not purchase were able to find new apartments within a short period of time. The developer also provided housing relocation assistance.

Market Considerations

Marketing to outside buyers was virtually all done by newspaper advertising. Eighteen of the purchasers had previously been renters. Twenty of the purchasers were single, and most purchasers were either young adults under 35 years old or older retirees. More than one-half of the buyers had been living within five miles of the project.

Condominium Association

A consultant was used by the developer to assist with the design phase of the condominium association as well as with the transition from developer control to

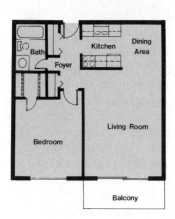

3-33 and 3-34 Floor plans.

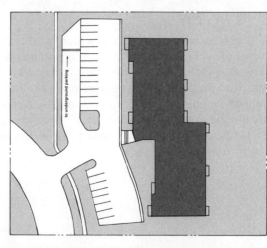

3-35 Site plan.

homeowner control. During the design phase, the consultant was responsible for the following: the review of legal documents to assure that they would be sound and workable; the review of the various plans for common areas to assess the impact of such plans on the association; the preparation of a fee study and the association's first annual budget; the preparation of a complete insurance program for the association; the preparation of a set of rules and regulations detailing use and architectural guidelines for the project; the review of marketing and sales materials; and the coordination of the preparation of the disclosure documents.

During the transition phase, the consultant prepared specifications for management requirements and recommended an ongoing management agent and procedures to efficiently operate the association. He also provided assistance to the board of directors, held informational sessions on the association for buyers, activated the association, and assisted with the final transition phase of acceptance of the common areas by the association.

The association bylaws call for a three- or five-member board of directors which has a variety of responsibilities including the care and maintenance of the common areas and facilities, the employment and removal of a manager, the adoption and implementation of uniform rules and regulations, the preparation of the annual budget, and the collection of assessment payments.

Experience Gained

- In other, larger conversions undertaken by the developer, an on-site caretaker/manager has been necessary in order to assure efficient management. This on-site management was provided by selling one of the units in the project to the condominium association for use by the caretaker/manager. However, due to this project's small size and the resulting cost impact, there was no need for a unit for a caretaker/manager.
- A project should not be purchased for conversion unless the developer has a commitment for both interim and permanent financing.
- In order to assure a smooth transition of control from the developer to the condominium association, the developer must make certain that the annual condominium association budget is adequate to cover operating expenses. He must set up a good condominium association budget and then adhere to it, making sure that he takes care of his responsibilities at the time of transition. The developer should also emphasize to the association that the budget will have to increase each year.
- It is imperative that the developer have the transition consultant involved in the formation of the condominium association from the outset. This will assure that the condominium association documents are drafted properly. The proper drafting of documents

will require that the attorney preparing the documents be advised by the transition consultant, who is familiar with the management and the transition process. The documents not only must meet the various legal requirements and requirements of the association but they also must be workable. Therefore, the documents should not follow a standard format but should vary according to the requirements of the particular project.

- Generally, it is advisable to give the board of directors of the condominium association as much authority as possible and to keep necessary quorums as low as possible. This will allow the association to function with maximum efficiency. However, while giving the board of directors a great deal of authority, it is important that owners be protected adequately. The documents need to provide these protections in the event of unwise decisions by the board of directors.
- The availability of underground parking was an important selling feature due to the harsh winter climate in the area. However, more underground spaces were available (42 spaces) than were actually needed for the 30-unit project. This excess supply was dealt with by including the price of a parking space or spaces in the total unit price.
- Some form of tenant relocation assistance should be provided, such as listings of available apartments and moving firms. While the individual providing relocation assistance should be employed by and work with the developer, he or she should not be involved in sales and should truly be helpful to those tenants requiring assistance.
- In a rental market with a relatively high vacancy rate, such as suburban Minneapolis, those tenants who do not wish to purchase units will usually begin to relocate immediately upon notification of the conversion, thereby significantly reducing cash flow from rentals. This loss of rental income as a result of immediate move-outs can be overcome by re-leasing units on a short-term basis. In addition, the developer has the option of taking legal action against those tenants who do not honor their leases. However, for public relations reasons such action generally is not advisable.
- The budget for the condominium association should be prepared based on the marketing's level of service guidelines for the project. For example, if the marketing for the project is middle-income and the sales theme is economy, then the association budget should be prepared keeping in mind that monthly unit dues will have to be relatively modest. Conversely, marketing should "sell" the adopted budget and its resulting level of service.

- Ideally, all capital improvements should be completed before sales are closed. This will avoid skepticism and complaints by buyers.
- The method used by the developer is to price the units first based on conversion costs and then determine if they are marketable, rather than determining what price the market will bear first and then attempting to adjust conversion costs accordingly.
- While the conversion of a small project is easy to handle operationally and does not require a large time commitment, it does not provide the flexibility which is present when converting a larger project.
- Units which are vacated by tenants upon notification of the conversion and then re-leased on a short-term basis in order to maintain cash flow should be rented furnished. If units are not rented furnished, there will be a conspicuous movement of furniture by short-term tenants. This in and out movement, when viewed by prospective purchasers who are visiting the project, can have a negative impact on sales and is irritating to residents.
- Maintaining good public relations is critical when undertaking conversions. In this regard, the developer should provide assistance for those tenants who relocate, with special assistance provided for elderly tenants who relocate.
- It is desirable for the developer to use the same sales staff from one project to the next in order to maintain sales continuity.
- A rule of thumb used by the developer is that a conversion should generally result in a $5,000 per unit net profit before taxes.
- It is generally advisable to select projects for conversion which require primarily cosmetic renovation and little rehabilitation.
- The developer should give those tenants who purchase the unit which they have been renting a redecorating allowance rather than attempting to renovate units while they are occupied.
- Undertaking a rental profile which focuses on tenants' incomes is useful in estimating the percentage of tenants who will purchase units. In the Minneapolis market, 20 to 25 percent is an extremely good rate of tenant purchases; the conversions undertaken by the developer have averaged about 15 percent.

PROJECT DATA

Land Use Information:

Site Area: 1.9 acres (.77 hectares)
Gross Density: 15.4 d.u. per acre
Total Dwelling Units: 30
Parking Spaces:
Underground 42
Surface 21

   Total 63
Parking Ratio: 2.10 parking spaces per unit

Unit Information:

D.U. Size	No.	Bedrooms	Bathrooms	"As Is" Sales Price[1]	"Decorated" Sales Price[1]
700–732 sq. ft.	11	1	1	$42,900–43,900	$45,500–46,500
958–993 sq. ft.	19	2	1	$50,900–54,900	$53,900–57,900

Land Use Plan:

	Acres	Percent
Building	.7	37.0
Open Space	.9	47.0
Parking	.3	16.0
Total	**1.9**	**100.0**

Economic Information:

Site and Building Cost: $900,000
Renovation Cost: $125,245
Marketing Costs: $93,028
Finance Costs: $98,400
Total Conversion Costs: $1,216,673

Renovation Budget:
Interior—Individual Unit/Repairs & Replacements:

Replacement of bathroom exhaust fans	$210
Replacement and adjustment of interior door	300
Bifold doors	
replacement	300
repair	150
Replacement of carpet pad	400
Renailing of floors allowance	400
Repair of porcelain chips in tubs and sinks	100
Replacement of porcelain sinks	700
Ceramic tile repair allowance	600
Wallpaper repair allowance	200
Installation of smoke detectors	800
Steam clean units ("as is" only)	1,700
Misc. maintenance supplies for units	3,100
Cleaning	
One bedroom	660
Two bedroom	1,520
Patio door replacement	500
Patio door adjustment	500
Repair of texture ceilings	1,800
Painting	
One bedroom 11 units × $300 . . .	3,000
Two bedroom 19 units × $340 . . .	6,460
Installation of kitchen lights	1,650
Contingencies	1,700
Total	**$27,950**

Interior—Individual Unit/Appliances/Repairs & Replacement

Air conditioning units				
replaced	10%	3@$295	$	885
repaired	30%	9@ 100		900
Refrigerators				
replaced	10%	3@$360		1,080
repaired	30%	9@ 95		855
parts replaced .	40%	12@ 30		360
Ranges/Ovens (gas, continuous cleaning)				
replaced	10%	3@$435		1,305
repaired	30%	9@ 95		855
parts replaced .	40%	12@ 30		360
Range exhaust hoods				
replaced	10%	3@$ 65		195
repaired	25%	8@ 30		240

Dishwashers

replaced	15%	5@$250	1,250
repaired	25%	8@ 85	680
parts replaced	40%	12@ 30	360

Garbage disposals

replaced	30%	9@$ 60	540

Countertops—kitchen

replaced	20%	6@$250	1,500
adjusted	25%	8@ 65	520

Cabinets—kitchen

replaced	20%	6@$350	2,160
adjusted	45%	14@ 20	280

Vanities

replaced	20%	6@$200	1,200
repaired	30%	9@ 30	270

Total $15,795

Mechanical And Electrical—Common:

Inspection of and adjust elevator, cab decorating allowance $850

Maintenance allowance for MATV and security systems 1,200

Maintenance allowance for fire emergency service 500

Engineering fees for inspection 750

Replacement of bleeder valves 500

Maintenance of boiler fan unit 150

Contingency allowance for mechanical systems 1,200

Construction of protective cage around fuel oil pump 300

Repair of rooftop noisy fan units 1,000

Contingencies 4,500

Total $10,950

Common Areas Interior:

Lobby decorating allowance $1,500

Decorating of front vestibule 500

Additional hallway lighting 600

Painting and repair of hall ceilings 775

Painting and repair of hallway walls . 6,500

Cleaning of carpet—hallways, entryways, and stairwells (twice) 800

Laundry room decorating allowance . 2,100

Sound proofing of laundry room 1,500

Sauna/exercise decorating, sauna/exercise repair allowance 1,000

Storage lockers 1,200

Emergency light system 800

Locksmith allowance 200

Exterminator 500

Clean windows 500

Guest room decorating 2,500
(paint, carpet, furniture, lights, drapes)

Garage repair 6,000
(waterproofing, ceiling)

Restriping of garage stalls, numbering garage stalls 300

Lighting added to garage 100

Contingencies 5,500

Total $32,875

Common Areas Exterior:

Additional landscaping $6,000

Exterior remodeling (paint/stain) 6,500

Exterior carpenter repair 500

Painting of outside barbeques 50

Servicing of outside barbeques 150

Repair of balconies 500

Concrete patio repairs 200

Weatherstripping 300

Adjusting of doors 300

Locksmith allowance 150

Patch bituminous and sealcoat 2,000

Degreasing of parking areas and garages 250

Garage door repair, garage door adjustment 700

Painting of curb 75

Roof repair contingency 4,000

Building caulking 5,000

Repair of exterior lighting allowance . . 500

Screen allowance 500

Masonry repairs 2,000

Tuck Pointing 1,500

Contingencies 5,000

Total $37,675

Common Areas Exterior	$37,675
Common Areas Interior	32,875
Mechanical and Electrical—Common	10,950
Interior Individual Unit/Appliances/Repairs and Replacement	15,795
Interior Individual Unit Repair and Replacement	27,950

Grand Total $125,245

Cost of Decorator Packages:

One-Bedroom Apt.

Carpet and installation	$640
Refrigerator	360
Gas range hood	485
Dishwasher	240
Garbage disposal	55
5 percent added for price increase	89

Total $1,869

Two-Bedroom Apt.

Carpet and installation	$865
Refrigerator	360
Gas range hood	485
Dishwasher	240
Garbage disposal	55
5 percent added for price increase	100

Total $2,105

Condominium Association—Projected Annual Budget of Common Area Expenses (Calendar Year 1980)

Administrative

Accounting/Legal	$1,000
Office Expense	200
Management Fee	4,500
Misc. Administration	275
Insurance[2]	2,773
License/Permits	200

Repairs & Maintenance

Misc. Grounds	$200
Heating Systems	1,500
Security	400
Supplies	475
General Repairs and Maintenance	2,170

Contract Services

Elevator	$850
Exterminating	120
Rubbish Removal	640
Lawn and Snow Removal	4,800
Cleaning Service	2,400

Utilities

Electric	$3,500
Fuel Oil[3]	4,000
Gas[3]	5,000
Water/Sewer	1,950
Unclassified/Emergency Account	$700
Total Operating Expenses	$37,653
Replacement Reserve	$1,500
Total Income Requirements	$39,153
Less Laundry Income	(600)
Less Guest Room Income	(240)
Net Common Areas Expenses	$38,313

Notes:

[1] The purchase price of each condominium unit includes one or two parking spaces valued at $3,000 each.

[2] Includes public liability and property insurance on building and individual apartments (not including personal liability or property such as furniture, clothing, etc.). Directors and Officers' liability insurance included.

[3] Includes heat and cooking fuel for individual apartments.

Developer:

Lanvesco Corporation
6600 France Avenue South #490
Edina, Minnesota 55435
(612) 927-4004

Permanent Financing:

Hennepin Federal
818 Marquette Avenue
Minneapolis, Minnesota 55402
(612) 371-5718

Management:

Community Management Co.
6400 Flying Cloud Drive
Eden Prairie, Minnesota 55344
(612) 941-9050

ATS (Creative Transitions, Inc.)
6600 France Avenue South #680
Edina, Minnesota 55435
(612) 926-8075

Structural Engineering:

Hage Construction Co.
142 West 61st Street
Minneapolis, Minnesota 55430
(612) 861-4243

Mechanical Engineering:

Owen Services
930 E. 80th Street
Bloomington, Minnesota 55420
(612) 854-3868

Laurel Tree

3-36 Attractive landscaping at the entrance is a feature of this 514-unit garden apartment conversion in San Pedro, California.

Laurel Tree, a 514-unit garden apartment complex, was originally completed in 1971 and was operated as a rental property until it was purchased by the developer for conversion in 1978. Located in San Pedro, California, in southern Los Angeles County, the project contains 27 separate buildings which are laid out in an irregular pattern. The development is divided into an adult section (359 units) and a family section (155 units) by a private street which runs the entire length of the site. The irregular siting of buildings, together with the use of grade differentials between buildings and extensive landscaping and other visual effects, has created an attractive private setting and has helped to minimize the impact of the project's relatively high density (22.2 dwelling units per gross acre).

In addition to its pleasant suburban ambiance, the project features spectacular views and a variety of amenities including three swimming pools, a wading pool, two recreation centers (with gyms, saunas, billiard rooms, kitchens, dance floors, and lounges), and two jacuzzis. The project also contains a security guard house with 24-hour security, five laundry rooms, and 908 covered and uncovered parking spaces (including a three-level parking facility).

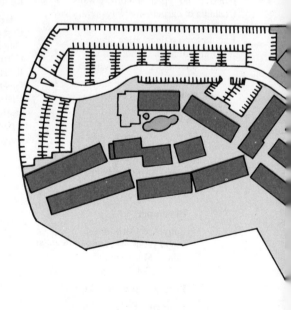

Adult Area
Family Area

3-37 Site plan.

76

The buildings have a California theme. The exteriors are tan stucco with dark brown wood trim and balconies and roofs of red concrete tile or asphalt shingles. Units are one, two, or three bedrooms and range in size from 694 to 1,272 square feet. The one- and three-bedroom units are all flats, while the two-bedroom units are all townhouses. Original sales prices to the public ranged from $48,138 to $74,023. The absorption rate was extremely high, with 437 units closed during the first year of the conversion. The final closing took place in February 1980.

The project's vacancy rate prior to conversion was relatively low (less than five percent). Fifteen tenants purchased units. (Tenant purchases for conversions in the southern California market average five to 10 percent.) All tenants were notified of the conversion by certified mail, and the notification and relocation process was coordinated by a relocation director on the developer's staff. In accordance with existing state legislation (as of 1979), tenants were given 120 days notice of the intent to convert and a 60-day right of first refusal. A 10 percent discount was given to all tenants and a five percent discount to outside buyers who purchased a unit in "as is" condition. As required by the subdivision tentative map, $200 in relocation assistance payments was provided to relocating tenants who presented itemized receipts of moving expenses to the developer.

3-38   A security guard house with 24-hour security is provided.

The Site

The 23.2-acre site is located on the east side of the Palos Verdes Peninsula immediately west of Long Beach and is readily accessible by freeways and major roadways. It is bordered on the west and east by Miraleste Drive and Western Avenue and on the north and south by First and Ninth Streets. The hillside site slopes from west to east and has dramatic ocean views as well as views of the San Pedro Harbor, the Palos Verdes bluffs, and a canyon which is located immediately to the south of the site. Many units have views of either the ocean, the harbor, or the canyon.

The city of San Pedro is a small community designed to accommodate a lifestyle of recreation and outdoor living, with the nearby marinas and beaches representing a major attraction for homeowners. Focal points close to the site include Marine Land, Cabrillo Beach State Park, the docked ocean liner the *Queen Mary,* Harbor Junior College, and the Ports 'O Call mall containing a variety of shops and restaurants. Laurel Tree is surrounded on all sides by high quality residential areas of Rancho Palos Verdes and San Pedro. These areas contain single-family detached homes which range in price from $125,000 to $750,000. Mixed residential and commercial uses are concentrated on and near Western Avenue to the east and in downtown San Pedro to the southeast.

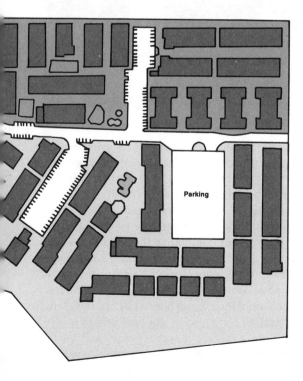

Parking

3-39 and 3-40   The project's irregular siting of buildings and extensive landscaping have created an attractive private setting and have minimized the impact of the project's relatively high density.

Conversion Feasibility

A market analysis was conducted by the developer in 1977 (prior to purchasing the project) in order to determine the feasibility of converting Laurel Tree to a condominium. This analysis identified a number of factors which indicated the feasibility of the conversion. These included:

- Significant growth in employment in Los Angeles County and a resultant shortage of ownership housing
- A pent-up demand of purchasers who had been priced out of the market but had the demographic characteristics to be homeowners
- A very high population density in the area surrounding the site
- Above average family incomes in the area, with an average family income in the area of approximately $21,000
- A generally favorable reaction to the area surrounding the site and to Laurel Tree, together with a high preference among residents of the area for purchasing a unit at Laurel Tree.

In addition to the factors identified in the market analysis, several other factors made the conversion feasible. First, the project is well situated, with easy accessibility, proximity to high quality single-family development and recreational opportunities, and scenic views. Second, the buildings were relatively new and were structurally sound, thus eliminating the need for extensive renovation. Third, the project featured sound land planning and design, mature landscaping, and a variety of outdoor and indoor recreational amenities. The existence of such amenities is considered by the developer to be imperative for a successful conversion in the Southern California market. Fourth, the project's unit mix and division into adult and family areas made it attractive to families as well as to singles and empty-nesters.

Renovation

The initial step in the renovation process was a detailed engineering and architectural inspection by the developer's staff. It was found that no systems or structural renovations were necessary. Renovation to the building's exteriors included the painting of the wood trim and balconies, the addition of stringers where necessary, and the installation of new drains, gutters, and downspouts. The building's stucco exteriors were in excellent condition and did not require refinishing.

Renovation of common areas included the laying out of a new parking plan (as required by the city) which provided 304 additional parking spaces. All parking areas were also restriped and resealed. Landscaping was refurbished throughout the project, and new sprinkler and drainage systems were installed. The existing recreational amenities were also upgraded. A new swimming pool and wading pool were added in the project's family section and an additional jacuzzi was installed in the adult section. The existing pools were replastered, and new pool decks were provided. Renovation of the two recreation centers included painting, new carpets and drapes, new pool equipment and furniture, and new gym equipment.

Both tenants and outside buyers had the option of purchasing units in "as is" condition. Renovation work on "as is" units was limited to major repairs, the installation of new air conditioners, and the refurbishing of appliances (with a one-year limited warranty provided on all appliances). Renovation work on "renovated" units included the following (in addition to the work done on "as is" units): new wall-to-wall carpeting and new kitchen floor tiles, new drapes, painting, and new dead bolt locks and viewers on front doors. Three options were offered for the carpeting and floor tiles.

Marketing

The marketing program was developed approximately 90 days before the opening of the project and relied primarily on advertising in the *Los Angeles Times,* as well as models and off-site signs. Advertising emphasized the project's excellent location, its quality design and sound land planning, its amenities, its 24-hour security, and the affordable sales prices (with 9 7/8 percent to 10 7/8 percent financing available). Sales were by the developer's own sales staff. A majority of the purchasers were first-time buyers and consisted primarily of singles, young marrieds, and middle-income families.

Condominium Association

The condominium association is governed by a five-member board of directors consisting of resident homeowners. The board works with the property management company and is responsible for running the association, establishing and enforcing rules and regulations, establishing committees, preparing an annual budget, and ensuring that enough money has been allocated for all reserve accounts. Association dues at the time of marketing were based upon individual unit square footages and averaged between $60 and $80 per month.

Experience Gained

- It is important for the developer to work with the existing tenants as much as possible and to be aware of their rights. An on-site tenant relocation director should be provided to meet with tenants and to assist them with relocation.
- Due to the extremely rapid absorption rate in 1979, the developer's objective when converting Laurel Tree was to have nonpurchasing tenants move out as quickly as possible. However, in other conversions which are currently being undertaken by the developer the objective has been to have a considerable number of nonpurchasing tenants continue renting for a period of time in order to maintain adequate cash flow. This has been necessary due to the slower absorption rates resulting from high interest.

3-41 The project features a variety of outdoor and indoor recreational amenities.

3-42 The buildings were designed to carry a California theme and have tan stucco exteriors with dark brown wood trim.

3-43 One-bedroom unit.

3-44 Two-bedroom unit.

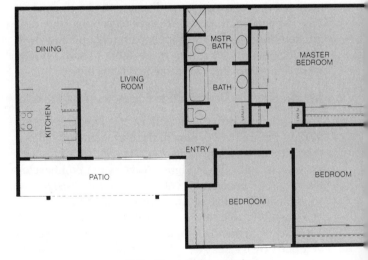

3-45 Three-bedroom unit.

- The extremely rapid absorption rate (437 units were sold in one year) made it impossible for the developer to complete the upgrading of all common areas and facilities prior to the first meeting of the board of directors of the condominium association. As a result, the board of directors has not released the developer's $500,000 bond covering the common area improvements, although this work was completed shortly after the first meeting of the board.

- Frequently, when control of the condominium association is transferred from the developer to the homeowners, the quality of the common area maintenance will decline, resulting in considerable dissatisfaction on the part of homeowners. Therefore, it is imperative that homeowners understand that following the transition the responsibility for all common area maintenance lies with the association and not with the developer, and that an increase in association dues may be necessary in order to allow common areas to be maintained to the quality desired by the homeowners.

- Although new kitchen appliances were not provided at Laurel Tree as part of the interior renovation, this did not have a negative impact on sales. However, it is the developer's belief that the dramatic changes which have occurred in the market since the conversion of Laurel Tree now make it necessary to provide new kitchen appliances as part of the renovation.

- In today's Southern California market, cosmetic renovation and recreational amenities are essential for a successful condominium conversion. Quality control and attention to detail are critical when undertaking the cosmetic renovation.

- Financing terms are much more critical to a successful conversion today than are the sales prices. Both interim and permanent financing must be secured by the developer before undertaking a conversion.

- Factors which must be considered in evaluating the general feasibility of a project for conversion include the project's location, the condition of the building or buildings, the common facilities and the landscaping, the size and the layout of the units, and the standards of tenants. The characteristics and standards of tenants (including factors such as the project's rent rolls, tenant incomes, and credit ratings of tenants) generally will indicate the standard of the project.
- The division of the complex into all adult and family sections has been a very successful feature.
- The ideal unit mix for a conversion in the Southern California market is 25 percent one-bedroom units, 50 percent two-bedroom units, and 25 percent three-bedroom units.
- Both tenants and outside buyers should have the option of buying units in "as is" condition. This can reduce renovation costs (thereby, reducing the amount of the construction loan) and make a more rapid sell-out possible.
- Interior design options available to buyers should generally be limited (except when dealing with the upper end of the market) in order to expedite the renovation process and thus reduce carrying costs. A design center will usually be very costly and, therefore, should not be provided in most cases.
- Many successful conversions undertaken by experienced converters involve a combination of "gut feeling" and staying power (that is, the ability to meet today's high carrying costs).

PROJECT DATA

Land Use Information:

Site Area: 23.2 acres (9.4 hectares)
Total Dwelling Units: 514
Gross Density: 22.2 d.u. per acre
Parking Spaces: 908

Economic Information:

Project Acquisition Cost:	$15,153,217
Renovation Costs:	$ 6,869,575
New Construction Costs:	$ 11,469
Amenities Costs:	$ 33,070
Marketing Costs:	$ 1,056,472
nance Costs:	$ 1,661,949
tal Costs:	$24,785,742
tal Sales:	$33,990,600
tal Rental Income:[1]	1,537,700
tal Revenue:	$35,528,300

Bathrooms	Sales Price[2]	Preconversion Rents[3]
1	$48,138	$265
1	$53,423	$275
1	$57,119	$285
2	$70,126	$310
2	$70,218	$325
2	$73,916	$335
2	$74,023	$400–410

Developer:

Daon Corporation
4041 MacArthur Boulevard
Newport Beach, California 92660
(714) 752-7855

Interim Financing:

Bank of Nova Scotia
San Francisco, California
(415) 986-1100

Permanent Financing:

Suburban Coastal Corporation
Newport Beach, California
(714) 640-4580

Sto-fed Mortgage Company
Newport Beach, California
(714) 752-6571

Structural and Mechanical Engineering:

Theodore Barry & Associates
Los Angeles, California 90017
(213) 413-6080

Civil Engineering

Psomas & Associates
Santa Monica, California 90405
(213) 450-1217

Stratford Green

3-46 and 3-47 The English Tudor theme of the 28, two-story brick buildings is apparent even in the recreational room (above).

Stratford Green is a 489-unit garden apartment conversion in suburban Chicago which has offered an exceptional home ownership opportunity for the first-time buyer of moderate income. Sales prices ranged from $23,500 for a one-bedroom, one-bath, 680-square-foot unit to $33,500 for a two-bedroom, one-bath, 920-square-foot unit. These low sales prices were made possible by limiting renovation work and by accepting lower profit margins than competitors. The low sales prices, together with attractive financing, resulted in extremely rapid sales which, in turn, resulted in lower than normal carrying costs (which are a significant part of overall conversion costs). In addition, the rapid sales rate has enabled the developer to undertake a larger volume of conversions than competitors, thus compensating for the reduced profit margins.

The project was purchased by the developer for conversion in September 1979. As a result of the low sales prices, more than one-half of the units were sold during the first quarter of 1980, representing one-fourth of all condominium conversion sales in the Chicago market during this period, and the entire project was sold out within 10 months. About 70 percent of the units were purchased by owner occupants and 30 percent were purchased by investors. Only units which were occupied by existing tenants were sold to investors.

The project was eight years old when it was purchased by the developer. It contains 28 two-story, brick buildings in an attractive English Tudor design. There are 236 one-bedroom units and 253 two-bedroom units. Buildings are sited around a man-made lake and courtyards. The floor plans are functional and units include features such as entries with guest closets, a patio or balcony adjoining the living room, air conditioning, carpeting, a ceramic bath with a separate vanity room, a fully applianced kitchen with an eating area and ample cabinet space, walk-in closets, and 24-hour maintenance.

Stratford Green also offers an amenity package. A recreation building on the premises includes a full basketball court, men's and women's locker rooms and saunas, an indoor whirlpool, party rooms, fully equipped exercise rooms, a lounge with a fireplace, and ping pong and game tables. An L-shaped outdoor pool with a sun deck adjoins the recreation building. Several playground areas for children have also been provided.

3-48 Site plan.

The Site

The 27-acre site has excellent access. It is located at the interchange of Interstate 55 and State Highway 83 in the Clarendon Hills area of DuPage County, Illinois, approximately 25 miles southwest of downtown Chicago. Both ''the loop'' and O'Hare International Airport are within convenient driving distance of the project. The Burlington commuter line is also nearby and offers service to downtown.

The surrounding area is a mixture of single-family detached homes, garden apartments, and commercial development. Several major shopping centers are a short drive from the site. A variety of recreational facilities are also nearby, including golf courses, a forest preserve with picnic areas, fishing, and tobaggan slides.

Renovation

As mentioned earlier, the developer's strategy was to limit renovation in order to allow sales prices to be kept low. An architect and structural and mechanical engineers were hired to inspect the project and make recommendations on the necessary renovation work. After reviewing these recommendations, the developer then made a decision on what renovation should be undertaken. The decision by the developer regarding the necessary renovation was made based on sound rental management principles—that is, what renovation would be necessary to compensate for deferred

3-49 The Stratford Green site features open space with a man-made lake and mature trees and landscaping.

maintenance and to place the project in optimum condition if it was to continue to operate as a rental property. Therefore, the renovation emphasized the completion of essential repair work, and cosmetic renovation was kept to a minimum. All units were sold in "as is" condition. However, the "as is" sale included the completion of all repair and painting as needed. Thus, the renovation of unit interiors was based upon the condition of the individual units.

Exterior renovation of buildings included repairing roofs, repairing gutters and downspouts, repairing damaged balconies, painting and staining of exterior wood trim and balconies, repairing exterior doors, and tuck-pointing and painting the exterior of the recreation building. Renovation of interior common areas included painting of hallways and replacement of worn carpeting, repairing of exhaust fans in the laundry areas, and repairing, cleaning, and adjusting boilers. Finally, renovation of the grounds included the patching of parking areas, the repair of a wooden fence along the western property line, the installation of safety fencing along the inlet to the man-made lake, the repair of children's play equipment, and the repair of light poles. The landscaping was in excellent condition and required only ordinary maintenance.

Financing

In addition to the low sales prices, the project's attractive financing was an important factor in its success and its affordability to moderate-income first-time buyers. Through a local savings and loan, the developer was able to offer financing to buyers at an 11.5 percent interest rate with as little as a five percent downpayment, thus making it possible for many buyers to have monthly payments following the purchases which were approximately the same as their previous monthly rent. For example, with a 20 percent downpayment on a $23,500 unit, monthly payments of approximately $290 covered the principal, interest, insurance, taxes, and condominium association dues. This was comparable to the monthly rent for the unit prior to conversion.

During the spring of 1980 when interest rates increased dramatically, the developer bought down the interest rate so that buyers could continue to get rates of about 12 percent. These buy-downs accounted for 20 percent of sales.

Handling of Tenants

In accordance with Illinois law, a letter stating the developer's intent to convert was mailed to all tenants providing them with 120 days notice of the conversion. Tenants were also given a 120-day right of first refusal. All tenants who purchased within 120 days were given a $500 discount on the sales price. Approximately 35 percent of the tenants purchased units.

3-50 Exterior renovation of the buildings included repairing damaged balconies and exterior doors as well as painting and staining the wood trim.

At the same time that tenants were notified of the conversion, they were also sent a letter giving them the option of renewing their lease for one year with a $10 increase in the monthly rent. In addition, 15 percent of all units were kept as rentals for senior citizens and hardship cases on a two-year lease at 1979 rents. All units which continued to be rented were sold to investors.

Tenants were not pressured to buy their units and only those tenants who were undesirable were evicted (that is, those tenants who could be legally evicted and should be evicted based on good rental management principles). A monthly newsletter sent to tenants reminded them of the opportunity to purchase their unit. Deposits of as little as $1,000 were accepted prior to the closing. If a tenant decided for some reason not to buy the unit following the signing of a contract, then the deposit was returned by the developer.

Marketing

The project's marketing program was limited. Furnished one- and two-bedroom models were used on-site to provide buyers with a full view of the units and the features of the two-story English Tudor buildings. Advertising, budgeted for $1,000 per week, was limited to the *Chicago Tribune*. The project also benefited from articles in the *Chicago Tribune*, the *Chicago Sun-Times*, and several other local suburban newspapers.

The majority of the units were purchased by younger buyers, although there were middle-age and retirement-age buyers as well. Sales were through the developer's own sales office.

Condominium Association

The condominium association bylaws were prepared by the developer's attorney during the initial stages of the conversion process. At the same time, surveys of each unit were made with a percentage of ownership assigned to each unit, and a budget was prepared for the operating expenses of the association. Following the sale of 75 percent of the units, control of the association was transferred from the developer, and officers of the association were elected by the owners. Prior to his departure, the developer signed over all association funds to the board of directors and presented them with all recorded documents and with a list of recommendations regarding the operation of the association. Finally, the developer appointed a management company to assist the board during the first two years of its operation.

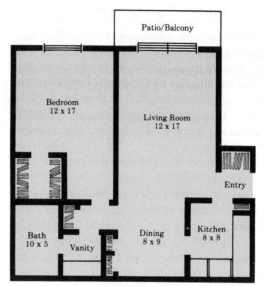

3-51 One-bedroom unit.

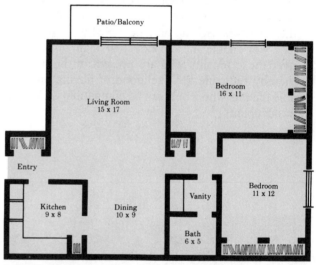

3-52 Two-bedroom unit.

85

Experience Gained

- Tenants should not be pressured to buy units. Only undesirable tenants should be evicted.
- Rental apartment projects which are approximately 10 years old are ideal for conversions. Generally, the acquisition cost for projects of this age will be reasonable, the quality of construction will be good, and a significant amount of structural and systems renovation will not be needed. Projects which are significantly younger than this may have poorer quality construction, while projects which are significantly older may require considerable renovation.
- The financial stability of the condominium association is important to the project's success. In this regard, it is advisable to set up an operating budget which includes reserves of 10 to 15 percent. Monthly association dues should be clearly stated to all purchasers.
- When selling units to both investors and owner occupants, it is wise not to sell unoccupied apartments to the investors. Selling only occupied units to investors will enable the developer to maintain control over those tenants who are present in the project, thereby reducing the likelihood of having undesirable tenants who would not be compatible with owner occupants.
- When market conditions are poor, one-bedroom units will generally be the best sellers. The developer believes that an ideal unit mix for conversions is two-thirds one-bedroom units and one-third two-bedroom units. Three-bedroom units are nearly always poor sellers.
- Garden apartment projects containing buildings with long corridors generally are not good candidates for conversion.
- Condominium conversions should be geared to the first-time buyer. Therefore, the emphasis should be on affordability and square footage instead of an extensive and costly cosmetic renovation.
- No more than 40 percent of the units should be sold to investors. Sales of more than 40 percent of the units to investors can present problems with regard to the smooth operation of the condominium association.
- Conversions can be profitable to the developer while at the same time being affordable to the moderate-income, blue-collar buyer. Performing only essential renovation will allow sales prices to be kept low without sacrificing profitability. The low sales prices combined with attractive financing will, in turn, encourage high sales volume, allowing a rapid sell-out and minimizing the project's carrying costs.

3-53   The landscaping was in excellent condition and required only ordinary maintenance as part of the conversion.

PROJECT DATA

Land Use Information:

Site Area: 27 acres
Total Dwelling Units: 489
Gross Density: 18.1 d.u. per acre
Parking: 1.75 spaces per d.u.

Unit Information:

Unit Type	D.U. Size	Number	Bathrooms	Sales Price	Preconversion Rents
One bedroom	680 sq.ft.	236	1	$23,500–$24,500	$285–315
Two bedroom	920 sq.ft.	253	1	$32,500–$34,500	$320–340

Economic Information:

Renovation Costs:

Exteriors and Common Areas . $600,000
Interiors 150,000

   Total .... $750,000[1]

Soft Costs (per unit):

Legal $150
Architect 50
Surveys 75
Advertising 100
Models 20
Sales fees 100
Operating costs 25

   Total ....$520 per unit[2]

Condominium Association Dues:

One-bedroom unit .. $ 75–80 per month
Two-bedroom
unit .... $105–110 per month

Developer:

Vigilante Realty, Builders and Management
425 Talcott Road
Park Ridge, Illinois 60068
(312) 825-6660

Notes:

[1] Per unit renovation cost was approximately $1,500. Hard costs only.

[2] Does not reflect total carrying costs for the project of $1 million.

1980 Condominium Association Budget:

Expenses

Management Services
   Expense $41,000.00
   Audit 3,000.00

Operating

Common Area Electric 45,000.00
Gas 120,000.00
Water and Sewer 47,000.00
Janitors (three full-time) 54,600.00
Union Welfare and Pension ... 10,500.00

Payroll Taxes Est. 22,000.00
Security Guard 27,500.00
Insurance 30,000.00
Licenses 500.00
Contingency or Reserve 28,000.00

Recreation Building

Recreation Director 14,000.00
Budget for Recreation Program .. 500.00
Life Guards and Pool
Supplies 4,500.00

Maintenance and Repair

Maintenance Engineer and
   Assistant 43,600.00
Exterminating 3,000.00
Scavenger 10,000.00
Landscaping 30,000.00
Snow Removal 11,000.00

   Total Expense $545,700.00

Income

Laundry (Estimate) 15,000.00
   Total Income 15,000.00

   Net Operating Expense $530,700.00

The Arlington

3-54 Exterior renovation has transformed the Arlington from its original row appearance to the varied appearance of individual townhouses.

3-55 Units are located in two- and three-story buildings which are clustered to form individual courtyards.

The Arlington is an example of an unsuccessful, deteriorating rental apartment complex which was converted to extremely successful condominiums. At the time the 518-unit, garden apartment project in Arlington, Virginia, was purchased for conversion, it was known as the Claremont Apartments and was characterized by high vacancy rates, comparatively low rents, and numerous building violations and safety hazards. Its assessed value at the time of purchase was less than $10,000 per unit. Those tenants remaining were predominantly lower-income families from a mixture of national origins. If left to continue as a rental complex, the project eventually would have been condemned, abandoned, and demolished. Any new housing which might have been constructed probably would have been affordable only to upper-income buyers.

Despite the project's deteriorating condition at the time of purchase, a number of factors indicated its potential success as a conversion. First, the project is strategically located. It enjoys a suburban location yet is within a short commute of downtown Washington, D.C. Second, although requiring significant renovation, the project's buildings are structurally sound and the site offers abundant open space and attractive mature landscaping. Third, the Washington, D.C., market is ideally suited for condominiums, with a high concentration of young, upwardly mobile, middle- to upper-middle-income residents. Finally, there is an acute demand in the market for affordable ownership housing for the first-time buyer which is being met, in part, by moderately priced condominium conversions.

3-56   The 28-acre site offers abundant open space and mature landscaping.

The project was originally completed in 1952 and was purchased by the developer for conversion in 1978. Sales began in March 1979, and as of December 1980 over 340 units had been sold. It is projected that The Arlington will be sold out by October 1981. The conversion has been undertaken in eight phases.

The project's 518 units are located in 54 two- and three-story buildings which are offset in clusters to form individual courtyards. Five different floor plans are offered which are geared toward sophisticated and upwardly mobile buyers. Units are either one or two levels and feature patios or balconies and fireplaces. They range in size from 755 to 1,576 square feet, and most have two bedrooms and one bath. Approximately 45 units have three bedrooms and two baths. Sales prices as of January 1981 ranged from $70,990 to $98,990 (with most units priced in the low- to mid-70s), compared to a price range of $46,990 to $69,990 when sales opened in March 1979.

Extensive exterior and interior renovation of the buildings has dramatically changed the project's character and appearance. In addition to the renovation of the buildings, the grounds were refurbished and new amenities were added, including two swimming pools, two bath houses, two lighted tennis courts, and two volleyball courts.

89

The Arlington has been significant not only for its creation of moderately priced ownership housing, but also for its role as a catalyst for neighborhood revitalization. The project's deterioration prior to conversion had a negative impact on the surrounding neighborhood. The area had become a high crime area, placing a financial burden on Arlington County. However, with the conversion this trend has been reversed completely and The Arlington has made a significant contribution to the county's tax base.

The Site

The 28-acre site is located at the intersection of Route 7 and South Walter Reed Drive, approximately five miles from downtown Washington, D.C. Access to downtown is provided along Interstate-395, and convenient bus transportation is available at the site. The area surrounding the site is a mixture of residential (single-family detached, townhouses, and condominiums) and commercial uses. The project is nestled between Fairlington Villages (a condominium conversion), Windgate (a new townhouse development), the King Street commercial center, and Jefferson Davis Memorial Hospital. In addition to Fairlington Villages, another conversion (Parkfairfax) is close by. Since the initial conversion sales in these two projects are, for the most part, complete, the only direct conversion competition to The Arlington is from their resales.

The site is irregular in shape. Its many mature trees and open areas provide an atmosphere of low density suburban living. Portions of the site contain wooded areas which offer buffers from the surrounding arterial roads and other uses. The site also offers topographic variety, with relatively steep slopes on its southern and eastern borders and flat areas to the north and west.

Exterior Renovation and Design

The extensive exterior renovation was designed to dramatically alter the project's image and character, as well as to provide the necessary repairs. The harsh row appearance and visual monotony of the buildings' original red brick exteriors has been transformed into the varied appearance of individual townhouse units. This variety in facades has been provided in a number of ways. In many areas, the red brick either has been painted white or light yellow, or has been covered with white or light yellow aluminum siding. Thus, the red brick now alternates with either clapboard exteriors or with white or yellow brick. Mansard roofs have also been added in some areas and help to break up the straight line of the buildings' facades. French doors, bay windows, iron balconies, and patios also have been provided to create even more of an individual appearance. Patios enclosed by red brick walls and white picket fencing were located to the front of some units, while patios enclosed with wood fencing were located to the rear.

3-57 Site plan.

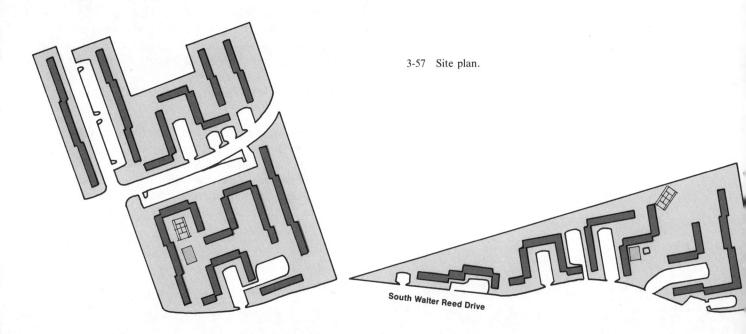

South Walter Reed Drive

3-58 Units feature balconies or patios as well as fireplaces.

Existing windows were replaced with new white aluminum windows which have helped to brighten the buildings' exteriors. Some windows were also added on end units to enhance unit views and to provide additional light for the interiors. Existing entrances to the buildings' foyers (four units per foyer) were replaced with a variety of wood frame, colonial-style entrances which have heightened the colonial theme of the exterior renovation. All of the new foyer entrances are painted white. The buildings' existing slate roofs were in poor condition and had to be replaced. This provided an opportunity to further emphasize the appearance of individual townhouses by using two kinds of roof surfaces (either metal or asbestos shingles) in a variety of colors.

In addition to the renovation of the buildings' exteriors, renovation of the project's common areas was needed. This renovation included the repaving of streets and parking areas, the repair of curbs, gutters, and sidewalks, the planting of new trees and shrubs, and the sprucing up of existing landscaping. As mentioned earlier, a variety of amenities was also provided.

3-59 French doors and bay windows have been added.

Renovation of Utility Systems

As part of the conversion, the project's original central boiler network was eliminated and replaced with individually metered electric heating and air conditioning systems for each of the units. A central hot water tank was provided for each group of buildings. The existing electrical and plumbing systems were also replaced, including some of the lateral plumbing lines from the buildings to the trunk sewers.

Unit Interiors

Five floor plans have been provided, including three different single-level plans and two two-level plans. Although the units are relatively small (most range in size from 755 to 875 square feet), the floor plans are creative. Woodburning fireplaces are available in most units. In some of the two-level units, old boiler rooms (which were no longer needed with the installation of the new heating and air conditioning system) were renovated for use.

Unit interiors prior to the conversion had bathroom floors of ceramic tile and bathroom walls of either ceramic tile or plaster. Interior walls in all other rooms were plaster, as were the ceilings. Floors in the kitchen were vinyl and all remaining floors were parquet wood. The use of concrete for the ground floor slabs as well as for the upper floors, together with thick walls, assured minimal sound transmission between units.

All unit interiors were extensively renovated. The focus in the interior renovation was on the kitchens and bathrooms. New kitchen appliances were provided, including a range and oven with a vented range hood, a refrigerator-freezer, a dishwasher, and a garbage disposal. Other standard kitchen features provided included a stainless steel sink, Formica countertops and cabinets, cushioned vinyl flooring, and designer lighting. A variety of options also were offered including microwave ovens and other alternate appliances, washers and driers (laundry areas with washer and drier connections were standard unit features), and a range of selections for kitchen flooring. Bathrooms were painted and provided with new sinks, bathtubs, shower enclosures, toilets, custom-quality vanity counters, designer lighting, mirrored medicine cabinets, and easy care vinyl flooring.

All units were painted white and the option of wall-to-wall carpeting (including full installation) for the living and sleeping areas was offered (with a wide selection of alternate carpeting available). A décor center and an interior decorator were provided at the sales office to assist buyers in the selection of optional features. All carpet and floor samples as well as the appliance options were displayed at the décor center.

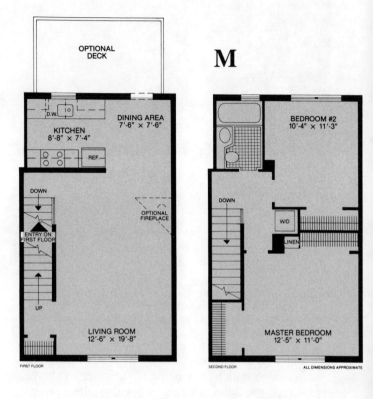

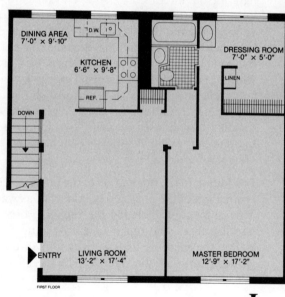

3-60 Floor plans.

92

Tenant Relations

The establishment and maintenance of good relations with tenants was an important consideration of the developer during the conversion. An ombudsman was hired by the developer to handle tenant relations and was available to tenants 24 hours a day. This proved to be particularly helpful in alleviating the fears and concerns of tenants. A major role also was played by the ombudsman in finding new housing for those tenants who did not purchase units, an extremely important factor since most tenants did, in fact, relocate.

In accordance with Virginia law at the time the condominium was registered, tenants were given 90 days notice of the conversion and the first rights of refusal (this legislation has since been changed and now requires 120 days notice). For foreign language tenants, these notices were translated into their native tongue. In addition to fulfilling the state requirements, the developer voluntarily offered an incentive program to allow tenants who would not normally buy an opportunity to do so. This program provided a $2,500 discount off the base price, plus an additional $25 per month discount for every month of tenancy and for every month a tenant was over the age of 62. Those tenants who did not purchase were given relocation assistance through the early refund of their security deposit (and, in some cases, the payment of security deposits for new apartments), help in finding alternative housing, and payment of their moving expenses. In addition, the developer and the ombudsman worked with the Arlington County Tenant Landlord Commission to provide special handling for foreign speaking, low-income, disabled, and elderly tenants.

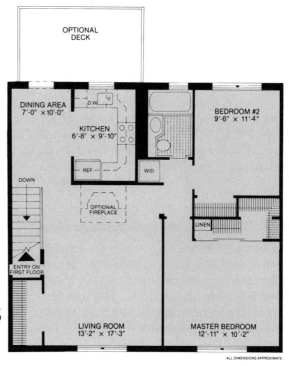

Market Considerations

Marketing to tenants was primarily through letters with invitations to visit the sales office to discuss questions, concerns, and purchasing. The general public was offered the opportunity to sign up on the waiting list by placing a refundable $250 deposit. Purchasers were called in turn as units became available for sale. The priority waiting list program lasted 1½ years with over 1,400 people registered.

Since this time marketing has been via *The Washington Post,* the local *New Homes Guide,* radio spots, and various magazines. The marketing program has emphasized the project's proximity to downtown Washington, D.C., its location within an established, suburban community, its open space, its attractive and mature landscaping, and its on-site parking. The long-range financial benefits of home ownership and the availability of below-market-rate financing have also been stressed, as have the buildings' sound construction and colonial-style architecture.

Most buyers have been young (the average age is about 30), single, professionals employed in Washington, D.C. The average buyer income is approximately $28,000. Approximately half of the buyers have been female.

Condominium Association

The bylaws of the condominium association were recorded in March 1979. Control of the association will remain with the developer until 75 percent of the units have been sold and settled. The five-member board of directors (terms range from one to three years) is responsible for governing the affairs of the association, entering into contracts on its behalf, making decisions regarding rules and regulations, and any other duties required for the smooth operation of the association. The association has an active network of committees, manned by individual homeowners, which provide input to the board on matters of finance, buildings and grounds maintenance, architectural integrity, and similar items. The association's monthly assessments for 1981 range from $57.61 to $123.08 per unit and are used for the payment of water bills, trash and snow removal, and the maintenance of recreational facilities and common areas. Electric service is metered and charged separately.

Experience Gained

- In order to eliminate unnecessary tenant fears and to avoid negative publicity, it is imperative that tenant concerns be carefully addressed and that the tenant notice/move-out cycle be controlled. This can best be done by hiring an ombudsman to handle tenant relations and communications. Typically, the ombudsman should be a public relations professional who is able to identify with the fears and concerns of tenants and who does not represent the developer. The ombudsman should basically be given a free rein by the developer, contacting the developer only when major problems arise, and should be available to tenants 24 hours a day. The additional cost of hiring an ombudsman will be more than compensated for by smooth tenant relations and the absence of adverse publicity.

- The ombudsman will be particularly important when dealing with poor, minority, and elderly tenants. An essential role will be played by the ombudsman during negotiations with tenants whose leases have not expired and when providing relocation assistance. Assistance by the ombudsman in these areas will tend to enable units to be vacated more quickly, expediting the conversion process. Therefore, both the tenants and the developer will benefit.

- Special relocation assistance should be provided by the developer to elderly, poor, and handicapped tenants. Such assistance might include paying for packing and moving and providing security deposits for the tenants' new apartments.

- A conversion should not be undertaken unless financing has been preselected and prepaid, particularly during periods of high interest rates. The availability of prepaid financing at below-market interest rates will allow sales to continue, thus enabling the developer to make the necessary payments on high-interest construction loans. The Arlington has been able to offer buyers who occupy the units 30-year conventional financing at below-market rates (10 5/8 percent to 11 7/8 percent during a period of 15 to 16 percent financing) with as little as a five-percent downpayment.

- With a conversion involving extensive renovation, it will usually be difficult to project realistic delivery dates for buyers. In most instances, unforeseen delays and hidden costs will be encountered during extensive renovation.

- When converting a previously unsuccessful rental project which has significant deterioration, it is essential that the project's image be completely changed. This new image can best be achieved by significantly altering the project's exterior appearance and by changing its name.

- A rule-of-thumb used by the developer is that for every $1,000 of renovation work per unit, the sales price of the unit will increase by approximately $5,000.

- Washer and drier connections will be important selling features, especially when a majority of the project's buyers are former apartment renters. After having to use laundry rooms for some time, former apartment renters will be greatly attracted by the opportunity to have washers and driers in their units.

- The condition of kitchens and bathrooms following the conversion will be a significant factor to many prospective purchasers. Therefore, kitchens and bathrooms should be made as attractive as possible by providing new kitchen appliances and cabinets, new sinks, new bathtubs, and new toilets.

- Although only five unit types were actually offered for sale, a total of 17 unit types were designed and recorded. The existence of these additional unit types offers the option of easily replacing any of the five unit types if they should begin to sell poorly.

- In the project's first phase, fireplaces were only offered as options in 50 percent of the units which could accommodate them (the "B" and "M" plans). However, these proved to be such popular selling features that they were offered as options in 90 percent of the "B" and "M" plan units in the second phase, and as options in all of the "B" and "M" plan units in the third and subsequent phases. The balconies/patios also proved to be popular selling features.

PROJECT DATA

Land Use Information:

Site Area: 28 acres (11.34 hectares)
Total Dwelling Units: 518
Gross Density: 18.5 d.u. per acre
Net Density: 43.2 d.u. per acre
Parking: 1.12 spaces per d.u.

Land Use Plan:

	Acres	Percent
Buildings	8.0	29.0
Parking/Circulation ...	4.0	14.0
Open Space	16.0	57.0
Total	28.0	100.0

Unit Information:

Unit Type	D.U. Size	Number	Bedrooms	Bathrooms	Sales Price[3]	Pre-conversion Rents
A–Garden	755 sq.ft.	105	2	1	$72,990	$250
B–Garden[1]	800 sq.ft.	147	2	1	$75,990	$260
C–Garden	810 sq.ft.	71	2	1	$70,990	$250
L–Townhouse[2]	1,576 sq.ft.	45	2-3	2	$98,990	N.A.
M–Townhouse[1,2]	875 sq.ft.	143	2	1	$79,990	$325
To be determined	N.A.	7	N.A.	N.A.	N.A.	N.A.

Economic Information:

Site and Building Cost: $9,616,174
Construction Cost: $15,058,653[4]
Marketing and Warranty Costs: $2,164,000
Finance Costs: $4,893,415
Conversion Fees: $1,481,557
Total Conversion Costs: $33,213,799
Total Sales Income: $37,101,264

Notes:
[1] Optional fireplace.
[2] Two-level unit.
[3] Sales prices as of January 1981.
[4] Includes $180,000 amenities cost.

Developer:

Klingbeil Management Group Company
5900 Prince James Drive
Springfield, Virginia 22152
(703) 569-4914

Engineering:

Delashmutt Associates
1327 North Court House Road
Arlington, Virginia 22201
(703) 527-2588

Architecture:

Brown and Page
1320 Prince Street
Alexandria, Virginia 22314
(703) 549-7474

Landscape Architecture:

The Berkus Group
1048 Potomac Street, N.W.
Washington, D.C. 20007
(202) 333-1440

Interim Financing:

Continental Bank and Trust
231 La Salle Street
Chicago, Illinois 60693
(312) 828-2345

Permanent Financing:

Dominion Federal Savings and Loan
8301 Greensboro Drive
McLean, Virginia 22102
(703) 734-9000

Washington Federal Savings and Loan
5101 Wisconsin Avenue, N.W.
Washington, D.C. 20016
(202) 537-8200

University Place

University Place is a 76-unit garden apartment conversion located approximately five miles north of the central business district of Dallas, Texas. The project was built in 1963 and contains six two-story, brick veneer buildings which are arranged in an irregular rectangle to form a spacious interior courtyard and are joined by covered passageways. This courtyard is heavily landscaped with mature trees and shrubs and features a swimming pool and deck area and outdoor barbeque grills.

One hundred and forty eight on-site parking spaces are provided, including 96 spaces covered by carports. All parking is to the rear of the buildings. One parking space was assigned to each unit purchaser and the remaining spaces are open parking.

3-61, 3-62, and 3-63   The buildings have brick-veneer exteriors, flat mansard-style roofs, and colonial-style enclosed foyer entrances. They surround an attractively landscaped interior courtyard.

The units range in size from 1,286 to 1,751 square feet and contain two bedrooms and two or two-and-one-half baths. All units were sold unfinished, although the option of interior renovation following the sale was offered by the developer and was requested by most buyers. Sales prices for the unfinished units ranged from $44,100 to $62,700 and the average interior renovation cost per unit was $3,725. Rents prior to conversion ranged from $340 to $380 per month. Unit features include front and rear entrances, either patios or balconies, walk-in closets, formal dining rooms, foyer entrances, fireplaces (in about half the units), dens, and crystal chandeliers.

The project had been successful as a rental complex and when it was purchased by the developer in December 1977, it was 100 percent occupied. Despite month-to-month tenancies, most tenants had occupied their apartments for five years or more. Seventeen of the 76 tenants, or 23 percent, purchased units. About 10 percent, on average, of the tenants had purchased their units in other Dallas area conversions by the developer. The developer provided elderly tenants with limited incomes the option of continuing to rent. All tenants were notified of the conversion with a personal visit 30 days in advance and carefully informed of their options. No general public notice of the conversion was required.

The conversion process for the project was initiated in September 1978 and most sales were completed by June 1979. The last unit was sold in December 1979. There are no conversion restrictions in Dallas and, in general, there is a favorable attitude in the market toward conversions. In addition, the market currently has a favorable supply and demand situation for conversions.

The Site

The project is ideally located and enjoys easy access to the central business district of Dallas as well as to other employment centers and shopping. The 4.37-acre site is situated at the southwest corner of University Boulevard and Skillman Avenue. University Boulevard is a major east/west arterial running through the neighborhood and the Southern Methodist University campus. Skillman Avenue is a major north/south arterial and, together with the North Central Expressway and Greenville Avenue, carries a high volume of daily traffic to and from the central business district. Bus transportation to downtown and other areas of the city is provided along University Boulevard.

The area surrounding the site consists primarily of well maintained, low density, garden apartments constructed during the 1960s and is 95 percent developed. There are over 20 garden apartment projects in the area, including 12 which have been converted to condominiums in recent years. The neighborhood is characterized by older, upper-middle-income residents. Two very successful regional shopping centers, North Park and Old Town, are a short drive from the site, as are several high-rise office buildings.

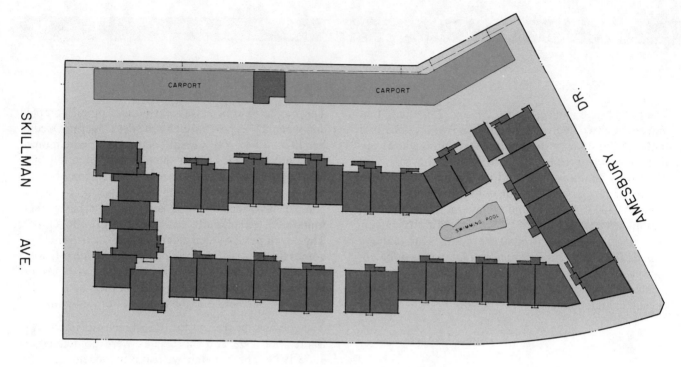

3-64   Site plan.

SKILLMAN AVE.

UNIVERSITY BLVD.

DR.

AMESBURY

CARPORT

CARPORT

SWIMMING POOL

Exterior Architecture and Renovation

The project's six two-story buildings have concrete pier and beam foundations, brick veneer exteriors, flat mansard-style roofs, and colonial-style enclosed foyer entrances (with one foyer for every four units). All of the buildings were structurally sound prior to the conversion and, therefore, no structural repairs were necessary. However, due to inadequate maintenance, a number of minor repairs had to be undertaken on the buildings' exteriors as part of the conversion process. The buildings' roofs were leaking in some spots and nearing the end of their economic life. Therefore, the original tar, gravel, and plywood surface on the flat portions of the roofs was completely removed and replaced with a new surface. The existing asbestos shingles on the roofs' sloping portions also were replaced with light grey asbestos shingles. All of the buildings' wood trim was caulked and repainted light grey (from its original green). Some of the wooden foyer entrance doors were rotting and had to be replaced, as did the wooden portion of one of the metal balconies. The buildings' buff colored brick was in good condition and required no work.

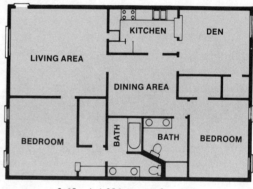

3-65   A 1,286-square-foot unit.

KITCHEN

DEN

LIVING AREA

DINING AREA

BEDROOM

BATH

BATH

BEDROOM

The project's grounds were also suffering from inadequate maintenance and required some repair work and sprucing up. The swimming pool had been leaking and required relining as well as the installation of a new filter system and new pumps. In addition, all pool pumps and filtering equipment were relocated away from the units to provide additional unit privacy. All driveways and parking areas were repaved and new sidewalks were installed where necessary. New fencing was erected to the rear of those buildings which are adjacent to the parking area, and an attractive iron gate was added at the project's front entrance. Also, landscape gardeners were used to treat and tidy up the site's many trees, shrubs, and lawn areas, and the outside sprinkler system was repaired.

98

Interior Architecture and Renovation

The units' spacious interiors and a variety of other features made them ideal for conversion. All units had separate front and rear entrances and most had either balconies (for second floor units) or enclosed patios (for ground floor units). Other features present before conversion included large windows, paneled dens (with patio or balcony doors off each den), brick fireplaces covering one wall of the den (in 40 of the units), separate formal dining rooms, crystal chandeliers, decorative moldings, and walk-in closets in the bedrooms. Kitchen features included a double stainless steel sink, a dishwasher, and a garbage disposal. All bathrooms had tile floors and vanity tops and double sinks in the master baths. Floors in the living room, dining room, den, and bedrooms were all carpeted. All roofs and walls were insulated at the time of construction and the buildings' solid construction eliminated the need for further soundproofing.

As part of the conversion process the project's central heating and air conditioning system was replaced with individually metered heating and cooling for each unit. Washer and drier connections were provided for each unit although two laundry rooms were also left. Since units were sold unfinished, interior renovation was left to the buyer's discretion. However, in most instances, buyers chose to take advantage of the interior renovation services offered by the developer. An estimated interior redecorating cost was given to each buyer at the time of purchase. A fairly standard package of interior design features, including new appliances, interior painting, and new carpeting, was made available. Buyers met with the project's interior designer to select from the various features available. Only a few buyers selected all of the available options and completely upgraded their units. In all cases, it was possible for the developer to undertake the interior renovation of these units purchased by tenants without the tenants having to vacate their units temporarily. Most interior renovations took approximately two weeks to complete.

Market Considerations

The project's most important selling feature was its location, with its proximity to downtown, its convenience to some of the best shopping in Dallas, and its attractive neighborhood setting. The upper-middle-income, adult character of the neighborhood was significant to many buyers. The project's many unit features and amenities, particularly the attractively landscaped courtyard, were also crucial to its marketability.

Approximately 70 percent of the buyers were over 55 and 30 percent were in their late 20s or early 30s. The average income was approximately $40,000. Children under the age of 16 were not permitted as permanent residents without the approval of the condominium association's board of directors.

3-66   All units have front and rear entrances and either patios or balconies.

Advertising was primarily in the classified ads, although some color display ads were used. A number of articles in the real estate sections of local newspapers were also helpful. Limited billboard advertising also proved successful. Model units were an integral part of the marketing program, since all units were sold with unfinished interiors.

Condominium Association

The condominium association is governed by a seven-member board of directors which is responsible for the maintenance, repair, and surveillance of the project's common elements, for the assessment and collection of dues, and for the maintenance of a detailed account of the receipts and expenditures affecting the project. Four of the board's initial members were appointed for two-year terms, while the three remaining members were appointed for one-year terms. All successors of the initial members are elected to two-year terms.

The board of directors was controlled by the developer until 50 percent of the units had been sold. Following the transfer of control from the developer to the unit owners, the developer maintained one seat on the board for approximately one year. This helped to assure a smooth transition period. In addition, the developer worked closely with the association during its formation in order to make certain that it would function as efficiently as possible. The developer set up the original ledger for the association and worked with the association through the first audit. The developer was

99

also available to suggest a certified public accountant to the association and to advise the association regarding legal problems. However, a professional project manager was not recommended to the association since it was the developer's experience that associations from several different projects in a neighborhood usually will hire the same manager.

Experience Gained

- In order to ensure adequate cash flow during the initial stages of the conversion process, it is essential to keep as many units as possible occupied by tenants. Since those tenants who do not wish to purchase will generally vacate their units as soon as possible, it will often be necessary to re-lease many of these vacated units to maintain the desired cash flow.
- While it is important to keep most units occupied by tenants prior to their conversion, it is also imperative that an adequate inventory of vacant units be maintained. This inventory will enable the conversion process to continue uninterrupted. The timing of leases will be a critical factor in maintaining this inventory and, therefore, should be thoroughly investigated before purchasing a project for conversion.
- The sale of unfinished units greatly reduced the project's front-end costs, an important consideration during a period of extremely high financing costs. However, since buyers frequently are unable to visualize the various possibilities for the finishing of unimproved units, the use of finished models will be an essential marketing tool.
- In general, model units should be sold last, since selling the units earlier will make it necessary to provide new models, thereby increasing conversion costs. However, the sale of model units at an earlier date may be advisable during bad market conditions.
- Detailed engineering reports should be prepared before purchasing a project for conversion. If any major renovation work is needed, engineering consultants should be hired to set all specifications.
- The establishment of good relations with tenants and the community will be important to the project's success as well as to the success of future conversions undertaken by the developer in the same market.

- Although University Place was fully occupied at the time it was purchased for conversion, it has been the developer's experience that projects with high vacancy rates can also be successful conversions if they are strategically located. Location is the most important factor in determining the feasibility of conversion. Other important factors are the project's physical condition, the unit design, the unit mix, and the amenities available.
- When renovating units purchased and occupied by tenants, it is generally advisable to work around the occupants rather than asking them to temporarily relocate during the renovation period. Although renovating occupied units will increase renovation costs somewhat (approximately $.20 per square foot more than renovating a vacant unit) and be more time consuming, it generally will be better received by buyers than having to relocate temporarily during renovation.
- In order to minimize the time required by buyers in the selection of interior design options, and thereby expedite the interior renovation process, it is important to have all options displayed in one location and a limited number of options available.

3-67 The courtyard features a swimming pool, deck area, and barbecue grills.

3-68 Wooden fences provide a buffer between the rear yards and the parking lot.

PROJECT DATA

Land Use Information:

Site Area: 4.37 acres (1.78 hectares)
Gross Density: 17.4 d.u. per acre
Net Density: 27.9 d.u. per acre
Total Dwelling Units: 76
Parking:
  Spaces: 148[1]
  Index: 1.94 per d.u.

Land Use Plan:

	Acres	Percent
Buildings	2.72	62.36
Carports	.34	7.79
Pavement/Open Space	1.31	29.85
Total	4.37	100.00

Economic Information:

Site and Building Cost: $1,995,000 (1977)
Construction Cost: $462,715[2]
Soft Costs: $1,146,445[3]
Total Conversion Costs: $3,604,160

Total Sales: $3,799,172
Total Rental Income: $175,330[4]
Miscellaneous Income: $7,937
Total Income: $3,982,439

Average Interior Renovation Cost Per
  Unit: $3,725[5]
Condominium Association
  Dues: $68.48–$93.24 per month

Unit Information:

D.U. Size	Number	Bedrooms	Bathrooms	Sales Price
1,286 sq.ft.	34	2	2	$44,100–$46,100
1,355 sq.ft.	20	2	2	$47,000–$49,500
1,409–1,462 sq.ft.	10	2	2	$48,500–$52,400
1,500–1,572 sq.ft.	6	2	2-2½	$51,800–$54,700
1,654–1,658 sq.ft.	4	2	2½	$57,200–$59,200
1,751 sq.ft.	2	2	2½	$60,700–$62,700

Notes:
[1] Includes 96 covered spaces and 52 uncovered spaces.
[2] Hard costs only. Includes interior and exterior renovation costs.
[3] Includes advertising costs, financing costs, property taxes, insurance, depreciation, administrative expenses, and property operations costs.
[4] During conversion.
[5] Average interior renovation cost to the unit purchaser. All units were sold unfinished.

Developer:

Real Condominiums, Inc.
3700 Cedar Springs
Dallas, TX 75219
(214) 522-2500

Union Wharf

3-69 and 3-70   As part of the conversion of the historic granite warehouse on the Boston waterfront to 64 residential and office condominiums (above), the building's granite and brick exterior had to be chemically cleaned (below).

Union Wharf in Boston, Massachusetts, may be accurately described as an atypical condominium conversion for several reasons. First, unlike most conversions, it was a warehouse, not a rental apartment. Second, it was converted to a mixture of both office and residential condominiums rather than just residential condominiums. Third, all of the units were sold as raw space with no interior finishing provided. Although the sale of raw space per se is not unique, in most instances when units are sold unfinished the developer offers interior renovation services following the sale. However, with Union Wharf the developer did not participate at all in the renovation of unit interiors. The sole responsibility for the finishing of interiors was left with the purchaser.

Located on a 2.6-acre site on Boston's waterfront, the project is a conversion of a historic granite warehouse built in the mid 1840s into 64 residential and office condominiums (31 residential units and 33 office units) ranging in size from 933 to 4,000 square feet. Amenities provided include an outdoor swimming pool, landscaping, plaza areas, a roof deck on the granite building, and a marina with approximately 400 feet of dock space. In addition to the conversion of the granite warehouse, the project included the construction of 23 new townhouse units and the conversion of an old tin shed structure to two office units.

The developer's decision to sell the units unfinished, together with the mixture of residential and office uses and the combination of renovation and new construction, resulted in some difficulty in obtaining a financing commitment. The financing commitment included conditions for presales as well as certain equity requirements. The developer was required to presell 30 percent of the total number of units to prove both pricing and marketability. A few units were sold at a substantial discount to provide the additional equity required.

The site was purchased by the developer in April 1978, and the conversion process was started shortly thereafter. The project was completed and all units were sold by late 1979. Approvals were required by the Boston Redevelopment Authority (BRA), the State Historic Commission, and the Massachusetts Turnpike Authority, the latter because the Callahan Tunnel runs beneath the site.

3-71 A typical office interior after finishing by the buyer. Both the office and residential condominiums were sold by the developer as raw space with no interior finishing provided.

The Site

Located along Commercial Street, Union Wharf is the last of the four historic wharfs on Boston's waterfront to be recycled. It is bordered by Lincoln Wharf to the north, site of a defunct Massachusetts Bay Transit Authority (MBTA) power station, and Sargent's Wharf to the south, currently used as a public parking lot. The site is conveniently located. It is approximately a 10-minute drive from Logan Airport, two minutes from the Southeast Expressway, and within a five-minute walk of an MBTA stop. Faneuil Hall Marketplace, the downtown financial district, Lewis Wharf, Commercial Wharf, Long Wharf, Government Center, and the North End are all within convenient walking distance. The project's location at the water's edge provides superb views of both the Boston Harbor and the city skyline. Three other large warehouses within three blocks of the site have been converted to residential, office, and retail uses.

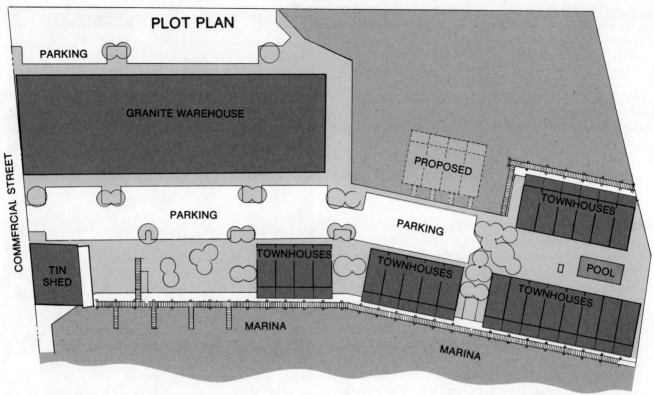

PLOT PLAN

PARKING

GRANITE WAREHOUSE

COMMERCIAL STREET

PARKING

PROPOSED

PARKING

TOWNHOUSES

TIN SHED

TOWNHOUSES

TOWNHOUSES

POOL

TOWNHOUSES

MARINA

MARINA

3-72   Site plan.

The irregularly shaped wharf extends 590 feet into the harbor and has approximately 1,200 feet of water frontage. At the time the site was purchased it contained two buildings: the historic granite warehouse occupied the northwestern portion of the wharf and a two-story tin shed of approximately 5,000 square feet was located at the entrance to the wharf. The remainder of the site was being used as a dirt parking lot and as a commercial marina landing.

Granite Building

The massive granite-faced warehouse was built in 1846–1847. Its overall dimension of 92 feet by 290 feet was divided into seven bays, each approximately 40 feet wide. Each bay of the building had a basement and, originally, four stories with a pitched roof. Sometime later, a fifth story with a modified pitched roof was added to the western portion. A fire in the eastern portion of the building in the early 1940s damaged the fourth floor, which was removed shortly thereafter. The remainder of the building showed no evidence of fire or serious structural problems. However, there was some interior water damage and roof and floor deterioration. There were also some cracks resulting from settlement following construction of the Callahan Tunnel under the eastern portion of the wharf.

The granite building is an outstanding example of the 1810–1860 Boston granite style and was one of only four remaining examples of its use for warehouses. The detail of the building is the same on all elevations. On the ground floor large windows and doors are framed by rock faced granite post and lintel architraves, with the areas between openings infilled with layers of granite blocks two feet high. The upper floors are ornamented with windows having post and lintel enframements of smoothly finished granite, which also is used decoratively in the staggered quoins in all four corners and for the cornice.

The building's interior was rough, warehouse-type space. Throughout the interior, brick party walls and wooden joists, measuring approximately four by 12 inches, were exposed. The flooring was heavy wooden planks, with the exception of the dirt basement floor. Small interior staircases connected the various floors along with floor openings for conveyor belts which were added during the 1930s. Each bay contained three large windows on both the north and south sides in addition to large double doors. Corner bays contained four to seven additional windows.

Development Strategy and Renovation

The basic development objective was to provide raw space for residential and office condominium units for a luxury market. The strong demand for space in a historic wharf setting on the waterfront, coupled with a dwindling supply of such space due to the earlier recycling of the three other historic wharfs, made it feasible to charge the highest possible prices within certain limits. Dealing with the top end of the market also meant that because buyers were paying a premium they would have definite ideas as to the end product. Therefore, the sale of finished units would have made it necessary for the developer to offer a wide variety of finishes and to be prepared to make considerable changes to satisfy buyers. In order to avoid this problem, it was decided to offer all of the units as raw space for complete inner finishing and customizing by buyers. Public restrooms were not provided for commercial areas; it was the responsibility of each owner to construct such facilities.

Raw space delivered to buyers in the granite building consisted of sandblasted exposed beam ceilings and brick walls, a concrete floor, and roughed-in plumbing and electricity. Each unit also was provided with a flue and hearth to permit the owner to have a brick fireplace, Franklin stove, or a modern free-standing fireplace unit. Floors were straightened and leveled somewhat by pouring about three inches of concrete over the existing wood floors. This provided fire protection and also helped to soundproof the building. Further soundproofing was provided by eliminating all vertical

3-73 Curving iron balconies were added.

penetrations between units except for the designed utility chase at the corridor wall. Electric heat pumps were installed by the developer to provide an efficient heating and cooling system with individual control of heating or cooling. Individual electric meters and hot water heaters also were provided for each unit to further enhance energy user responsibility.

The granite and brick exterior of the building was chemically cleaned, bringing it back from a very dark grey to its original light grey and red brick. A sixth floor was constructed on the building's western portion as a dormer opening onto private roof decks. Graceful, curving iron balconies measuring six by 12 feet were added for each unit above the first floor, and mahogany French doors were installed for access to the balconies using existing openings. The balconies, together with white vinyl clad windows, helped to accent the massiveness of the granite, an important consideration in the exterior renovation.

Market Considerations

Since the project includes both residential and office condominiums, the developer was selling to two distinct markets. The residential market was upper-income professionals, primarily childless couples in the 35–55 age bracket. About 50 percent of the buyers were individuals renting or owning in Boston, primarily in the waterfront area. Most buyers were seeking more space and/or an ownership position. Also, the concept of designing one's own home greatly enhanced sales. The remaining half of the buyers were from the suburbs or from outside of Massachusetts. Typically, these were empty-nesters no longer needing a large single-family detached home.

The largest market for office condominiums was for attorney's offices, followed closely by investment and management consultants. All of the office buyers were attracted by the benefits of owning as opposed to renting, especially with the increasingly tight downtown rental market. Also, the sale of rough space appealed to office users since it allowed them to design the space to meet their own particular needs.

Through a discount presale program, 50 percent of the units were under contract prior to construction. A sales office was established at an adjacent wharf property. Advertising for both the residential and office condominiums was handled through direct mailings and weekly ads in two local papers and various trade publications. A full-time broker was employed by the developer along with two other sales/administrative people. Outside broker participation also was encouraged.

Condominium Association

The condominium association was formed in November 1978 and was controlled by the developer until June 1979 (as stipulated in a contract approved by the unit owners). The association is governed by a five-member board of trustees (made up of unit owners) which is responsible for hiring and removing personnel required to manage and administer the condominium, for modifying rules and regulations as necessary, and for the operation, maintenance, and repair of common areas.

Common area charges are based on a percentage of ownership derived from a percentage of the market value, as required by state law. They range from $68 per month for a 1,000-square-foot first floor and basement commercial unit to $491 per month for a fifth and sixth floor 4,000-square-foot residential unit. All operating costs are covered by these charges, with the exception of individual unit electricity, personal property insurance, and real estate taxes.

Experience Gained

- The sale of all units as raw space reduced the time cost of the project by allowing units to be conveyed at the earliest possible time and by eliminating the necessity of waiting to do detail work and having to make last-minute finishing changes for buyers. The sale of raw space resulted in the lowest net project cost and presented the opportunity, through marketing, to maximize the profitability to the developer. This resulted in a project that was able to return approximately 20 percent of gross sales as a profit.
- The sale of raw space is particularly successful when dealing with a luxury market. Upper-income buyers generally want to add their own design touches and can afford to do so.
- In the sale of raw space, it is imperative that extreme care be exercised regarding major structural or systems changes which are contemplated by buyers. The developer should clearly identify to buyers those changes which are not permitted and should carefully review the changes proposed for each unit.

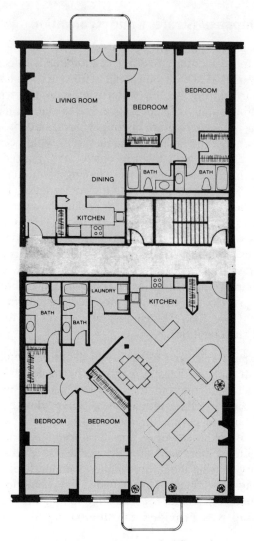

3-74 Granite warehouse typical floor plans.

- The mixture of residential and office uses in the same building has worked very well. Reserving certain portions of the building for only residential use or for limited office use also helped to assure compatibility between the two uses.
- The individual metering of units has not only encouraged energy responsibility by purchasers, but also assured that the five day per week office users will not be burdened with the costs of the seven day per week energy use of residents.
- A complex, short-term rehabilitation project will generally require greater than ordinary supervision by the general contractor of his employees. It will also require that quick, on-site decisions be made by the development team as the project proceeds. It sometimes will be necessary for actual construction to deviate from construction drawings.

PROJECT DATA

Land Use Information:

Site Area: 2.61 acres (1.06 hectares)[1]
Total Units: 64[2]
Gross Density: 34.10 units per acre[3]
Parking: 112 spaces

Land Use Plan:

	Acres	Percent
Buildings	1.15	44.06
Parking/Circulation ...	.96	36.78
Landscaping/Pool	.50	19.16
Total	2.61	100.00

Economic Information:

Site Cost: $1,350,000 (1978)
Site Improvement Cost: $500,000[8]
Construction Cost: $23 per square foot[9]
Total Conversion Costs: $5,415,000
Total Revenue: $6,312,286

Unit Information:[4]

Unit Type	Size	Number	Sales Price[5]	Bedrooms[6]	Bathrooms[6]
First Floor/ Basement	933–4,000 sq.ft.	15	$33,000–155,000	N.A.[7]	N.A.[7]
Second and Third Floors	1,264–2,000 sq.ft.	28	$55,000–150,000	2	2
Fourth, Fifth, and Sixth Floors	1,275–4,000 sq.ft.	21	$65,000–252,000	2	2

Notes:
[1] This does not include water rights in the marina area covering 1.65 acres of water surface.
[2] Total units in the granite building (31 residential units and 33 office units). This total does not include the 23 new townhouse units and the conversion of an old tin shed structure to two office units.
[3] The calculation of gross density includes the new townhouse units and those in the shed structure as well as those units in the converted granite building.
[4] For granite building only.
[5] All sales prices are for raw space.
[6] Typical unit information. Residential units only.
[7] These areas contain only commercial space.
[8] Cost for pool, parking, utilities, plaza areas, and landscaping.
[9] Hard costs only. Site improvement costs are also not reflected in these figures. Total hard construction costs for the conversion of the granite building were $2.25 million. Soft costs were $1.2 million.

Developer:

James S. Craig and Austin A. Heath, Partners
Union Wharf Development Associates
54 Lewis Wharf
Boston, Massachusetts 02110
(617) 227-3710

Architecture:

Moritz Bergmeyer Associates, Inc.
118 South Street
Boston, Massachusetts 02110
(617) 542-1025

Engineering:

David M. Berg, Inc.
570 Hillside Avenue
Needham, Massachusetts
(617) 444-5156

Management:

Hunneman Management Company
One Winthrop Square
Boston, Massachusetts 02110
(617) 426-4260

Financing:

Schroder Bank and Trust
One State Street
New York, New York 10015
(212) 269-6500

CBT Realty Corporation
One Constitution Plaza
Hartford, Connecticut 06115
(203) 244-5069

Four Lakes Village

3-75 Many of the units have lakefront views.

3-76 Extensive landscaping was part of the project's renovation.

Four Lakes Village is a 1,547-unit garden apartment conversion on a 200-acre site in suburban Chicago. The project is the second largest conversion in the Chicago market, topped only by the 2,610-unit Carl Sandburg Village. Its 77 buildings consist primarily of two- and three-story walk-ups, although there are also some mid-rise (five and six stories) elevator buildings. The original development was built in five phases over a 15-year period. At the time the conversion was started in 1979, the buildings ranged in age from 15 years to brand new. The project also contains land for two additional phases which will allow up to 300 to 400 additional units to be constructed.

The buildings were carefully designed and sited so that they complement the site's attractive wooded setting. They are of a rustic design and feature exteriors of brick and rough-sawn wood. Most of the units are one- and two-bedrooms and range in size from 720 to 1,200 square feet. Units feature woodburning fireplaces, floor-to-ceiling sliding glass doors leading to large balconies or patios, use of natural brick walls, private entrances from outside, and efficient, contemporary floor plans. The buildings were sited to provide attractive lake and hilltop views.

In addition to its rustic design and wooded setting, the project featured an outstanding variety of amenities at the time it was purchased for conversion. These included a ski slope and ski lodge; four lakes available for sailing, rowboating, and canoeing; three swimming pools; lighted tennis courts; an indoor tennis and racquetball club; a health club; wooded paths for jogging, hiking, and biking; volleyball courts; an archery range; a pub and restaurant; and a convenience store.

At the time the conversion was initiated the project was neat but included some deferred maintenance in the buildings and considerable deferred maintenance on the landscaping. The occupancy rate was about 89 percent with an annual turnover of 50 to 60 percent. Most tenants were single, in their late 20s, and had modest incomes. The conversion is being undertaken in four phases, with 483 units in the first phase. Sales to tenants began in October 1979, and sales to the public began in November 1979.

3-77 Signage throughout the project directs residents and visitors to the various facilities.

The Site

The project is located 32 miles west of downtown Chicago, yet has easy access to both suburban and urban amenities. Many of the major expressways of the Chicago metropolitan area are readily accessible. The East-West Tollway is approximately two miles north of the site and both Interstate 294 and the Stevenson Expressway (I-55) are within a short drive. O'Hare International Airport is 30 minutes away via I-294 and driving time to the Loop is approximately 40 minutes. The site is also just a five-minute ride from the Burlington Northern Line train station which provides express train service (36 minutes) to downtown. Two arterials are contiguous to the site (Maple Avenue and Route 53) and contain shopping facilities for day-to-day needs. In addition, three major regional shopping centers are convenient to the project.

Residential development close to the site consists of single-family detached homes as well as several major rental projects. Two golf courses are adjacent to the site, and forest preserves and other recreational attractions are nearby. The site features rolling, wooded terrain with mature trees and shrubs and a variety of scenic lake and hilltop vistas. Seventy percent of the site is open space.

Conversion Feasibility

The attractive site, the size of the units, and the layout of the units and the buildings made the project suitable for conversion. Unit sizes (primarily one- and two-bedrooms with some studios) dictated that the project would be appropriate for first-time homebuyers—a major component of the conversion market.

The key to the feasibility of the conversion was a phased closing of the property over a five-year period with a negligible carrying cost, computed in the price. The initial phase of the takedown was "front-end loaded" both in price and in size. The first phase contained 483 units, subsequent phases will have approximately 100 to 200 units per phase. However, there is the possibility of combining subsequent phases if the market warrants it.

The physical layout of the units and the buildings is such that the physical phasing of the conversion can be readily achieved. There are a number of shared amenities which are maintained by an umbrella homeowners association which is comprised of the individual condominium associations representing the various phases.

3-78 Site plan.

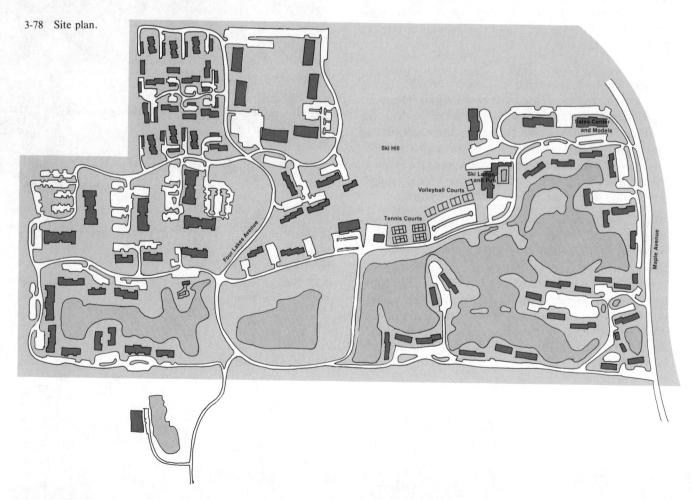

3-79   The project features a full complement of amenities and rolling, wooded terrain.

The feasibility of the conversion has also rested, in part, with the ability of the developer to improve the rental situation to the point where it is a profit making operation on its own and not a burden on the conversion process. This has been possible by having the developer manage the remaining rental phases until the title is exchanged for these final phases.

Interim Financing

The interim financing for the conversion was obtained at one of the top 10 money center banks which has had extensive experience in financing conversions. The financing was obtained by paying a combination of points over the floating prime rate and front-end fees. It was secured by the first mortgage and backed by certain guarantees of the borrowing entity and the sponsors. As a result of accelerated repayments as units sold, the interim lender's loan-to-value position improved as the sales program progressed. In addition, certain accommodations and restructuring were provided by the interim lender during the program.

Permanent Financing

Permanent financing was provided by a number of savings and loans in the Chicago area. Due to the skyrocketing interest rates at the end of 1979 and the beginning of 1980 when the project was opened, permanent financing became critical to the success of the project. A number of innovative financing programs were initiated at this time. These included buy-downs and subsidies to lower the interest rate and, therefore, the qualifying level for first-time buyers. In addition, a program was established which enabled tenants to continue renting for a period of time with an option to purchase.

3-80   Custom-made sliding glass storm doors were installed on patios and balconies to increase energy efficiency.

This was the first program of this type to be established in the marketplace for several years. A sale-leaseback program for investor purchasers was also established, whereby units were leased from the buyer for 18 months and concurrently subleased. This assured the investor of either a break-even or positive cash flow at the time of purchase and at least for the first 18 months.

There was a continuing process of identifying, negotiating, and working with savings and loans in order to provide the best financing available in the market. The focus was on minimizing buyers' downpayments and making monthly payments as low as possible in order to allow first-time buyers to qualify for a mortgage. The developer also took applications for financing from buyers and processed them for the permanent lenders. This proved to be a tremendous advantage, especially with first-time buyers who were not familiar with this financing process.

Renovation

Since the project had been built in phases over a 15-year period, the condition of units and buildings varied widely, with the older structures requiring a great deal of work to offset some deferred maintenance. The initial renovation focused on immediately correcting problems which were going to deteriorate even further, providing better and more intensive service to tenants in order to encourage them to purchase, and refurbishing those common areas which were most visible.

Common area renovation involved the resurfacing of roads, parking areas, and tennis courts, the refurbishing of laundry rooms, the remodeling of the ski lodge and other recreational facilities, and the extensive upgrading of the project's 200 acres of landscaping, including the planting of attractive flower beds and the trimming and removal of trees and other vegetation to provide views of the lakes.

Renovation of the buildings' exteriors consisted of some roof repairs, painting, and considerable repair of the wooden balconies and wood trim, along with new light fixtures and signage. Custom-made sliding glass storm doors for patios and balconies were installed to complement the existing single pane glass doors, and the chimneys were cleaned and new energy-efficient dampers were installed. The installation of the sliding glass storm doors is expected to reduce heat loss during cold weather by up to 30 percent, while the installation of new dampers should result in an energy savings of up to 15 percent.

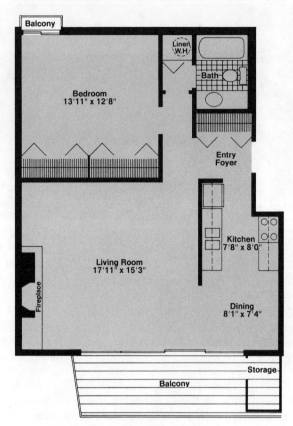

3-81   A 720-square-foot unit.

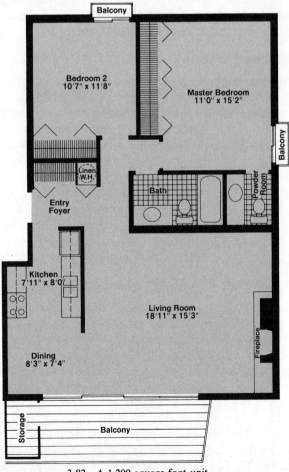

3-82   A 1,200-square-foot unit.

Buyers had three purchasing options: "as is," with a basic refurbishment package, or with upgraded refurbishment. Basic repair and maintenance of unit interiors was quite extensive and was included in the "as is" package. It included bathroom work, tile replacement, some floor work, door repairs, and kitchen cabinets and appliances repairs. The basic refurbishment package was included in the base price and was obtainable in part or in whole and included new wall-to-wall carpeting and pads, new kitchen and bathroom flooring, painting, new living room and bedroom drapes, new garbage disposals, new kitchen and bathroom light fixtures, and refinished kitchen cabinets. Optional upgrades included new kitchen appliances, upgraded carpeting and pads, upgraded kitchen and bathroom floors, new kitchen cabinets and countertops, a new bathroom vanity and countertop, mirrored sliding glass doors, custom installed molding in the living room, custom designed fluorescent wall lighting in the living room, and upgraded lighting fixtures in the bathroom, kitchen, and dining areas.

A program of third party warranty of the appliances was contracted, and 24-hour maintenance was available on all appliances. This was a one-year renewable warranty.

Marketing

The marketing program to tenants was launched with a major party held for tenants and their friends. During the day-long party, food and a band were provided and there were tours of the project with a double-decker bus. Over 1,000 tenants attended and over 150 made appointments with sales people. Following the party, there were follow-up phone calls and sales promotions. A sliding scale of discounts acted as an incentive for tenants to buy, and over 23 percent of the units in the 438-unit first phase were sold to tenants. In the suburban Chicago market, an average of 10 to 15 percent of the tenants will normally purchase units.

The marketing program to outside buyers was initiated just before the conclusion of the tenant program. It included a full spectrum of marketing initiatives and a major advertising agency was used. The backbone of the program was advertising in the major newspapers in the real estate section. Other advertising media were used including major magazines on a zip code area basis, direct mail to renters in the geographic area, offsite signage, and radio and television promotions. There was also some brokerage participation, but it was a minor part of the marketing program and an in-house sales staff on the site did the actual selling and closings.

Public relations was a major part of the marketing effort. On a per dollar basis, the public relations effort had far greater results than any other aspect of the marketing program. It gave the project tremendous credibility in the marketplace and was the best traffic generator of the entire marketing program.

Experience Gained

- In determining the economic feasibility of a conversion, the renovation budget should be based solely on the renovation work which is required to put the project in top shape and not on a maximum amount of renovation which can be undertaken if the desired profit margin is to be realized. Once the renovation budget for a conversion has been prepared, it should not be revised based on the sales prices which the market will bear. If there is not an adequate profit margin based on the required renovation budget and the projected sales revenue, then a "no-go" decision should be made. In no case should the converter revise the renovation budget or skimp on renovation in order to make the desired profit.

- Since tenants represent a prime market for the converter and can be an important factor in achieving a rapid sell-out, the converter should focus on obtaining a high percentage of sales from tenants. A professional sales approach should be used with tenants and they should be given discounts and the opportunity to buy their unit in "as is" condition.

- A large-scale complex which is converted in phases and has a relatively high tenant turnover presents the advantage of having a large number of new prospective purchasers each year.

- The financing package is critical to the success of a conversion. In today's market there is nothing more important than having the right financing to enable prospects to buy. It is advisable for the developer to take applications for financing from buyers, since this will give the developer an opportunity to educate the buyers on their financial situation and can be an important factor in enabling buyers to qualify for loans. The ability of the developer's staff to work directly with buyers and savings and loans can make it possible for a significant number of buyers to qualify for financing who ordinarily would not be able to do so.

- When undertaking a phased conversion, it is important that the first phase of buyers be satisfied and happy. Referrals will be one of the best sources of sales in future phases.

- If the market is slow during the latter phases of a conversion, sales prices should not be reduced below those in earlier phases in order to increase the absorption rate. Such a reduction in sales prices would upset those who bought in the earlier phases. Instead, a good way to increase the absorption rate in a slow market is to offer additional refurbishment of unit interiors without increasing prices—in other words, provide more rather than cutting prices.
- When converting a large-scale complex, it can be advantageous from the viewpoint of property taxes to file a separate condominium declaration for each phase of the project rather than filing one declaration for the entire project. Filing a separate declaration for each phase will assure that the entire project is not assessed at its higher value as a condominium when in reality only a portion of the project has been converted.
- The project's phases should be kept small enough to allow the developer to meet any presale requirements of the permanent lenders.
- It is imperative that the rental management office be physically separated from the condominium sales office. The failure to provide separate rental management and sales offices will have a negative impact on sales.
- Timing is a critical variable in the economic feasibility of a conversion. That is, the longer it takes for the market to absorb the units, the higher the cost to carry the project. With the higher cost of money, this is all the more true.
- The renovation strategy should be designed to encourage tenants to purchase units. In this regard, the initial renovation should focus on correcting problems which have resulted from deferred maintenance, providing more intensive service to tenants, and on completing renovation of the most visible, high impact areas. The initial renovation should focus on spending the up-front renovation money where it will generate the greatest return.
- A public relations program, if well organized and executed, has tremendous credibility in the marketplace and is an excellent traffic generator.
- Due to the size of the first phase, the condominium association is still under the control of the developer. Major meetings are held periodically and a good response from residents has been achieved. The policy is to have open communication and to promote participation in the belief that this will avoid problems with homeowners and tenants. Thus far, this policy has proven to be most effective.
- In determining assessments for the condominium association, great care was taken to make sure that the assessments would be adequate to cover all expenses and that they would not have to be increased substantially in future years. It was recognized that any substantial increase in association dues would be a deterrent to future sales in subsequent phases.

PROJECT DATA

Land Use Information:

Site Area: 200 acres (81 hectares)
Total Dwelling Units: 1,547
Gross Density: 7.7 d.u. per acre
Parking Spaces: 3,008

Economic Information:[2]

Site Acquisition Costs: $16.25 million
Renovation Costs: $2.15 million[3]
Marketing Costs: $1.75 million
Finance Costs: $7.50 million
Projected Gross Sales Volume (all phases): $75 million

Notes:

[1] Unit information for phase one only. Sales prices as of 6/30/81.
[2] Phase one costs only.
[3] Includes $1 million for renovation of common areas, $1 million for renovation of units, and $150,000 for renovation of landscaping. The renovation budget for the entire project is $7 million.

Developer:

Four Lakes Development Company (a joint venture between Regis Homes, Inc. and Daon Development Corporation)
5540 East Lake Drive, Apt. A
Lisle, Illinois 60532
(312) 963-5211

Engineering/Planning:

Balsamo-Olson
1S 376 Summit Avenue
Suite 1F
Oakbrook Terrace, Illinois 60181

Unit Information:[1]

Unit Type	D.U. Size	Bedrooms	Bathrooms	Sales Price
Arbor	720 sq.ft.	1	1	$45,500–49,000
Birch	960 sq.ft.	2	1	$54,500–62,200
Cedar	1,036 sq.ft.	2	1½	$69,000–73,000
Deerpath	1,200 sq.ft.	2	1½	$57,500–65,500
Evergreen	720 sq.ft.	1	1	$45,500–51,500
Forest View	420 sq.ft. (efficiency)	1	1	$26,000
Greenbriar	720 sq.ft.	1	1	$44,500–49,500
Hawthorne	755 sq.ft.	1	1	$39,500–41,000
Indian Trail	1,200 sq.ft.	2	1½	$56,500–63,000
J (Penthouse)	1,586 sq.ft.	3	2	$95,000

Landscape Architecture:

Merrick Hoshl
525 Pfingsten Road
Northbrook, Illinois 60062
(312) 272-3460

Management:

Lolli & Jara Realty & Management, Inc.
497 Main Street
Glen Ellyn, Illinois 60137
(312) 858-9680

Interim Financing:

Continental Bank
231 South LaSalle Street
Chicago, Illinois
(312) 828-6277

Permanent Financing:

Talman/Home Federal
State Street
Chicago, Illinois
(312) 922-9600

Cragin Federal
Fullerton Street
Chicago, Illinois
(312) 889-1000

Public Relations:

Taylor-Johnson Associates
244 East Ogden Avenue
Hinsdale, Illinois 60521
(312) 655-0202

Appendices

Appendix A—Condominium Declaration

Declaration Establishing A Condominium

This Declaration of Condominium (hereinafter "Declaration") is made and executed in _____ County, state of _____ this _____ day of _____, 1979, by _____ Corporation, a _____ corporation (hereinafter "Declarant"), pursuant to the provisions of the _____ Condominium Act (hereinafter "Act").

W I T N E S S E T H :

WHEREAS, Declarant is the contract vendee of a certain parcel of real property, located in the city of _____, county of _____ , state of _____, and legally described herein by reference, and made a part hereof; and

WHEREAS, the land described has been improved and there is constructed thereon one multifamily building and certain other improvements described below; and

WHEREAS, it is the desire and the intention of Declarant to divide the building situated upon the property described in Exhibit ___ into individual residential apartments as hereinafter defined and to sell the apartments to various purchasers pursuant to a plan for the individual ownership of the apartments and the co-ownership by the individual owners thereof, as tenants in common, of all of the "common areas and facilities" (as hereinafter defined), subject to the covenants, conditions, and restrictions herein reserved to be kept and observed; and

WHEREAS, Declarant desires and intends by filing this Declaration to submit the property described in Exhibit ___ and the improvements thereon to the aforesaid Act as condominium property to be known as "The _____ Condominium" (hereinafter "Condominium").

NOW, THEREFORE, the Declarant, for the purposes set forth above, does hereby publish and declare as follows:

1. Submission of Condominium. All of the real property described above and the improvements heretofore and hereafter constructed thereon are hereby submitted to the provisions of the Act, and shall be held, conveyed, encumbered, leased, rented, used, and occupied subject always to all covenants, conditions, restrictions, uses, limitations, and obligations codified in the Act, expressed hereinafter in the Articles of Incorporation of The Association, Inc. (hereinafter Articles), the Declaration, and contained in the bylaws of The Association, Inc. (hereinafter "bylaws"), incorporated herein by reference, and made a part hereof. All of such covenants, conditions, restrictions, uses, limitations, and obligations are declared and agreed to be in furtherance of a plan for said Condominium, and shall be deemed to run with the land and shall be a burden and a benefit to Declarant, its grantees, successors, and assignees and any person acquiring or owning an interest in the Condominium, their grantees, successors, and assignees. The Condominium is hereby divided into the following separate freehold estates:

A. Thirty (30) separately designated and legally described freehold estates constituting residential apartments and forty-two (42) separately designated and legally described freehold estates constituting garage apartments (as hereinafter defined).

(1) The fee title to each apartment shall include:

(i) The areas contained within the perimeter boundaries of each of the residential and garage apartments in the Building (as hereinafter defined); and

(ii) An undivided interest in the common areas and facilities and the "limited common areas and facilities," said undivided interest to be deemed to be conveyed or encumbered with its respective residential apartment and garage apartment. Any attempt to separate the fee title to a residential apartment or a garage apartment from the undivided interest in the common areas and facilities and limited common areas and facilities appurtenant to such apartment shall be null and void, and all future acquisitions of common areas and facilities or limited common areas and facilities shall be owned by all apartment owners in the percentages of undivided interest appurtenant to their respective residential apartments and garage apartments. The term "common areas and facilities," when used throughout this Declaration, shall mean both common areas and facilities and limited common areas and facilities, unless the context otherwise specifically requires.

B. Said apartments and the percentage interest in the common areas and facilities appurtenant to each are separately designated on Exhibit ___, incorporated herein by reference and made a part hereof. Said apartments are depicted on the floor plans for The Condominium, recorded simultaneously with the recording of this Declaration.

C. Each of the aforesaid percentages of undivided interests, as designated in Exhibit ___, shall be equivalent to the percentage which the value of the residential apartment or the garage apartment bears to the value of all of the residential apartments, all of the garage apartments, and all of the common areas and facilities.

2. Description. The real estate described above and all improvements thereon, shall be Condominium property.

The improvements consist of one (1) building containing a total of thirty (30) residential apartments, forty-two (42) below grade, heated garage apartments, and twenty-one (21) outdoor parking spaces, all as more specifically described in exhibit attached hereto and made a part hereof.

3. Name and Purpose. The property is to be identified by the name "The Condominium" and will be used for residential purposes, subject to the provisions of Paragraph 10 hereof.

4. Definitions. Unless the context indicates otherwise, for purposes of this Declaration and annexed bylaws, the following words and terms have the meaning attributed to them:

A. "Apartment" shall hereafter refer to and include both residential apartments and garage apartments, unless the context otherwise specifically requires. Apartments are depicted on the floor plans recorded simultaneously with the recording of this Declaration.

(1) "Residential apartment" means a part of the Condominium, including one or more rooms or enclosed spaces, or part or parts thereof, in the building, with a direct exit to a common area leading to a public street or highway, intended for residential use.

(2) "Garage apartment" means a part of the Condominium on the garage level of the building, including the space enclosed within the upper surface of the floor, the lower surface of the ceiling, and inner surface of any perimeter walls or doors separating garage apartments, and the planes rising vertically from the inner lines or stripes painted or marked on the floor. A garage apartment has a direct exit to a common area leading to a public street or highway, and is intended for the parking of vehicles belonging to apartment owners or other occupants of a residential apartment.

B. "Apartment owner" means the record owner, whether one or more persons, owning an apartment in fee simple absolute, including the undivided interest in the fee simple estate of the common areas and facilities appurtenant to that apartment in the percentages specified and established in the Declaration. "Apartment owner" also means and includes a contract purchaser of such apartment.

C. "Apartment number" means the number, letter, or combinations thereof, designating the apartment in the Declaration.

D. "Building" means the building containing the apartments and comprising a part of the Condominium.

E. (1) "Common areas and facilities," unless otherwise provided in the Declaration or lawful amendments thereto, means the portions of the Condominium not included in the apartments and includes:

(a) The land on which the building is located;

(b) The foundations, columns, girders, beams, supports, main walls, roofs, halls, corridors, lobbies, stairs, stairways, fire escapes, and entrances and exits of the building;

(c) The yards and gardens, if any;

(d) Installations of central services such as power, light, gas, hot and cold water, and heating;

(e) The elevator, tanks, pumps, motors, fans, ducts, furnaces and furnace rooms, and all other apparatus and installations existing for common use;

(f) The 21 outdoor parking spaces;

(g) The laundry rooms located on all floors of the building;

(h) The exercise room, sauna, and restroom located on the garage level of the building;

(i) The guest/party room located on the garage level of the building;

(j) The equipment storage areas located on the garage level of the building and the store rooms located throughout the building for use by the association for storage purposes;

(k) All other parts of the Condominium necessary or convenient to its existence, maintenance, and safety, or normally in common use.

(2) The common areas and facilities shall not include, however, any areas within partition walls, floors, or ceilings which are removed for the purpose of making those areas a part of two or more adjoining residential apartments used together as an integrated whole, nor hallways used as a part of two or more adjoining residential apartments so used together, provided that such removal was done pursuant to subparagraph C(4) of paragraph 12 hereof, with certification of the Board as required therein, so long as such wall areas, floors, ceilings, or hallways are used as part of such integrated apartments, and as long as so used, such areas shall be a part of the integrated residential apartments, anything herein to the contrary notwithstanding.

F. "Common expenses" means and includes:

(1) All sums lawfully assessed against the apartment owners by the association;

(2) Expenses of administration, maintenance, repair, or replacement of the common areas and facilities;

(3) Expenses declared to be common expenses by the association;

(4) Expenses declared to be common expenses by this Declaration, the bylaws, or the Act.

G. "Common profits" means the balance of all income, rents, profits, and revenues from the common areas and facilities remaining after the deduction of the common expenses.

H. "Declarant" means _____ , or any successor to the entire then interest in the apartments herein defined upon transfer, assignment, conveyance, or otherwise, including but not limited to any contract vendor or mortgagee who succeeds to such entire then interest upon contract cancellation, mortgage foreclosure, or acceptance of a deed in lieu of foreclosure. "Declarant" shall not mean, however, any person acquiring apartments in the ordinary course for residential purposes.

I. "Declaration" means the instrument by which the Condominium is submitted to the provisions of _____, as amended, and such amended Declarations as may be lawfully authorized and recorded in the office of the County Recorder of _____ County.

J. "The Association, Inc." (hereinafter "Association") means the nonprofit corporation organized and existing in accordance with the laws to administer the Condominium. The membership of the Association consists of all the apartment owners who shall act through their duly elected Board of Directors in accordance with the bylaws of the association and this Declaration.

K. "The Condominium" (hereinafter sometimes "Condominium") means and includes the land, the building, all improvements and structures thereon, all easements, rights, and appurtenances belonging thereto, and all articles of personal property intended for use in connection therewith, which have been or are intended to be submitted to the provisions of this Declaration.

L. "Holder of an interest" means the apartment owner, contract vendee, life tenant, tenant under a lease for more than three (3) years, or any combination thereof.

M. "Limited common areas and facilities" means and includes those common areas and facilities designated in the Declaration as reserved for use of a certain apartment or apartments to the exclusion of the other apartments.

N. "Majority" or "Majority of Apartment Owners" means those apartment owners holding more than fifty (50) percent of the votes in accordance with the percentages assigned to the apartments for voting purposes as shown in Exhibit __ to this Declaration.

O. "Occupant" means any person or persons, other than an apartment owner or the Declarant, in possession of or residing in an apartment.

P. "Person" means individual, corporation, partnership, association, trustee, or other legal entity.

Q. "Recording officer" means the County Recorder of _____ County.

5. Boundaries of Apartments. The boundaries of each apartment shall be as follows:

A. *Upper and Lower Boundaries.* The upper boundary of each residential and garage apartment shall be the horizontal plane of the undecorated, finished ceiling, and the lower boundary of each apartment shall be the horizontal plane of the undecorated finished floor, as such planes intersect with the perimetrical boundary planes.

B. *Perimetrical Boundaries of Residential Apartments.*

(1) *Interior Walls.* The perimetrical boundaries of each residential apartment shall include the vertical planes of the undecorated, finished interior of the interior walls bounding the apartment as such planes intersect (i) with each other, (ii) with the perimetrical boundary planes of the exterior walls, and (iii) with the upper and lower boundary planes.

(2) *Exterior Walls.* The perimetrical boundaries of each residential apartment shall include (i) the vertical planes of the undecorated, finished interior of the exterior walls and (ii) the vertical planes of the outside face of all glass windows and glass doors and air conditioning units, if any, bounding the apartment, as such planes in (i) and (ii) intersect with each other, with the perimetrical boundary planes of the interior walls bounding the apartment, and with the upper and lower boundary planes.

C. *Perimetrical Boundaries of Garage Apartments.* The perimetrical boundaries of each garage apartment shall include the vertical planes of the undecorated, finished perimeter walls or doors separating garage apartments, if any, and the vertical planes rising from the inner lines or stripes painted or marked on the floor of the garage level of the building.

6. Rights and Benefits of Apartments. The rights and benefits accruing to each apartment shall be as follows:

A. *Voting Percentages.* The proportionate representation of the separate owners of the respective apartments for purposes of this Declaration and for the purposes of the bylaws of the Association and for voting purposes in the Association shall be the percentages established for each apartment set forth in Exhibit __ hereof.

B. *Appurtenances.* The ownership of each apartment shall include, and there shall pass with each apartment as appurtenances thereto, whether or not separately described, all of the rights, title, and interest of an apartment owner in the Condominium, which shall include but not be limited to the following:

(1) *Common Areas and Facilities, Limited Common Areas and Facilities, and Common Expenses and Profits.* An undivided interest in the common areas and facilities, the limited common areas and facilities set forth in Paragraph 7 hereof, and the common expenses and profits, which percentages of undivided interest are set forth in Exhibit __ of this Declaration.

(2) *Association.* The membership of each apartment owner in the Association and in the funds and assets held by the Association.

(3) *Cross Easements.* Perpetual, nonexclusive easements from each apartment owner to each other apartment owner and to the Association, as follows:

(a) *Maintenance, Repair, and Replacement.* Easements through the apartments and common areas and facilities for maintenance, repair, and replacement of the apartments and common areas and facilities during reasonable hours, except that access may be had at any time in case of an emergency.

(b) *Support.* Each portion of an apartment contributing to the support of the building shall be burdened with an easement for support for the benefit of all other apartments and common areas and facilities in the building.

(c) *Utilities.* Easements through the apartments and common areas and facilities for conduits, ducts, plumbing, wiring, and other facilities for the furnishing of utility services.

(d) *Easements for Shifting.* Easements to the extent that walls depicted on the floor plans as being partly in one apartment and partly in an adjacent apartment may deviate from the vertical by reason of any shifting of the building.

(e) *Easements Through Garage Apartments.* Easements through garage apartments to permit temporary passage through or crossing of the boundary lines of garage apartments while entering or exiting a garage apartment or parking a vehicle therein.

(4) *Sharing Common Expenses and Profits.* Each apartment owner shall be liable for a proportionate share of the common expenses and entitled to ownership in a share of the common profits, such share being equal to the undivided interest appurtenant to said owner's residential apartment and garage apartment as set forth in Exhibit __ hereof.

(5) *Easement to Air Space.* An exclusive easement for the use of air space occupied by the apartment and its patio or balcony as it exists at any particular time and as the apartment may be altered or reconstructed from time to time, which easement shall be terminated automatically in any air space which is vacated from time to time.

7. Limited Common Areas and Facilities. The limited common areas and facilities allocated herein for use only by the owner or owners of a certain apartment or group of apartments and their family members, guests, invitees, and lessees are designated on Exhibit _____ attached hereto and made a part hereof and are as follows:

A. Balconies and patios appurtenant to the residential apartments.

B. Storage lockers located on the garage level of the building.

8. Conveyance of Apartments. The individual apartments which shall be individually conveyed, together with their respective numbers, their location, approximate area, and immediate common area to which each has access, are depicted on the floor plans. The respective undivided interest to be conveyed with each apartment, as indicated above, cannot be changed, except as provided in the Act, and the Declarant and all grantees, and their respective heirs, representatives, successors, and assignees, covenant and agree that the fee title to each freehold estate shall include both the area described in Paragraph 5 hereof and the respective undivided interest in the common areas and facilities, which shall not be separated or separately conveyed. Each undivided interest shall be deemed to be conveyed or encumbered with its respective apartment even though the description in the instrument of conveyance or encumbrance may refer only to the fee title to the apartment, and all future acquisitions of common areas and facilities and limited common areas and facilities shall be owned by all apartment owners in the percentages of undivided interest appurtenant to their respective apartments.

9. Membership in The Association, Inc. An owner of an apartment shall automatically upon becoming such owner be a member of the Association, Inc. Said owner shall remain a member of the Association until such time as his ownership ceases for any reason, at which time his membership in the Association shall automatically cease. When more than one person holds an interest in an apartment, all such persons shall be members. The administration of the Condominium shall be governed by the bylaws of the Association. Every member of the Association shall enjoy the privileges and be bound by the obligations contained in the Association's articles and bylaws.

A. *Registration of Owner and Occupant.* It shall be the duty of each owner, and any occupant residing in the apartment if the owner is not residing therein, to register with the Secretary of the Association in writing (i) the name and address of such owner or occupant; (ii) the nature and satisfactory evidence of such owner's or occupant's interest or estate in the apartment, if any; (iii) the addresses at which such owner or occupant desires to receive notice, if entitled to such notice, of any duly called meeting of the members; (iv) the name and address of the first mortgagee, if any, of the apartment owned by said owner; and (v) the name of the owner or occupant, if there is more than one owner or occupant with respect to an apartment, who shall be authorized to cast the vote with respect to such apartment owned by said owner. If an owner or occupant does not register as provided in this paragraph, the Association shall be under no duty to recognize the rights of such person hereunder, and shall not recognize such person's right to vote as provided herein, but such failure to register shall not relieve an owner or occupant of any obligation, covenant, or restriction under the governing documents. If there is more than one owner or occupant of an apartment, each must execute the registration as provided in this paragraph.

B. *Restrictions on Ownership and Transfer.* The interests, rights, and obligations of a member in the Association may not be assigned, pledged, encumbered, or transferred in any manner, except as an appurtenance to such member's apartment.

10. Further Covenants and Agreements of the Parties. By and through this Declaration, Declarant, its successors, assignees, all present and future owners of the apartments, all first mortgagees of the individual apartments, and the Association further covenant and agree as follows:

A. *Partition, Subdivision, Abandonment, Encumbrance, or Transfer.*

(1) The common areas and facilities shall remain undivided, and neither the owners, the Declarant, the first mortgagee, nor the Association shall seek to partition or subdivide the same unless the Condominium has first been removed from the Act pursuant to Paragraph 25 hereof.

(2) The Association shall not seek to partition or subdivide any apartment, unless the Condominium has first been removed from the Act pursuant to Paragraph 25 hereof.

(3) As used in this Paragraph 10, the terms "partition" and "subdivide" shall not include the physical combination, separation, or restoration of residential apartments contemplated in Subparagraph C(4) of Paragraph 12 hereof.

B. *Use of Residential Apartments.* The residential apartments shall be occupied and used by the respective owners only as a private dwelling; provided, however, that an owner may pursue any home vocation that does not violate this Declaration or the Act, nor adversely affect other apartment owners, if otherwise allowed by applicable zoning codes and restrictions; the owner may use the apartment as a place of temporary residence for his guests or lessees, and for private meetings or conferences held by the owner, his lessees or guests; provided, further, that Declarant may use one or more of the apartments for display purposes, sales promotion, construction of offices, and temporary storage purposes. The apartments shall not be rented by the owners thereof for transient or hotel purposes, which shall be defined as (i) rental for any period less than six (6) months; or (ii) any rental if the occupants of the apartment are provided customary hotel services, such as room service for food and beverage, maid service, furnished laundry and linen, and bellboy service. Other than the foregoing obligations and the provisions of Paragraph 22A of this Declaration, the owners of the apartments shall have the absolute right to lease the same provided that said lease is made subject to the convenants and restrictions contained in this Declaration and the bylaws and such rules and regulations as may be promulated by the Association, and provided further that the owners of the apartments assume absolute responsibility for ensuring that their tenants are fully aware of and abide in all respects by the same.

C. *Use of Garage Apartments.* The garage apartments may be used for the parking of vehicles and related purposes which do not conflict with rules and regulations promulgated by the Board of Directors governing use of the garage apartments. Garage apartments may be owned only by apartment owners and may be sold independently of the owner's residential apartment, but only to another apartment owner. Garage apartments may be leased, but only to another apartment owner, or to an occupant, as herein defined, and only if there are no delinquent assessments or other charges against such garage apartment on the effective date of such lease. Any such lease shall terminate when the lessee ceases to be an apartment owner or occupant. The Board of Directors of the Association may promulgate such additional reasonable rule and regulations as it deems necessary to implement the provisions of this Declaration or the bylaws relating to the ownership and use of, and the transfer of interests in, garage apartments. Any transfer, assignment, conveyance, or lease of a garage apartment in violation of the restrictions contained in this paragraph shall be void.

D. *Ownership of Apartments.* The owners of the apartments shall own that portion of the building defined herein as an "Apartment," the boundaries of which are described previously. The owners of the apartments shall not own the undecorated perimeter walls, floors, and ceilings surrounding their respect apartments, nor shall said owners own pipes, wires, conduits, or other public utility lines running through the apartments, which serve more than one apartment, except as tenants in common with the other apartment owners.

E. *Control and Administration of Condominium.* Control and administration of the Condominium shall be vested in the Association and its Board of Directors in accordance with the provisions of this Declaration, the Articles of Incorporation of the Association (the "Articles"), the bylaws of the Association, and such rules and regulations as may be promulgated by the Association. The Association, through its Board of Directors, may establish and amend such rules, regulations, and procedures to govern and operate the Condominium as it deems reasonable and necessary.

F. *Compliance and Binding Effect.* Each owner, tenant, or occupant of an apartment, or any other person having a present or future interest therein, shall be bound by and comply with the provisions of this Declaration, the Articles, the bylaws, and such rules, regulations, determinations, and resolutions as may be promulgated and made by the Association from time to time, and failure to comply with any such provisions, rules, regulations, determinations, or resolutions shall be grounds for action, legal or otherwise, by the Board of Directors to enforce the rights of the Association.

G. *Obligation for Common Expenses.* No owner of an apartment may exempt himself from liability for his contribution toward the common expenses by waiver of the use of enjoyment of any of the common areas and facilities or by the abandonment of his apartment(s).

H. *Encumbrances.* The interests of the owner and mortgagee of each apartment in the apartments shall be subject to any encumbrance set out on the deed executed in connection with the purchase of such apartment.

I. *Pets.* No dogs, cats, or other animals or reptiles may be brought into or kept, bred, or raised in or about the residential apartments, the garage apartments, the common areas and facilities, or the limited common areas and facilities of the Condominium except for small birds and fish. Any apartment owner or occupant who violates this covenant shall have the following responsibilities:

(1) Each owner of a pet shall assume full responsibility for personal injuries or property damage caused by such pet and shall be responsible to indemnify the Association, its Board of Directors, the managing agent of the Condominium, and owners and occupants of the apartments, and shall hold them harmless against any loss, claim, or liability of any kind or character arising from or growing out of any act of such pet.

(2) Any apartment owner or occupant who violates this covenant shall be required to pay, and hereby agrees to pay, in addition to the assessment described in Paragraph 13 hereof, a charge in the amount equal to twice the Association assessment for his apartment(s) for each month in which the violation occurs. In addition, any apartment owner or occupant who violates this covenant shall be subject to all legal remedies available to the Association, its Board of Directors, and to all other residents, as provided to such parties in this Declaration, in the bylaws, or by law.

11. Amendment of Declaration. This Declaration may be amended by the owners of apartments having at least seventy-five (75) percent of the voting interest in the Association and by at least seventy-five (75) percent of the holders of first mortgages of record covering the apartments (based upon one vote for each first mortgage owned); provided, however, that any change in the respective undivided interests established herein shall only be made pursuant to the Act.

When voting for or against a proposed amendment, owners of apartments shall vote as members of the Association, and amendments passed by the members of the Association shall not be valid unless and until an instrument setting forth the provisions of the amendment and certified by the President and Secretary of the Association as to the requisite voting percentages cast in favor of the said amendment is duly recorded in the office of the _____ County Recorder.

12. Maintenance and Alterations. The responsibility for the maintenance of the Condominium, and the obligations related thereto, are as follows:

A. *The Association.* All maintenance, repairs, and replacements of the common areas and facilities, the limited common areas and facilities, and all painting and decorating of the exterior doors of the apartments shall be made by the Association and shall be charged to all apartments owners as a common expense, except to the extent that the same are caused or permitted by the negligence, misuse, or neglect of an apartment owner or occupant, in which case such expense shall be charged to such apartment owner. All damage caused to an apartment by the Association as a result of its authorized work on the common areas and facilities, limited common areas and facilities, or exterior doors of apartments shall be promptly repaired at the expense of the Association. All apartment owners and occupants shall promptly report to the Board any defect or need for repairs, the responsibility for the remedying of which is that of the Association.

B. *The Apartment Owner.* Except for the portions to be maintained, repaired, and replaced by the Association, the apartment owner shall maintain, repair, and replace at his expense all portions of his apartment as defined and delineated in Paragraphs 4 and 5 hereof, including but not limited to all glass windows, all sliding glass doors, all window air-conditioning units, heating apparatus, and gas connections to ranges located within each apartment. All the repairs of internal installations of the apartment, including but not limited to water, light, gas, power, sewage, telephone, sanitary installations, heating apparatus, air-conditioning units, doors, windows, lamps, and all other accessories which are a part of the apartment shall be at the owner's expense. Such maintenance shall be performed without disturbing the rights of other apartment owners and in such manner as not to affect the safety or soundness of the Condominium. All apartment owners and occupants shall promptly report to the Board any defect or need for repairs, the responsibility for the remedying of which is that of the Association.

Every owner shall perform promptly all maintenance and repair work within his own apartment which, if omitted, would cause injury or damage to any part of the Condominium belonging to another owner, and each owner shall be expressly responsible for the damages and liabilities arising from his failure to so maintain and repair his apartment. The Association shall specifically not be responsible for injury or damage to an apartment or to an apartment owner or occupant, his tenants, guests, or invitees caused by the failure of the owner or occupant of another apartment to so maintain and repair his apartments.

An owner shall reimburse the Association for any expenditures incurred by the Association in repairing or replacing any of the common areas and facilities or limited common areas and facilities damaged through the negligence, misuse, or neglect of such owner or of an occupant of such owner's apartment, and such amount to be reimbursed may be levied against that owner's apartment in addition to any annual or special assessment and may be collected in a lump sum or on a monthly basis, as determined by the Board of Directors, and shall be a lien upon the apartment of the owner enforceable in the same manner as an annual or special assessment.

Limited common areas appurtenant to an apartment shall be for the exclusive use of the owner or occupant of such apartment. All such areas shall be kept free and clear of snow, ice, and other accumulations by the owner or occupant of such apartment, who shall also make all repairs thereto caused or permitted by such owner's or occupant's negligence, misuse, or neglect. All other repairs in, to, or with respect to such limited common areas shall be made by the Association and the cost thereof shall be a common expense.

C. *Alterations, Modifications, and Improvements.*

(1) *Of the Common Area.* Subject to Subparagraph C(4) hereof, no apartment owner shall make or cause to be made any structural modifications or alterations in the portions of the Condominium which are to be maintained by the Association, or remove any portion thereof without first notifying the Association in writing and obtaining approval of at least seventy-five (75) percent of the voting interest in the Association.

No apartment owner shall modify, decorate, or change the appearance of any portion of the exterior of the building, the hallways, the windows, whether part of the apartment or not, sliding glass doors, whether part of the apartment or not, the doors, or the balconies or patios so as to cause any apartment to violate the architectural scheme of the Condominium or to appear in any way different from any other apartment, without first notifying in writing the Design Review Committee, if any, or if no such committee exists, the Board of Directors of the Association. Unanimous approval of the members of the Design Review Committee must be obtained, or approval of the Board of Directors, as the case may be.

(2) *Of the Apartments.* Subject to Paragraph C(4) hereof, no apartment owner shall make or cause to be made any installations, modifications, or alterations in his apartment or installations located therein which touch or connect with a common area or limited common area or which are structural in nature or which would jeopardize the safety or soundness of the Condominium or impair any easements, without first notifying the Association in writing and obtaining approval of the Board of Directors.

(3) *Notices.* All notices required in Paragraph 12C shall be delivered in writing to the President of the Association at the registered office of the Association, with a copy to the President at his home address. Such notice shall not be deemed to have been given unless and until plans, in form and detail acceptable to the Board of Directors, showing the modification, alteration, or change to be made, have also been delivered to the President of the Association, and such modification, alteration, or change, if and when made, shall be made pursuant to such plans as delivered.

Where required by this paragraph, and within thirty-five (35) days after receipt of notice, the President of the Association shall have the responsibility of securing the approval or objections of the members of the Board of Directors to the proposed modification or alteration and of delivering the decision of the Board to the apartment owner giving notice. Where required by this paragraph, and within sixty (60) days after receipt of notice, the President of the Association shall have the responsibility of calling a special meeting of the members of the Association to vote upon the proposed modification, alteration, or improvement.

Anything herein to the contrary notwithstanding, the Board of Directors, in its discretion, may submit to the members of the Association for vote any proposal submitted to it by an apartment owner, whose proposal is not required by this paragraph to be submitted to the members of the Association. In the event that the Board of Directors in its discretion determines that a proposal should be voted upon by the members of the Association, the Board shall authorize the President of the Association to call a special meeting of the members of the Association to vote upon the proposal. At any such meeting, the decision of the apartment owners holding a majority of the voting percentages present in person or by proxy at the meeting shall in all instances control.

(4) *Residential Apartment Combinations.* Subject to (i), (ii), (iii), and (iv) of this subparagraph, the owner of adjoining residential apartments may remove, at the owner's expense, any ceilings, floors, or nonload-bearing partition walls between the owned apartments for the purpose of using the apartments together as an integrated whole, and may also make such mofidications and alterations inside the owned apartments, and to installations therein, as are shown on the plans previously delivered to and approved by the Board of Directors. If any such commonly owned adjoining apartments are at the end of a hallway as originally constructed within the building, then such owner may remove, at his expense, any nonload-bearing partition walls between the owned apartments and the hallway for the purpose of using said hallway area as a part of such apartments as an integrated whole, and may construct a new entrance from the hallway to serve such owned apartments, provided, however, that such entrance shall not be constructed beyond the point where the apartments on both sides of the original hallway are under common ownership or so as to block access to fire exits. The work on such new entrance shall be done in a good and workmanlike manner and in compliance with the applicable governmental regulations and shall conform to the architectural scheme, color, and décor of the remaining hallway.

Any such removed partition walls, floors, or ceilings may be restored, and such new hallway entrances may be removed, all at the expense of the owner of the affected apartments. All such restorations and removals shall be done with materials at least equal in quality to the original materials, and shall be done in a good and workmanlike manner and in compliance with all governmental regulations, and, as to such hallway, shall conform to the architectural scheme, color, and décor of the remaining hallway.

If the Board of Directors, in its sole discretion, shall determine that such new hallway entrance, or such restored partition walls, floors, ceilings, or hallway are not constructed as herein required, it may make such changes and additions as it deems desirable, and deduct the costs so incurred from the security deposit required herein, and if the deposit is insufficient, the deficiency amount may be levied against that owner's said apartments in addition to any annual or special assessments, and said amount may be collected in a lump sum or in monthly or other installments, on dates designated by the Board of Directors. Such amount shall be a lien upon said apartments effective as of the date the amount of the levy is fixed by the Board, shall have the same priority as the lien of annual assessments, and may be enforced in the same manner as an annual assessment.

No physical removal of ceilings, floors, or nonload-bearing partition walls, or construction of new hallway entrances, for the purpose of combining adjoining apartments, and no modifications or alterations inside such apartments or to the installations therein, and no separation or restoration of same may be commenced or completed until the following conditions have been complied with: (i) No such work shall be undertaken until the person desiring the same shall notify the Board of Directors of his desire and shall deliver to the Board plans and specifications of the work desired, as aforesaid; (ii) No such work shall be undertaken until after the Board of Directors has determined and resolved that the implementation of said plans and specifications will not adversely affect the structural soundness of the building or the functioning of any common pipes, conduits, wiring, or other utilities; (iii) No such work shall be undertaken until the person desiring the same shall have received the written consent of the holders of all first mortgages of record against the affected apartments; (iv) No such work shall be undertaken until reasonable security, as determined by the Board of Directors, shall have been deposited with the Treasurer of the Association, to be held by the Treasurer, without interest, as security for payment of all labor and materials employed in the work and for completion of the work pursuant to the plans as herein required.

13. Assessments. Assessments against the apartment owners shall be made by the Association for the common expenses. Payments to the Association for assessments shall commence on the date of the first conveyance of an apartment from the Declarant to an apartment owner, and the due dates therefor shall be established by the Board of Directors. Assessments shall be levied pursuant to the bylaws and subject to the following provisions:

A. *Share of Common Expenses.* Each apartment owner shall be liable for a proportionate share of the common expenses, and shall share in the common profits, in the percentage assigned to his apartment(s) in Exhibit ___. The common expenses shall include but not be limited to the expenses of operation, maintenance, repair, or replacement of the common areas and facilities, costs of carrying out the powers and duties of the Association, costs of fire and extended coverage insurance and other insurance, costs incurred in connection with emergencies, the expenses incurred in funding operating deficits, payments to a reserve fund for maintenance, repairs, and replacement of those common areas and facilities which must be replaced on a periodic basis, and other expenses designated to be common expenses in this Declaration, in the bylaws, and in such rules and regulations as may be promulgated by the Association.

B. *Payment.* All sums assessed by the Association pursuant to this Declaration and the bylaws shall be paid in lump sums or as otherwise designated by the Board. All sums assessed by the Association for payments to a reserve fund for operating costs and a reserve fund for maintenance, repairs, and replacement of the common areas and facilities which must be replaced on a periodic basis, shall be payable in regular installments rather than by special assessments.

C. *Service and Handling Fee.* Any assessments and installments thereon not paid when due shall be deemed delinquent. If an assessment is not paid within ten (10) days after the due date, a service and handling fee of $10.00, or such other amount as may be designated by the Board of Directors from time to time, shall be imposed on the person liable for the delinquent assessment. All payments on accounts shall first be applied to the service and handling fee due and then to the assessments due.

14. Liability of Transferee for Assessments. In a voluntary conveyance of an apartment, the grantee of the apartment shall be jointly and severally liable with the grantor for all unpaid assessments by the Association against the latter for his share of the common expenses up to the time of the grant or conveyance, without prejudice to the grantee's right to recover from the grantor the amounts paid by the grantee therefor. However, any such grantee shall be entitled to a statement from the Board of Directors setting forth the amount of the unpaid assessments against the grantor due the Association, and such grantee shall not be liable for, nor shall the apartment conveyed be subject to, a lien for any unpaid assessments made by the Association against the grantor in excess of the amount therein set forth.

15. Assessment Liens and Foreclosures. All sums assessed by the Association for annual and special assessments for the share of the common expenses chargeable to any apartment shall constitute a lien on such apartment for the full amount of the assessments, effective as of the date the amount of the assessment is fixed by the Board, prior to all other liens except only (i) tax liens on the apartment, including special assessments for public improvements, in favor of any governmental assessing authority or taxing authority, and (ii) all sums unpaid on any first mortgage of record against such apartment. All such assessments and all taxes, assessments, and charges imposed pursuant to law by any governmental assessing or taxing authority which may become liens prior to the mortgage on any apartment shall relate only to such apartment and not to other apartments or to the Condominium as a whole. Such assessment, while it or any installment is so delinquent for more than thirty (30) days, may be declared due and payable in full by the Board and such assessment lien, with interest at the maximum legal rate, may be foreclosed by suit by the Board or its agent, acting on behalf of the owners of the apartments, in like manner as a mortgagee of real property. In any such foreclosure the apartment owner shall also be required to pay the costs of such foreclosure, including reasonable attorney's fees and reasonable rental for the apartment if so provided by the Board, and the lien shall also secure such costs and attorney's fees. The Board, acting on behalf of the owners of the apartments, shall have power to bid in the apartment at foreclosure sale, and to acquire and hold, lease, mortgage, and convey the same. Suit to recover the money judgment for unpaid common expenses, with interest as above stated, shall be maintainable without foreclosing or waiving the lien securing the same, or the right to foreclose said lien, and in such event, the owner liable therefor shall also pay all costs of collection, including reasonable attorney's fees.

16. Liability Upon Mortgage Foreclosure. Where the mortgagee of a first mortgage of record or other purchaser of an apartment obtains title to the apartment as a result of foreclosure of the first mortgage, or by transfer of title in lieu of foreclosure, such acquirer of title, its (or his) heirs, representatives, successors, and assignees shall not be liable for the assessments by the Association chargeable to such apartment which accrue prior to the acquisition of title to such apartment by such acquirer. All unpaid assessments shall accrue as a common expense collectible from the owners of all of the apartments, including such acquirer, its (or his) heirs, representatives, successors, and assignees. For purposes hereof, title to such apartment shall be deemed acquired by foreclosure upon expiration of the applicable period of redemption or upon delivery of a deed in lieu of foreclosure.

17. Insurance. Insurance other than title insurance which shall be carried upon the Condominium and upon the apartments shall be governed by the following provisions:

A. *Responsibility and Benefit.* The Board shall have the authority to and shall obtain and continue in effect blanket property insurance for the Condominium, with coverage as set forth in Paragraph 17B hereof, for one hundred (100) percent of the replacement costs of the common areas and facilities and the apartments. Such insurance coverage shall be written on the Condominium in the name of, and the proceeds thereof shall be payable to, the Association as trustee for each of the apartment owners, and their respective mortgagees, as their interests may appear in the percentages established in Exhibit ___. Provision for such insurance shall be without prejudice to the right of each apartment owner to insure his own apartment and his personal property at his own expense, and insurance coverage obtained and maintained pursuant to the requirements of this Paragraph 17 may not be brought into contribution with insurance purchased by apartment owners or their mortgagees. All insurance coverage authorized to be purchased shall be purchased by the Association for itself and for the benefit of all of the owners of all of the apartments. Insurance premiums for the insurance coverage authorized in this Paragraph 17 shall be a common expense to be paid by monthly assessments levied by the Association.

B. *Coverage.* The following insurance coverage shall be maintained in full force and effect by the Association covering the Condominium and the operation and management thereof, to-wit:

(1) Casualty insurance covering all of the apartments, common areas and facilities, and limited common areas and facilities, in an amount equal to not less than one hundred (100) percent of the replacement value (exclusive of land, foundation, excavation, and other items normally excluded from coverage) thereof (including all building service equipment and any fixtures or equipment within the apartments which are financed under any mortgage covering an apartment), with an agreed amount endorsement or its equivalent, if available, or any inflation guard endorsement. Such coverage shall afford protection against the following:

(i) Loss or damage by fire and other hazards covered by the standard extended coverage endorsement, and by sprinkler leakage, debris removal, cost of demolition, vandalism, malicious mischief, windstorm, and water damage;

(ii) If the project contains a steam boiler, a broad form policy of repair and replacement boiler and machinery insurance of at least fifty thousand dollars ($50,000) per accident per location; and

(iii) Such other risks as are customarily covered in similar projects.

(2) Public liability insurance covering all of the common areas and facilities. Coverage shall be for at least one million dollars ($1,000,000) per occurrence, for personal injury and/or property damage. Such policy shall contain a "severability of interest" endorsement which shall preclude the insurer from denying the claim of an apartment owner because of negligent acts of the Association or another apartment owner. Such policy shall also contain cross-liability endorsements to cover liability of all owners of apartments as a group to each apartment owner. Such coverage shall include protection against water damage liability, liability for nonowned and hired automobiles, liability for the property of others, and elevator collision coverage.

(3) Worker's Compensation insurance to meet the requirements of law.

(4) Personal liability insurance covering all members of the Board of Directors and officers of the Association in the management of the Association's affairs. The premiums on such insurance shall be paid by the Association and shall be a common expense. The Association shall indemnify such persons, for such expense and liabilities, in such manner, under such circumstances, and to such extent as permitted by the state statutes, as now enacted or hereafter amended.

(5) Such other insurance coverage, other than title insurance, as the Board, in its sole discretion, may determine from time to time to be in the best interests of the Association and the apartment owners.

(6) All policies of insurance covering the Condominium shall provide that the insurance carrier shall notify in writing all holders of first mortgages of record covering the apartments and all other insureds at least thirty (30) days in advance of the effective date of any substantial modification or cancellation of the said policies.

(7) All policies of insurance covering the Condominium shall provide that, despite any provisions giving the carrier the right to elect to restore damage in lieu of a cash settlement, such option shall not be exercisable without the prior written approval of the Association or when in conflict with the provisions of any Insurance Trust Agreement to which the Association may be a party, or any requirement of law.

(8) All policies of insurance covering the Condominium must contain a waiver of subrogation by the insurer as to any and all claims against the Association, any apartment owner, and/or their respective agents, employees or tenants, and of any defense based on co-insurance or on invalidity arising from the acts of the insured.

(9) No insurance coverage provided for herein shall be prejudiced by (i) any act or neglect of the apartment owners when such act or neglect is not within the control of the Association; or (ii) any failure of the Association to comply with any warranty or condition regarding any portion of the Condominium over which the Association has no control.

C. *Insurance Trustee.* All policies of casualty insurance covering the Condominium shall provide for the insurance proceeds covering any loss to be payable to the Board of Directors of the Association, as trustee, as hereinafter provided, and the insurance proceeds from any casualty loss shall be held and distributed for the use and benefit of the Association and the owners of the apartments, and their respective mortgagees, as their interests may appear. The Association is hereby declared to be and appointed as authorized agent for the owners of all apartments for the purpose of negotiating and agreeing to a settlement as to the value and extent of any loss which may be covered under any policy of casualty insurance, and is granted full right and authority to execute in favor of any insuror a release of liability arising out of any occurrence covered by any policy or policies of casualty insurance and resulting in loss of or damage to insured property.

(1) The Association shall have the right to designate a reputable corporate trustee to act as trustee hereunder in its place, and all parties beneficially interested in such insurance coverage shall be bound thereby.

(2) The sole duties of the insurance trustee shall be to receive such proceeds of insurance as are paid and to hold the same in trust for the purposes herein stated, and for the benefit of the Association and the owners of all apartments and their respective mortgagees, and to disburse such insurance proceeds as hereinafter provided. In the event the Association appoints a corporate trustee, the Association, as a common expense, shall pay a reasonable fee to said trustee for its services rendered hereunder, and shall pay such costs and expenses as said trustee may incur in the performance of any duties and obligations imposed upon it hereunder. The trustee shall be liable only for its willful misconduct, bad faith, or gross negligence, and then for only such money which comes into its possession. Wherever the trustee may be required to make distribution of insurance proceeds to owners of apartments and their mortgagees, as their respective interests may appear, the trustee may rely upon a Certificate of the President and Secretary of the Association, executed under oath, certifying the name or names of the owners of each apartment, the name or names of the mortgagee or mortgagees who may hold a mortgage or mortgages encumbering each apartment, and the respective percentages of any distribution which may be required to be made to the owner or owners of any apartments and their respective mortgagee or mortgagees, as their respective interests may appear. Where any insurance proceeds are paid to the trustee for any casualty loss, the holder or holders of any mortgage or mortgages encumbering an apartment shall not have the right to elect to apply insurance proceeds to the reduction of any mortgage or mortgages, unless such insurance proceeds represent a distribution to the owner or owners of any apartments, and their respective mortgagees, after such insurance proceeds have been first applied to repair, replacement, or reconstruction of any loss or damage, or unless such casualty insurance proceeds are authorized to be distributed to the owners of any apartments and their respective mortgagee or mortgagees, by reason of loss of or damage to personal property constituting a part of the common areas and facilities and as to which a determination is made not to repair, replace, or restore such personal property.

18. Damage to or Destruction of Property. In the event all or any portion of the Condominium property is damaged or destroyed, the restoration or disposition of the said property shall be determined in the following manner:

A. *Less Than Total or Substantial Destruction of Insured Property.* If a majority of the total number of apartments are tenantable after damage or destruction and the property is insured against the peril causing the loss or damage, then the damaged portion of the improvements shall be restored, provision for reconstruction to be made not later than one hundred eighty (180) days from the date of damage or destruction, and the obligations of the parties shall be as follows:

(1) *Contract for Restoration.* The Board shall, within one hundred eighty (180) days from the date of damage or destruction, enter into a firm contract with a qualified builder providing for the restoration of the damaged or destroyed portion of the Condominium to substantially the same condition as existed immediately prior to the insured loss; provided, however, that no contract shall be entered into by the Board for an amount in excess of the insurance proceeds then held in trust in accordance with Paragraph 17C above until the Board has provided, through assessment of common expenses or otherwise, for funds sufficient to cover such excess costs. Said restoration shall be commended and completed with due diligence, and the owners of all apartments agree to cooperate with the Board in all matters affecting such restoration. The Board is hereby expressly authorized to assess as additional common expenses such amounts in excess of insurance proceeds as are necesary to repair, restore, or rebuild damaged apartments.

(2) *Failure to Contract.* In the event the Board fails to enter into a contract as provided in Paragraph 18A(1) above, then any apartment owner or mortgagee of record of an apartment, with the consent of the trustee, shall have the right, but not the obligation, within thirty (30) days after the expiration of the one hundred eighty (180)-day period specified in Paragraph 18A(1) to enter into those contracts which it deems necessary to complete said restoration, and shall have the right to have said insurance proceeds applied in satisfaction of any obligations incurred pursuant to said contracts, without liability of any kind to the Board or any owner of an apartment, and without liability for interest on said insurance proceeds.

(3) *Disbursement of Funds.* Disbursement of funds on deposit for contracts for restoration entered into by the Board shall be made by the trustee in substantially the same manner and with substantially the same safeguards as in the repair and reconstruction of like buildings, including but not limited to receipt by the trustee of written consents of the mortgagees of record of apartments affected by the construction work, receipt by the trustee of such sworn construction statements, lists of subcontractors, lien waivers and receipts as it shall determine to be appropriate, and subject to such inspections as it deems necessary to insure completion in accordance with the plans and specifications for the restoration. Nothing contained in this Paragraph 18 shall be construed to make the mortgagee or mortgagees, if any, responsible for collection or noncollection of any insurance proceeds, said mortgagees being responsible solely for the insurance proceeds which come into their hands.

B. *Total or Substantial Destruction or Uninsured Damage or Destruction.*

(1) If less than a majority of the total number of apartments are tenantable after the damage or destruction, or in the event the property is not insured against the peril causing the loss or damage, provision for reconstruction of the damaged portion of the property shall be made within one hundred eighty (180) days from the date of damage or destruction unless within said one hundred eighty (180) days at least seventy-five (75) percent of the first mortgagees of the apartments or their assignees (based upon one (1) vote for each first mortgage owned), and at least seventy-five (75) percent of the owners (other than Declarant) of the individual apartments, based upon the percentages set forth in Exhibit ___ hereto have given their prior written approval of a decision not to restore.

(2) Upon total or substantial destruction or uninsured damage or destruction of any apartment or any part of the common areas, any institutional holder of a first mortgage on an apartment, who has previously registered with the Association, will be entitled to timely written notice of any such damage or destruction.

C. *Non-Restoration.* If, by reason of the above, the damaged improvements are not to be restored, then the Board of Directors of the Association shall record with the Office of the _____ County Recorder a notice setting forth such facts, and upon the recording of such notice:

(1) The property shall be deemed to be owned in common by the apartment owners, each in the percentage of undivided interest previously owned by such owner in the common areas and facilities; and

(2) Any liens affecting any of the apartments shall be deemed to be transferred in accordance with the existing priorities to the percentage of undivided interests of the apartment owners in the property as above provided; and

(3) The property shall be subject to an action for partition at the suit of any holder of an interest, as herein defined, in which event, the net proceeds of sale, together with the net proceeds of the insurance on the property, if any, shall be considered as one fund and shall be divided among all holders of an interest in a percentage equal to the percentage of the undivided interest held by such owner as their respective interests may appear, after first paying out of the respective shares, to the extent sufficient for the purpose, all liens on the undivided interest on the property.

19. Eminent Domain. In the event all or any portion of the property is taken by exercise of the power of, or in the nature of, eminent domain, or by an action or deed in lieu thereof, (i) the institutional holder of any first mortgage on an apartment who has previously registered with the Association will be entitled to timely written notice of any such proceeding or proposed acquisition, and (ii) disposition of the awards and of the remaining property shall be determined in the following manner:

A. *Total or Substantial Taking of an Apartment.* If an entire apartment is acquired by eminent domain, or if a portion of an apartment is acquired by eminent domain leaving the apartment owner with a remnant which may not practically or lawfully be used for any purpose permitted by this Declaration, the award shall compensate the apartment owner, and/or his mortgagees, as their interests may appear, for the apartment and its interest in the common areas and facilities, whether or not any interest in the common areas and facilities is acquired. Upon acquisition, unless the decree otherwise provides, the apartment's entire interest in the common areas and facilities, voting percentage in the Association, and the common expense liability shall be automatically reallocated to the remaining apartments in proportion to the respective interests, votes, and liabilities of those apartments prior to the taking, and the Association shall promptly prepare, execute, and file an amendment to this Declaration reflecting the reallocation. Any remnant of an apartment remaining after part of the apartment is taken under Paragraph 19A shall thereafter be a common area.

B. *Less than Total or Substantial Taking of an Apartment.* Except as provided in Subparagraph A of this Paragraph 19, if a portion of an apartment is acquired by eminent domain, the award shall compensate the apartment owner, and/or his mortgagees, as their interests may appear, for the reduction in value of the apartment and its percentage interest in the common areas and facilities. Upon acqusition, that apartment's interest in the common areas and facilities, its votes in the Association, and its common expense liability shall be reduced in proportion to the reduction in the size of the apartment, and the portion of the interest in the common areas and facilities, votes, and common expense liability divested from the partially acquired apartment shall automatically be reallocated to that apartment and to the remaining apartments in proportion to the respective interests, votes, and liabilities of those apartments prior to the taking, with the partially acquired apartment participating in the reallocation on the basis of its reduced interest, votes, and liabilities.

C. *Partial Taking of the Common Areas and Facilities.* If a portion of the common areas and facilities is acquired by eminent domain, the award shall be paid to the Association. The Association shall divide any portion of the award not used for any restoration or repair of the remaining common areas and facilities among the apartment owners and/or their respective mortgagees, as their interests may appear, in proportion to their respective interests in the common areas and facilities before the taking. Provision for restoration, reconstruction, or repair of the remaining common areas and facilities shall be made within one hundred eighty (180) days from the date of the taking unless within said one hundred eighty (180) days at least seventy-five (75) percent of the first mortgagees of the apartments or their assignees (based upon one (1) vote for each first mortgage owned), and owners of the individual apartments based upon the percentages set forth in

Paragraph 6 hereof have given their prior written approval of a decision not to restore, reconstruct, or repair.

D. *Taking of Limited Common Area.* If part or all of a limited common area is acquired by eminent domain, the award shall be equally divided among the owners of the apartments to which that limited common area was allocated, and/or their respective mortgagees, as their interests may appear, at the time of the acquisition.

20. Individual Insurance Coverage. The owner of each apartment may, at his own expense, obtain insurance coverage for loss of or damage to any furniture, furnishings, personal effects, and other personal property belonging to such owner, and may at his own expense and option obtain insurance coverages against personal liability for injury to the person or property of another while within his apartment or upon the common areas and facilities or limited common areas and facilities. All such insurance obtained by the owner of each apartment shall, wherever such provision shall be available, provide that the insuror waives its right of subrogation as to any claims against other owners and occupants of apartments, the Association, and the respective servants, agents, and guests of said other owners, occupants, and Association. Risk of loss of or damage to any furniture, furnishings, personal effects, and other personal property (other than such furniture, furnishings, and personal property constituting a portion of the common areas and facilities) belonging to or carried on the person of the owner of each apartment, or which may be stored in any apartment, or in, to, or upon common areas and facilities or limited common areas and facilities, shall be borne by the owner of each such apartment. All furniture, furnishings, and personal property constituting a portion of the common areas and facilities and held for the joint use and benefit of all owners of all apartments shall be covered by such insurance as shall be maintained in force and effect by the Association as hereinafter provided. The owner of an apartment shall have no personal liability for any damage caused by the Association in connection with the use of the common areas and facilities or limited common areas and facilities. The owner or occupant of an apartment shall be liable for injuries or damages resulting from an accident in his own apartment to the same extent and degree that the owner or occupant of a single-family dwelling would be liable for an accident occurring within the dwelling.

21. Other Liens. All taxes, assessments, and charges which may become liens prior to the first mortgage under local law shall relate only to the individual apartments and not to the Condominium as a whole. All liens against an apartment other than for permitted mortgages, taxes, or special assessments shall be satisfied or otherwise removed by the owner of the apartment within sixty (60) days from the date of the lien attachment. All taxes and special assessments upon an apartment shall be paid by the owner of the apartment before they become delinquent.

A. *Notice of Lien.* An apartment owner shall give notice to the Board of Directors of every lien against his apartment other than permitted mortgages, taxes, and special assessments within thirty (30) days after the lien attaches, or after he has reason to believe or notice that the lien has attached. An apartment owner shall also give notice to the Board of satisfaction of such lien.

B. *Notice of Lawsuit.* An apartment owner shall give notice to the Board of Directors of every suit or other proceeding which may affect the title to his apartment, such notice to be given within five (5) days after the apartment owner receives notice thereof.

22. Declarant's Rights and Privileges. Notwithstanding anything herein to the contrary, Declarant shall have the following rights and privileges:

A. *Sales Activity.* The Declarant is irrevocably empowered to sell, lease, or rent apartments to any persons approved by it, including any apartments reacquired by the Declarant. Said Declarant or its successors or assignees shall have the right to transact on the Condominium any business necessary to consummate sales of apartments, including but not limited to the right to maintain models, post signs, maintain employees in a sales office, use the common areas and facilities, and show apartments. For so long as the Declarant owns any apartments, neither the apartment owners nor the Association nor their use of the Condominium shall interfere with the Declarant's disposition of the apartments. A sales office, signs, and all items pertaining to sales shall not be considered or used as common areas and facilities, and shall remain the property of the Declarant. In the event that there are unsold apartments, the Declarant retains the right to be the owner thereof, under the same terms and conditions as other owners save for this right to sell, lease, or rent, as contained in this paragraph.

23. Remedies for Breach of Covenants, Restrictions, and Regulations.

A. The violation of any restriction or condition or regulation adopted by the Board of Directors or the breach of any covenant herein contained or contained in the articles, bylaws, or such rules and regulations as may be promulgated by the Board shall give the Board the following rights, in addition to any other right herein contained: (i) to enter upon that part of the Condominium where such violation or breach exists and summarily abate and remove at the expense of the defaulting party, any structure, thing, or condition that may exist thereon contrary to the intent and meaning of the provisions hereof; or (ii) to enjoin, abate, or remedy by appropriate legal proceedings, either at law or in equity, the continuance of any such breach. All expenses of the Board in connection with such actions and proceedings and all court costs and attorneys' fees and other fees and expenses, and all damages, liquidated or otherwise, together with interest at the maximum legal rate until paid, shall be charged to and assessed against such defaulting party and shall be made a part of his respective share of the common expenses and a lien shall be held for all the same upon the apartment of the defaulting party and upon all of his additions and improvements thereto and upon all the personal property in his apartment or located elsewhere on the premises of the Condominium. Any and all such rights and remedies may be exercised at any time and from time to time, cumulatively or otherwise, by the Board.

24. General Provisions.

A. Each apartment owner and each subsequent grantee by the acceptance of a deed of conveyance, or each tenant under a lease, and all occupants of apartments accept the same subject to all restrictions, conditions, covenants, reservations, liens and charges in the jurisdiction, rights and powers created or reserved by this Declaration, and all rights, benefits, and privileges of every character hereby granted, reserved, declared, or imposed by this Declaration, the Articles, or the bylaws, or by such rules and regulations as may be promulgated or amended by the Association from time to time. These shall be deemed and taken to be covenants running with the land and shall bind any person having at any time any interest or estate in an apartment and in the Condominium and shall inure to the benefit of such owner in like manner as if the provisions of the Declaration, Articles, bylaws, or such rules and regulations as may be promulgated or amended by the Association from time to time, as the case may be, were recited and stipulated at length in each and every deed of conveyance.

B. No covenants, restrictions, conditions, obligations, or provisions contained in this Declaration, the Articles, bylaws, or contained in such rules and regulations as may be promulgated by the Association shall be deemed to have been abrogated or waived by reason of any failure to enforce the same regardless of the number of violations or breaches which may occur.

C. The invalidity of any covenant, restriction, condition, limitation, or any other provision of this Declaration or of the Articles, bylaws, or of such rules and regulations as may be promulgated by the Association, or any part of the same shall not impair or affect in any manner the validity, enforceability, or effect of the rest of this Declaration.

D. The provisions of this Declaration shall be liberally construed to effectuate its purpose of creating a uniform plan for the operation of a condominium apartment building.

25. Termination. The Condominium may be removed from the Act in the following manner:

A. *Agreement.* The termination of the Condominium may be effected by the unanimous written agreement of the apartment owners and all lienholders, or assignees, pursuant to the provisions of the State Act, as amended from time to time.

B. *Destruction.* In case of total or substantial destruction or uninsured damage or destruction, if within one hundred eighty (180) days from the date of the damage or destruction, at least seventy-five (75) percent of the first mortgagees of the apartments or their assignees (based upon one (1) vote for each first mortgage owned) and at least seventy-five (75) percent of the owners (other than Declarant) of the individual apartments, based upon the percentage set forth in Exhibit _____ hereto have given their prior written approval of a decision not to restore, then the condominium form of ownership shall be terminated in accordance with the provisions of the Act, as amended from time to time.

26. Notices. All notices to be given pursuant to this Declaration shall be in writing and shall be mailed by U.S. mail, postage prepaid, or personally delivered to the intended recipient at his or its address as set forth on the owners' register maintained by the Association.

27. Construction of Declaration. The provisions hereof shall be deemed independent and severable, and the invalidity or partial invalidity or unenforceability of any one provision or portion thereof as to any person or circumstance, as may be determined by a court of competent jurisdiction, shall not affect the validity or enforceability of any other provisions hereof, or of the invalid or unenforceable provision or portion thereof as to any other person or curcumstances.

IN WITNESS WHEREOF, Declarant has caused this instrument to be executed the day and year first above written.

State of _____

County of _____

On this _____ day of _____, 19_____, before me, a Notary Public, within and for said county, personally appeared _____, to me personally known, who, being by me duly sworn, did say that they are respectively with the _____ corporation named in the foregoing instrument, that the seal affixed to said instrument is the corporate seal of said corporation, and that said instrument was signed and sealed in behalf of said corporation by authority of its Board of Directors, and said persons acknowledged that said instrument was the free act and deed of said corporation.

                                        Notary Public

Appendix B—Condominium Association Bylaws

Article I
General

Bylaw 1. Submission. These are the bylaws of The _____ Association, Inc., a _____ nonprofit corporation (hereinafter "Association"), the Articles of Incorporation of which were filed in the Office of the Secretary of State of the state of _____ on _____, 19_____. This Association is organized for the purpose of being and constituting the association of apartment owners for the _____ Condominium (sometimes hereinafter referred to as "Condominium"), a condominium to be organized pursuant to the provisions of the state Condominium Act, (hereinafter referred to as the "Act") by Declaration of apartment ownership dated _____ (hereinafter referred to as the "Declaration").

(a) No apartment owner shall have any severable right or interest in any property, funds, or reserves of the Association but merely a right to the joint use and enjoyment thereof so long as he continues as an apartment owner.

Bylaw 2. Name. The name of the Association shall be "The _____ Association, Inc."

Bylaw 3. Principal Office. The principal office of the Association shall be at the offices of _____ or at such other place as may be subsequently designated by the Board of Directors.

Bylaw 4. Definitions. All terms as used herein, where applicable, shall have the same definitions as those attributed to them in the Declaration establishing the _____ Condominium, to which these bylaws shall be attached as an exhibit and which shall be recorded in the Office of the County Recorder.

Bylaw 5. Applicability. The provisions of these bylaws shall be applicable to the Condominium, and all present and future owners and tenants, and any other persons who might occupy or use the facilities of the Condominium in any manner, are subject to the provisions of the Declaration, these bylaws, and the Articles of Incorporation of The Association, Inc. (hereinafter "Articles"). The mere acquisition, rental, or occupancy of any of the apartments located in the Condominium will signify that the person exercising such rights has accepted and will comply with the provisions of the Declaration, these bylaws, and the Articles.

Bylaw 6. Association Responsibilities. The Association shall have the responsibility of administering the Condominium through its duly elected Board of Directors (sometimes hereinafter referred to as the "Board") and of approving the annual budget, establishing and collecting monthly assessments, and arranging for the management of the property of the Condominium.

Bylaw 7. Limitations on Rights of Association.

(a) Unless at least seventy-five (75) percent of the holders of first mortgages then of record against the apartments (based upon one vote for each mortgage owned) and owners having seventy-five (75) percent of the voting interest in the Association, or such greater percentage as may be required by the Act (excluding Declarant), have given their written approval, the Association shall not be entitled to:

(1) Petition or subdivide any apartment (which shall not include the combination, separation, or restoration of residential apartments contemplated in Subparagraph C(4) of Paragraph 12 of the Declaration);

(2) Use hazard insurance proceeds for losses to any Condominium property (whether to apartments or to common areas) for other than the repair, replacement, or reconstruction of such Condominium property, except as provided by the Act in case of substantial loss to the apartment and/or common areas of the Condominium.

(b) Unless one hundred (100) percent of the holders of all liens affecting any of the apartments and owners having one hundred (100) percent of the voting interest in the Association, as established by the Declaration, have given their prior written approval, the Association shall not be entitled to:

(1) Change the pro rata interest or obligations of any individual apartment for the purposes of (1) levying assessments or charges or allocating distributions of hazard insurance proceeds or condemnation awards; or (ii) determining the pro rata share of ownership of each apartment in the common areas;

(2) By act or omission, seek to abandon, partition, subdivide, encumber, sell, or transfer the common areas and facilities.

Article II
Membership and Voting

Bylaw 1. Membership. Every person who is a record owner of a fee or undivided fee interest in any apartment (as defined in the Declaration) of the Condominium, including contract for deed sellers and purchasers, shall be a member of the Association. Membership shall be appurtenant to and may not be separated from ownership of an apartment.

(a) *Registration of Owner and Occupant.* It shall be the duty of each owner, and any occupant residing in the apartment if the owner is not residing therein, to register with the Secretary of the Association in writing (i) the name and address of such owner or occupant; (ii) the nature and satisfactory evidence of such owner's or occupant's interest or estate in the apartment, if any; (iii) the addresses at which such owner or occupant desires to receive notice, if entitled to such notice, of any duly called meeting of the member; (iv) the name and address of the first mortgagee, if any, of the apartment owned by said owner; and (v) the name of the owner or occupant, if there is more than one owner of occupant of an apartment, who shall be authorized to cast their vote with respect to such apartment. If an owner or occupant does not register as provided in this Article, the Association shall be under no duty to recognize the rights of such person hereunder, and shall not recognize such person's rights to vote as provided herein, but such failure to register shall not relieve an owner or occupant of any obligation, covenant, or restriction under the governing documents. If there is more than one owner or occupant of an apartment, each must execute the registration as provided in this Article.

(b) *Restrictions on Ownership and Transfer.* The interests, rights, and obligations of a member in the Association may not be assigned, pledged, encumbered, or transferred in any manner, except as an appurtenance to such member's apartment.

Bylaw 2. Voting. Voting shall be on a percentage basis, and the percentage which the owner of each apartment is entitled to vote is the percentage assigned by the Declaration to that apartment for voting purposes. No vote in the Association shall inure to any apartment during the time when the apartment owner thereof is the Association. When more than one person is the owner of an apartment, all such persons shall be deemed owners, and the vote for such apartment shall be exercised as they, between or among themselves, determine, but if such persons cannot determine how to cast the vote for their apartment, such vote shall not be counted. In no event shall more than the percentage assigned in the Declaration for that apartment be voted.

Bylaw 3. Majority of Apartment Owners. As used in these bylaws, the term "majority" or "majority of apartment owners" shall mean those apartment owners holding more than fifty (50) percent of the total authorized votes of all apartment owners present in person or by proxy and voting at any meeting of the apartment owners.

Bylaw 4. Quorum. Except as otherwise provided in the Act, the Declaration, or these bylaws, the presence in person or by proxy of apartment owners holding, in the aggregate fifty-one (51) percent or more of the votes in accordance with the percentages assigned in the Declaration to the apartments for voting purposes shall constitute a quorum for the transaction of business of the Association. If, however, such quorum shall not be present or represented at any meeting of the owners, those entitled to vote thereat, present in person or represented by written proxy, shall have the power to adjourn the meeting, until a quorum shall be present or represented. At such adjourned meeting at which a quorum shall be present or represented, any business may be transacted which might have been transacted at the meeting originally called.

Bylaw 5. Proxies. An owner may cast the vote to which such owner is entitled and be counted as present at any meeting of the members of the Association by written proxy naming another person or persons entitled to act on that owner's behalf, delivered to the Secretary before the commencement of any such meeting. Unless otherwise provided in writing between an owner and occupant, the transfer of possession of an apartment to an occupant thereof under a contract for deed shall, during the actual, lawful possession and occupancy of such apartment by the occupant, serve to automatically grant to such occupant an irrevocable proxy authorizing such occupant to exercise the vote accruing to such apartment at all duly called meetings of the members of the Association held during such period; provided, however, that no such grant shall be deemed effective with respect to any meeting of the members of the Association unless such occupant has, prior to such meeting, registered with the Secretary of the Association as provided in Bylaw 1(a) of Article II of these bylaws. An occupant who has been granted a proxy and has registered with the Secretary of the Association as provided in this bylaw shall be entitled to notice of any duly called meeting of the members of the Association. Except for proxies which may be granted in favor of occupants specifically provided for in this bylaw, all proxies granted by a member of the Association shall be revocable by that member by written notice or by personally attending and voting at a meeting of the members of the Association, and shall in any case be invalid after one year from the date of such proxy.

Bylaw 6. Cumulative Voting. Cumulative voting is prohibited.

Article III
Membership Meetings

Bylaw 1. Place. All meetings of the Association shall be held at the office of the Association or such other place in _____ County, convenient to the owners, as may be designated by the Board of Directors in the notice.

Bylaw 2. Annual Meetings. The first annual meeting of the Association shall be held within one year from the date of incorporation of the Association, but in no event later than one hundred twenty (120) days after completion of the transfer to purchasers of title to apartments representing one hundred (100) percent of the votes of all apartment owners. Thereafter, the annual meetings of the Association shall be held on the same day of the same month of each year thereafter. If the day for the annual meeting of the Association is a legal holiday, the meeting will be held at the same hour on the first day following which is not a legal holiday.

Bylaw 3. Annual Report. An Annual Report shall be prepared by the Association. A copy of said Annual Report shall be provided to each apartment owner and, upon written request, to any institutional first mortgage holder, at least ten (10) days before every Annual Meeting of the Association. The report shall contain the following:

(a) A statement of any capital expenditures in excess of one thousand dollars ($1,000) anticipated by the Association during the current year or succeeding two fiscal years;

(b) A statement of the status and amount of any reserve for replacement fund and any portion of the fund designated for any specified project by the Board of Directors;

(c) A copy of the Statement of Financial Condition for the Association for the last fiscal year;

(d) A statement of the status of any pending suits or judgments in which the Association is a party;

(e) A statement of the insurance coverage provided by the Association; and

(f) A statement of any unpaid assessments by the Association on individual apartments, identifying the apartment number and the amount of the unpaid assessment.

Bylaw 4. Membership List. At least ten (10) days before every meeting of the Association, a complete list of apartment owners entitled to vote at said meeting, arranged numerically by apartments, with the voting percentage of each, shall be prepared by the Secretary. Such list shall be produced and kept at the office of the Association and shall be open to examination by any member.

Bylaw 5. Special Meetings.

(a) Special meetings of the Association for any purpose, or purposes, unless otherwise prescribed by statute, may be called by the President, and shall be called by the President or Secretary at the request, in writing, of a majority of the Board of Directors, or at the request, in writing to the Secretary, of the apartment owners holding one-third of the voting percentages. Such request shall state the purpose or purposes of the proposed meeting.

(b) Business transacted at all special meetings shall be confined to the subjects stated in the notice thereof.

Bylaw 6. Notice of Meetings.

(a) Written notice of all meetings of the Association stating the time, place, and complete agenda thereof shall be sent by the Secretary, by United States mail, to all apartment owners of record, and, upon written request, to any institutional holder of a first mortgage on a residential apartment, at the address of their respective apartments and to other addresses as any of them may have designated in writing to the Secretary. Said notices shall be mailed by him at least twenty-one (21) days in advance of the Annual Meetings and at least seven (7) days in advance of special meetings.

(b) Any institutional holder of a first mortgage will be permitted to designate a representative to attend all such meetings.

Bylaw 7. Right to Vote. At any meeting of the Association, each owner having the right to vote shall be entitled to vote in person or by proxy, pursuant to the provisions of Article II hereof.

Bylaw 8. Vote Required to Transact Business. When a quorum is present at any meeting, a majority of the voting percentage of such quorum shall decide any question brought before the meeting, unless the question is one upon which, by express provision of the Act, the Declaration, or of these bylaws, a different vote is required, in which case such express provision shall govern and control the decision of such question.

Bylaw 9. Action by Consent. Whenever the vote of apartment owners at a meeting is required or permitted by any provision of the Act, the Declaration, or these bylaws to be taken in connection with any action of the Association, the meeting and vote of members may be dispensed with if all the apartment owners who would have been entitled to vote at such meeting if such meeting were held shall consent in writing to such action being taken.

Article IV
Board of Directors

Bylaw 1. Interim Board of Directors. Until such time as the successors to the Interim Board of Directors shall have been elected and shall have qualified, the affairs of the Association shall be governed by an Interim Board of three (3) persons, none of whom need be members of the Association. The term of office of the Interim Board of Directors shall be from the date of adoption of these bylaws until the first annual meeting of the Association. The Interim Board shall have the same powers, duties, rights, and obligations enumerated in these bylaws and the Declaration as the Board elected by the Assocation. Vacancies in the Interim Board shall be filled by appointment made by the remaining member or members of the Interim Board of Directors. The members of the Interim Board shall serve without compensation except for reimbursement for out-of-pocket expenses incurred in the performance of their duties hereunder.

Bylaw 2. Number and Qualifications. At all times after the election and qualification of successors to the Interim Board of Directors, the affairs of the Association shall be managed by a Board of Directors composed of at least three persons who must be members of the Association. The number of persons comprising the Board of Directors may be increased to five by vote of members holding at least fifty-one (51) percent of the voting interest in the Association, at an annual meeting or at a special meeting called for that purpose.

Bylaw 3. Term of Office. The terms of office of directors comprising a three-member Board and a five-member Board, as the case may be, are as follows:

(a) *Three-Member Board.* Subject to Bylaw 4 of this Article IV, below, at the first annual meeting of the Assocation, or other annual meeting held subsequent to the events specified in Bylaw 4, the members shall elect one director for a term of one (1) year, one director for a term of two (2) years, and one director for a term of three (3) years. At the expiration of the initial term of office of each director, his successor shall be elected for a three-year term, subject to Bylaw 4 of this Article IV, below. A director shall hold office until his successor has been elected and shall have qualified, or until he has been removed in accordance with the provisions of these bylaws.

(b) *Five-Member Board.* Subject to Bylaw 4 of this Article IV, below, at the first annual meeting of the Association, or other annual meeting held subsequent to the events specified in this bylaw, the members shall elect two directors for a term of one (1) year, two directors for a term of two (2) years, and one director for a term of three (3) years. At the expiration of the initial term of office of each director, his successor shall be elected for a three-year term, subject to Bylaw 4. A director shall hold office until his successor has been removed in accordance with the provisions of these bylaws.

Bylaw 4. Limitation on Term of Office. At the annual meeting held subsequent to the earlier of (i) five (5) years from the date of filing of the Declaration, or (ii) when three-fifths (3/5ths) of the apartment owners are other than the Declarant, the terms of office of all then existing officers and directors shall terminate. Election of new directors at such meeting shall be conducted as provided in Bylaw 3, above, and Bylaw 9, below.

Bylaw 5. Limitation of Declarant's Board of Director Members. The term of the Interim Board of Directors and any Declarant representatives elected to the Board at any annual or special meeting called for the purpose of election of Board members shall terminate at the annual meeting following March 30, 1981. Declarant representatives cannot be re-elected to the Board unless approved by owners holding seventy-five (75) percent of the voting interests, other than Declarant.

Bylaw 6. Meetings of Directors. Regular meetings of the Board of Directors shall be held at least quarterly without notice, at such place within _____County, and at such hour as may be fixed from time to time by resolution of the Board. Special meetings of the Board of Directors shall be held within said county when called by the President of the Association or by the Secretary upon written request of any two directors, after not less than three (3) days' written notice to each director. Written notice of all special meetings of the Board of Directors shall state the time, place, and complete agenda thereof and shall be sent by United States mail to all directors at their home addresses.

Bylaw 7. Quorum. A majority of the directors shall constitute a quorum for the transaction of business. Every act or decision done or made by a majority of the directors present at a duly held meeting at which a quorum is present shall be regarded as the act of the Board. If, at any meeting of the Board of Directors, there be less than a quorum present, the meeting shall be adjourned, from time to time until a quorum is present. At any such meeting, any business which might have been transacted at the meeting as originally called may be transacted without further notice.

Bylaw 8. Action Taken Without a Meeting. The directors shall have the right to take any action in the absence of a meeting which they could take at a meeting when authorized in writing signed by all the directors.

Bylaw 9. Election of Directors. The election of directors comprising a three-member Board or a five-member Board, as the case may be, shall be conducted as follows:

(a) *Three-Member Board.* Directors of the Association shall be elected by vote as provided for in Article II hereof at the annual meeting of the Association. At the first annual meeting, and at the annual meeting subsequent to the events specified in Bylaw 4 of this Article IV, above, the one candidate receiving the greatest number of voting percentages shall serve a three-year term; the candidate receiving the second greatest number of voting percentages shall serve a two-year term; and the candidate receiving the third greatest number of voting percentages shall serve a one-year term of office. At all other annual meetings, the number of candidates to be elected shall equal the number of vacancies in the Board of Directors as of the date of the annual meeting, and the candidates receiving the highest voting percentages at such meetings shall be declared elected to serve three-year terms. Cumulative voting is not permitted.

(b) *Five-Member Board.* Directors of the Association shall be elected by vote as provided for in Article II hereof at the annual meeting of the Association. At the first annual meeting, and at the annual meeting subsequent to the events specified in Bylaw 4 of this Article IV, above, the two candidates receiving the greatest number of voting percentages shall serve three-year terms; the two candidates receiving the third and fourth greatest number of voting percentages shall serve two-year terms; and the candidate receiving the fifth greatest number of voting percentages shall serve a one-year term of office. At all other annual meetings, the number of candidates to be elected shall equal the number of vacancies in the Board of Directors as of the date of the annual meeting, and the candidates receiving the highest voting percentages at such meetings shall be declared elected to serve three-year terms. Cumulative voting is not permitted.

Bylaw 10. Vacancies. Vacancies in the Board of Directors, except for the Interim Board of Directors, shall be filled by a majority vote by the remaining directors even though they may constitute less than a quorum. Each person so elected shall serve as a director for the unexpired term of his predecessor.

Bylaw 11. Removal. After the first annual meeting of the Association, any director may be removed from the Board, with or without cause, by a majority vote of the members of the Association. Neither a director nor the entire Board may be removed unless the notice of the annual or special meeting at which removal is to be considered states such purpose, and the director whose removal has been proposed shall be given an opportunity to be heard at the meeting. In the event of removal of a director by the members, his successor shall be elected at the same meeting at which removal occurred, and such successor shall serve for the unexpired term of his predecessor.

Bylaw 12. Compensation. No director shall receive compensation for any service he may render to the Association. However, any director may be reimbursed for his actual expenses incurred in the performance of his duties.

Bylaw 13. Powers and Duties. The Board of Directors (or Interim Board of Directors, when operative) shall conduct and manage the business of the Association and shall have all powers and duties granted, or not specifically prohibited, by statute, the Declaration, the Articles, or these bylaws. In addition to the foregoing, the Board shall be responsible for and have the power to administer the following:

(a) The care, upkeep, and surveillance of the common areas and the limited common areas and facilities, all as defined in the Declaration.

(b) The employment and removal of a manager, managing agent, independent contractors, and other such employees as it deems advisable; entering into contracts and agreements for the purpose of providing for the performance of its powers and duties. The Board may further delegate any of its powers and duties to such persons or entities as the directors may determine, provided, however, that no contract, lease, management contract, employment contract, or lease of recreational areas or facilities, which is directly or indirectly made by or on behalf of the Association shall be entered into for a period exceeding two (2) years, and provided, further, that any management contract, or any other contract providing for services by the Declarant, shall provide for termination by either party (i) without cause or payment of a termination fee on ninety (90) days' written notice, or (ii) with cause and without payment of a termination fee on thirty (30) days' written notice.

(c) The adoption and implementation of uniform rules and regulations governing conduct within the apartments, the use of the common areas and facilities, the limited common areas and facilities, and the personal conduct of owners and lessees and their guests therein and thereon; the establishment of reasonable penalties for the infraction of such rules and regulations and reasonable means to enforce such rules and regulations by administrative or legal means, provided, however, that nothing in the Declaration, these bylaws, or any of said rules and regulations shall deny the owner of an apartment, or his family members, guests, invitees, or lessees, the right of ingress to or egress from the owner's apartment, nor the right to use any and all common utilities furnished to all apartments.

(d) The ownership, conveyance, encumbrance, lease, or otherwise of apartments conveyed to it or purchased by it as the result of enforcement of the lien for assessments or otherwise.

(e) The preparation of the annual budget, which shall include reserve funds for operating costs and for replacement and establishment of the annual assessment period and the amount of annual assessments against each apartment pursuant to the percentage interest of said apartment as established by the Declaration.

(f) Determination, subject to Article VI, Bylaw 1 hereof, of the annual and special assessments for common expenses required for management of the affairs of the Condominium, including but not limited to, the operation and maintenance of the property of the Condominium, maintenance of an adequate reserve fund for maintenance, repairs and replacement of those common elements that must be replaced on a periodic basis, funding of operating deficits, and payment of unforeseen costs and expenses arising out of emergencies.

(g) The collection of assessment payments, including in the discretion of the Board the foreclosing of liens against any apartment for which any assessment installment is more than thirty (30) days delinquent or the bringing of an action at law against the owner of an apartment during any period which a default by that owner exists in the payment of any assessment or installment thereof.

(h) The notification of Federal Home Loan Mortgage Corporation in writing of any loss to, or taking of, the common areas and facilities if such loss or taking exceeds $10,000, or damage to an apartment covered by a mortgage purchased in whole or in part by the Federal Home Loan Mortgage Corporation exceeds $10,000.

(i) The issuance of written notification to a first mortgagee of any default in the performance by an individual apartment owner of any obligation under the Declaration, these bylaws, or such rules and regulations as may be promulgated by the Board of Directors, which is not received within sixty (60) days.

(j) The issuance, upon demand of a person, of a certificate setting forth whether or not any assessment made by the Association has been paid or is delinquent and, if delinquent, the amount thereof. This certificate when issued to mortgagees or when issued for use at the closing of a sale of an apartment shall be binding upon the Association. A reasonable charge may be made by the Board for issuance of such certificate.

(k) The establishment of a fiscal year for the Association, which shall be the calendar year unless otherwise established by the Board.

(l) The selection and retention of certified public accountants to perform an annual examination of the books and records of the Association, including annual income and expense statements.

(m) The opening of bank accounts on behalf of the Condominium and designation of signatories required therefor.

(n) The obtaining of insurance for the Condominium, pursuant to the provisions of the Declaration.

(o) The making of repairs, additions, and improvements to, or alterations of, the property of the Condominium, and repairs to and restoration of the property of the Condominium in accordance with the Declaration and the other provisions of these bylaws.

(p) The dedication or transfer of any part of the common areas to any governmental subdivision or public agency or utility; provided, however, that such dedication or transfer is assented to by the owners of apartments holding seventy-five (75) percent or more of the voting interest in the Association, or such greater percentage as may be required by the Act (excluding Declarant), and seventy-five (75) percent or more of the holders of first mortgages covering the apartments then of record against the apartments (based upon one vote for each first mortgage owned).

(q) The preparation and delivery to each apartment owner of an annual report as provided in Artile III, Bylaw 3 above.

(r) The decision whether or not to elect to have Section 528 of the Internal Revenue Code, as added by Section 2101 of the Tax Reform Act of 1976, apply for each taxable year, and if such decision is made to have said section apply, the election will be at such time and in such manner as is prescribed in regulations promulgated by the Secretary of the United States Treasury Department.

(s) The appointment of a Design Review Committee composed of three (3) or more persons to whom plans and specifications showing the nature, kind, shape, heights, materials, and location of contemplated structures, or additions or alterations to existing structures, shall be submitted by the persons contemplating the same.

(t) The appointment of an Acceptance Committee to be created at the time of the election of members of the Board of Directors other than the Declarant. The Acceptance Committee shall be created, and its members appointed, by the successors to the Interim Board of Directors within sixty (60) days after the election of the successors to the Interim Board of Directors. The purpose and function of the Acceptance Committee shall be to review the books and records of the Association and to review the maintenance and condition of the common areas and facilities and limited common areas and facilities and to accept, approve, and receive the same within one hundred fifty (150) days from the date of the election and qualification of such successors. If such written acceptance, approval, and receipt is not received by the Declarant within said 150-day period, and if no report of the Acceptance Committee containing explanations or objections is received by the Declarant within said 150-day period, the Committee shall be deemed to have accepted, approved, and received the books and records of the Association and the maintenance and condition of the common areas and facilities and limited common areas and facilities.

(u) Appointment of other committees as the Board deems appropriate in carrying out its purposes.

Bylaw 14. Fidelity Bonds. All directors, managers, trustees, officers, employees, or volunteers of the Association responsible for handling funds belonging to or administered by the Association shall furnish adequate fidelity bonds. The premiums on such bonds shall be paid by the Association and be a common expense. Such fidelity bonds shall name the Association as obligee and be written in an amount equal to at least one hundred fifty (150) percent of the estimated annual operating expenses and reserves of the Condominium project. An appropriate endorsement to the policy to cover any persons who serve without compensation shall be added if the policy would not otherwise cover volunteers. All such bonds shall provide that they may not be cancelled or substantially modified (including cancellation for nonpayment of premium) without at least thirty (30) days' prior written notice to the Association and to the holders of all first mortgages of record covering the apartments.

Bylaw 15. Liability Insurance. All Board members and officers of the Association shall be protected from personal liability in the management of the Association's affairs by personal liability insurance. The premiums on such insurance shall be paid by the Association and be a common expense. The Association shall indemnify such persons, for such expenses and liabilities, in such manner, under such circumstances, and to such extent as permitted by the state statutes, as now enacted or hereafter amended.

Bylaw 16. Public Liability Insurance. The Association shall have a comprehensive policy of public liability insurance covering all of the common areas and facilities, as defined in the Declaration. Coverage shall be for at least one million dollars ($1,000,000) per occurrence, for personal injury and/or property damage. Such insurance policy shall contain a "severability of interest" endorsement which shall preclude the insurer from denying the claim of an apartment owner because of negligent acts of the Association. Such policy shall also contain cross-liability endorsements to cover liability of all owners of apartments as a group to each apartment owner. The premiums on such insurance shall be paid by the Association and be a common expense.

Article V.
Officers

Bylaw 1. Principal Officers. The principal officers of the Association shall be a President, a Vice-President, a Secretary, and a Treasurer, all of whom shall be elected by the Board and all of whom must be members of the Board. The directors may appoint an Assistant Treasurer, and an Assistant Secretary, and such other officers as in their judgment may be necessary, and such other officers so appointed need not be members of the Board. Any person may hold more than one office, except that the office of President and Vice-President shall be held by separate persons, and those persons shall not hold any other office in the Association.

Bylaw 2. Election of Officers. The officers of the Association shall be elected annually by the Board at the organizational meeting of each new Board and shall hold office at the pleasure of the Board.

Bylaw 3. Removal of Officers. Upon an affirmative vote of a majority of the members of the Board, any officer may be removed, either with or without cause, and his successor elected at any regular meeting of the Board, or at any special meeting of the Board called for that purpose.

Bylaw 4. President. The President shall be the chief executive officer of the Association and shall be a member of the Board. He shall preside at all meetings of the Association and of the Board. He shall have all of the general powers and duties which are usually vested in the office of president of an association, including but not limited to the power to appoint committees from among the owners from time to time as he may in his discretion decide is appropriate to assist in the conduct of the affairs of the Association. He shall have such other duties as may from time to time be prescribed by the Board.

Bylaw 5. Vice President. The Vice President shall be a member of the Board and shall take the place of the President and perform his duties whenever the President shall be absent or unable to act. If neither the President nor the Vice President is able to act, the Board shall appoint some other member of the Board to do so on an interim basis. The Vice President shall also perform such other duties as shall from time to time be prescribed by the Board.

Bylaw 6. Secretary. The Secretary shall keep or cause to be kept the minutes of all meetings of the Board and the minutes of all meetings of the Association; he shall have charge of such books and papers as the Board may direct; and he shall, in general, perform or cause to be performed all the duties incident to the office of Secretary.

Bylaw 7. Treasurer. The Treasurer shall have the responsibility for Association funds and securities and shall be responsible for keeping or causing to be kept full and accurate accounts of all receipts and disbursements in books belonging to the Association. He shall be responsible for the deposit by himself or his designee of all monies and other valuable effects in the name, and to the credit, of the Association in such depositories as may from time to time be designated by the Board.

Article VI
Responsibilities and Obligations of Owners

Bylaw 1. Assessments. All apartment owners are obligated to pay annual assessments imposed by the Association to meet all common expenses of the Condominium, including but not limited to: heat; gas for cooking; any central air-conditioning charges; water bills; all costs for maintaining, repairing, and replacing the common areas and facilities; liability and building insurance premiums for extended risk insurance to cover repair and reconstruction work in case of windstorm, fire, or earthquake; and such other and additional coverage as the Association deems necessary or desirable. The assessments shall be made pro rata according to the percentage of undivided interest appurtenant to each apartment in the Declaration and shall be payable in monthly installments or otherwise as designated by the Board. Such assessments shall include adequate monthly payments to a reserve fund for operating costs and a reserve fund for maintenance, repairs, and replacement of those common areas and facilities that must be replaced on a periodic basis. All income to the Association from fees and dues and all other sources shall be applied to reduce the amounts otherwise to be paid by assessments.

All apartment owners are also obligated to pay special assessments imposed by the Board of Directors to fund operating deficits and to pay for unforeseen expenses and costs arising out of situations the Board determines to be emergencies. Such special assessments shall be enforceable in the same manner as annual assessments and may be payable in installments or in a lump sum, as designated by the Board.

In addition to the special assessments which may be imposed by the Board, special assessments and the methods of payment and collection thereof may be approved and authorized by the holders of at least a majority of the voting percentages represented in person or by proxy at a meeting called for such purpose (including Declarant) and by fifty-one (51) percent or more of the holders of first mortgages then of record against the apartments.

Bylaw 2. Repairs and Maintenance. The responsibility for the maintenance of the Condominium, and the obligations related thereto, are specified in Paragraph 12 of the Declaration.

Bylaw 3. Use of Apartments. All apartments shall be utilized only for such purposes as are allowed by the Declaration.

Bylaw 4. Right of Entry. Owners and occupants shall and hereby do grant the right of entry to the manager or to any other person authorized by the Board of Directors or the Association in case of an emergency originating in or threatening his apartment, whether the owner or occupant is present at the time or not. Should such owner or occupant refuse entry to the manager or to any other person authorized by the Board or the Association in case of an emergency, such owner or occupant shall be solely responsible for any damage to his apartment incurred by such manager or other person in attempting to gain entry to such apartment.

Owners and occupants shall permit other owners, or their representative, to enter their apartment when so required, for the purpose of performing reasonable installations, alterations, or repairs to the mechanical or electrical services serving the apartment of the owner or occupant making such entry, provided that requests for entry be made in advance and that such entry is at a reasonable time, convenient to the owner or occupant. In case of an emergency, such right to entry shall be immediate. The owner or occupant making such entry into the apartment of another shall repair and restore such apartment to as near as possible the same condition such apartment was in prior to entry. All such entries shall be made and done so as to cause as little inconvenience as possible to the owners or occupants of the entered apartment.

Bylaw 5. Notice of Mortgages. Any owner who mortgages his apartment shall notify the Association in writing through the Board of the name and address of the mortgagee.

Bylaw 6. Children. The responsibility and obligations of apartment owners and occupants with respect to children are specified in Paragraph 10 (l) of the Declaration.

Bylaw 7. Pets. The responsibility and obligations of apartment owners and occupants with respect to pets are specified in Paragraph 10 (j) of the Declaration.

Article VII.
Books and Records

The books, records, and papers of the Association shall at all times, during the normal business hours, be subject to inspection by any apartment owner or any first mortgagee thereof at the principal office of the Association.

Article VIII.
Amendment to Bylaws and Resolution of Conflicts

Bylaw 1. Amendment. Subject to Article I, Bylaw 7 of these bylaws and the State Condominium Act, and unless specifically provided to the contrary herein, these bylaws may be amended by the owners of apartments having at least seventy-five (75) percent or more of the voting interest in the Association, as established in the Declaration, and by at least seventy-five (75) percent of the holders of first mortgages of record covering the apartments (based upon one vote for each first mortgage owned).

When voting for or against a proposed amendment, owners of apartments shall vote as members of the Association, and amendments passed by members of the Association shall not be valid unless and until an instrument setting forth the provisions of the amendment and certified by the President and Secretary of the Association as to the requisite voting percentages cast in favor of the said amendment is duly recorded in the office of the County Recorder.

Bylaw 2. Conflicts. In the case of any conflict between the State Condominium Act, the Declaration, or these bylaws, the Condominium Act shall control over all other provisions and the Declaration shall control these bylaws.

The foregoing bylaws of The Association were adopted by the Directors of said Association on the _____ day of _____, 19____.

Appendix C—Condominium Association Budget

Budget for The Arlington, A Condominium

Comparison of Expenses as A Rental Property and A Unit Owners Association

Items	Projected Operating Budget for 1/1/79 through 12/31/79	Actual Operating Expenses As A Rental Property For: 1975	1976	1977
Management	$48,228	$44,308	$50,003	$67,749
Building and Ground Maintenance	87,522	170,457	221,004	258,304
Utilities.........	42,252	214,907	243,951	266,568
Insurance	36,216	7,237	8,579	13,609
Legal and Auditing	5,000	–0–	–0–	–0–
Reserves........	68,575	–0–	–0–	–0–
Recreational Facilities........	30,180	–0–	–0–	–0–
	$317,973	**$436,909**	**$523,537**	**$606,230**

Notes on Budget:

1. Prior to the Condominium conversion, The Arlington condominium was known as Claremont Apartments. The actual costs shown for the annual periods of 1975, 1976, and 1977 reflect operations of this complex as a rental complex.

The above comparison is presented in the main to comply with the provision of the Condominium Act of Virginia and is not intended to create the impression that the actual expenditures reflected above for the years 1975, 1976, and 1977, in operating the complex as a rental apartment complex, are comparable to the expenditures to be anticipated in operating the complex as a condominium. It should be further noted that the buildings and grounds maintenance figures shown above for the years 1975, 1976, and 1977 include maintenance of the interior of the units as rental units, while the projected budget provides for buildings and ground maintenance only for the exterior of the buildings and the common elements, inasmuch as in the condominium form of ownership the obligation to maintain the interior of the condominium unit is the obligation of the individual owner.

The actual anticipated annual condominium budget from January 1, 1979 through December 31, 1979 can essentially be determined by multiplying the monthly assessment chargeable to each unit type, times the number of that type unit included in the condominium during the period, times the number of months that each such type unit was included in the condominium during the period, and adding the results for each type unit together.

2. The utilities category encompasses the costs of fuel oil during the rental period which does not reflect the true costs of the condominium because the centralized boiler system will be eliminated on the conversion, but it also must be noted that on the conversion plan common metering of electric and gas will continue for the site and entry lighting and for hot water.

3. In the projected budget shown for the period from January 1, 1979 through December 31, 1979 the Declarant has provided for a reserve in the amount of $68,575. This reserve is being established for the purpose of repairing or replacing in a major way the parking lots, the roofs, potential recreation facilities, and whatever other repairs may become necessary to the common elements of the condominium. This reserve further takes into consideration that the exterior of the buildings in The Arlington, A Condominium, will require repainting approximately every three (3) years.

4. This projected budget assumes that all 520 units and all proposed recreational facilities were included in the Condominium for the full period.

| Unit Type | Actual Operating Expenses As a Rental Property for: | | | Projected Operating Budget (Based on 520 Units) The Arlington 1/1/79–12/31/79 |
	1975	1976	1977	
A	61.90	74.20	85.88	45.05
B	61.90	74.20	85.88	45.05
C	58.25	69.80	80.85	42.40
D	58.25	69.80	80.85	42.40
E	69.20	82.90	96.00	50.35
F	69.20	82.90	96.00	50.35
G	51.00	61.10	70.75	37.10
H	51.00	61.10	70.75	37.10
J	61.90	74.20	85.88	45.05
L	131.10	157.10	181.90	95.40
M	69.20	82.90	96.00	50.35
N	69.20	82.90	96.00	50.35
O	105.60	126.50	146.50	76.85

The table above reflects the estimated initial monthly assessment for each type of unit, based on the percentage interest each such unit bears to the whole. The assessment reflected in columns two, three, and four represent the monthly amount which a unit owner would have paid under rental operation during the periods indicated to cover what would have been common expenses if the project had been under the condominium form of ownership. The rental operation did not include, however, the projected cost of operation of the proposed recreational facilities. The monthly rate as a rental is arrived at by taking the monthly expenses as a rental property and multiplying by the percentage interest for each unit type.

Table of Reserves
(Exterior Maintenance and/or Replacement Costs)

Item	Estimated Replacement Costs in Current Dollars	Useful Life	Annual Reserve
Roofing	$162,500	10 yrs	$16,250
Gutters & Downspouts	30,000	20 yrs	1,500
Wood Trim	61,500	20 yrs	3,075
Painting	100,600	3 yrs	35,000
Streets & Grounds .	180,000	20 yrs	9,000
Recreational Facilities	75,000	20 yrs	3,750
Total			**$68,575**

Note: The above includes reserves which are estimated to be needed if all recreational facilities contemplated by Declarant are constructed.

Appendix D—Management Agreement ▬▬▬▬

Management Agreement
Between

Association:_____

and

Management Company:_____
for Property Located at
(Street Address, City, State)
_____

Beginning: _____
Ending: _____

THIS AGREEMENT is made and entered into this _____ day of _____, 19___, by and between _____ a _____ corporation (hereinafter the "Association"), organized and established in accordance with the "Declaration Establishing (name of condominium)," filed in the office of the Registrar of Titles for the county of _____ in the state of _____ (hereinafter "Declaration") and with _____, hereinafter the "Management Company".

W I T N E S S E T H :

WHEREAS, the Declaration provides in Paragraph 10, E thereof that the control and administration of the _____ (hereinafter "Condominium") shall be vested in the Association and its Board of Directors; and

WHEREAS, the bylaws of the Association provide in Bylaw _____ of Article I thereof that the Association shall have the responsibility of managing the property of the Condominium and shall discharge this responsibility and its other duties through its duly elected Board of Directors; and

WHEREAS, the Board of Directors of the (association), deems it in the best interests of the Condominium to employ the Management Company to manage the property of the Condominium; and

WHEREAS, the Management Company is desirous of performing services for the management of the property of the Condominium.

NOW, THEREFORE, in consideration of the terms, conditions, and covenants hereinafter set forth, the parties hereto mutually agree as follows:

1. Employment. The Association hereby employs the Management Company, and the Management Company hereby accepts employment on the terms and conditions hereinafter provided, as exclusive managing agent of the Condominium located at _____, city of _____, county of _____, state of _____, consisting of one (1) building containing _____ apartments and _____ outdoor parking spaces.

2. Term of Employment. Unless cancelled pursuant to subparagraphs a, b, or c of this Paragraph 2, this Agreement shall be in effect for a term of two (2) years from the date of its execution, and thereafter for renewal periods of two (2) years each, unless thirty (30) days prior to the expiration of this Agreement, written notice is given of a party's intention not to renew.

a. This Agreement may be terminated by either party without cause and without termination fee on ninety (90) days' written notice.

b. In the event a petition in bankruptcy is filed by or against the Management Company, or in the event that the Management Company shall make an assignment for the benefit of creditors or take advantage of any insolvency act, either party hereto may terminate this Agreement, and such termination shall be effective upon the dispatch of written notice from one party to the other.

c. In the event it is alleged or charged that any act or failure to act by the Association or its Board of Directors fails to comply with or is in violation of the requirements of any constitutional provision, statute, ordinance, law, rule, order, or regulation of any governmental body or of any public authority or official thereof having or claiming to have jurisdiction over the Association and its Board, and the Management Company in its sole and absolute discretion considers that the action or position of the Association with respect thereto may result in damage or liability to the Management Company, the Management Company shall have the right to cancel this Agreement, which cancellation shall not release the indemnities of the Association set forth in Paragraph 5 below and shall not terminate any liability or obligation of the Association to the Management Company for any payment, reimbursement, or other sum of money then due and payable to the Management Company hereunder.

d. Upon termination and within thirty (30) days of the date of termination of this Agreement unless extensions of time are agreed upon by both parties in writing, the parties hereto shall account to each other with respect to all matters outstanding as of the date of termination.

3. Scope of Employment. The Management Company hereby agrees to perform the following services in the name of and on behalf of the Association, and the Association hereby gives the Management Company the authority and powers required to perform the following services:

a. *Financial Management.*

(1) The Management Company shall maintain the Association's records and files and books of account;

(2) The Management Company shall collect all monthly assessments and other charges due to the Association. The Association hereby authorizes the Management Company to request, demand, collect, and receive all such assessments which may at any time be or become due to the Association by way of legal process or otherwise as may be required for the collection of same, and the Association shall reimburse the Management Company for all costs of legal action, court fees, and related expenses incurred in the collection of same. The Management Company shall furnish the Association with an itemized list of all delinquent accounts immediately following the fifteenth (15th) day of each month.

(3) From the funds collected and deposited in the special accounts hereinafter provided, the Management Company shall prepare drafts for payment of all charges or obligations incurred by the Association after receipt of the same at the Management Company's office, provided, however, the Management Company shall not be obliged to make any advance to or for the account of the Association, nor shall the Management Company be obliged to incur any liability or obligation for the account of the Association without assurance that necessary funds for the discharge thereof will be provided. From the funds collected and deposited in the special accounts hereinafter provided, the Management Company shall cause to be disbursed regularly and punctually in any order that may be specified by the Board of Directors of the Association:

(a) Salaries and any other compensation due and payable to the employees of the Association, and the taxes payable under subparagraph (9) below:

(b) Insurance premiums in amounts specified by the Board of Directors of the Association for payment or for allocation to reserve accounts; and

(c) Sums otherwise due and payable by the Association as operating expenses authorized to be incurred under the terms of this Agreement, including the management fee payable to the Management Company.

(4) After disbursement, any balance remaining in the special accounts may be disbursed or transferred to other accounts from time to time, but only as specifically directed in writing by the Board of Directors of the Association. Such balances of account shall be within the limits of the fidelity bond provided in Subparagraph (11) below unless the handling of additional funds is specifically authorized in writing by the Board of Directors of the Association.

(5) The Management Company shall maintain office records, books, and accounts which shall be subject to examination by agents authorized by the Association during reasonable business hours. The Management Company shall promptly submit to the Board of Directors of the Association a financial statement indicating account balances and budget figures for the current month and year-to-date for the preceding month, on or before the fifteenth (15th) day of each month.

(6) The Management Company shall monitor the Association's checking and savings accounts and reconcile its checking accounts each month. The Management Company shall not reduce any of the Association's accounts below zero at any time.

(7) The Management Company shall prepare and submit to the Board of Directors of the Association, 60 days prior to the fiscal year-end of the Association, a preliminary budget for the next fiscal year showing anticipated expenditures for such year.

(8) Within forty-five (45) days after the end of each fiscal year, the Management Company shall submit to the Association a final financial statement for the preceding fiscal year. This service is not to be construed to require the Management Company to supply an audit or tax preparation. The audit or tax preparation required by the Association shall be prepared at the expense of the Association by accountants selected by the Association.

(9) The Management Company shall prepare and file all forms, reports, and returns required by law in connection with the employment of on-site Association personnel, including but not limited to unemployment insurance, worker's compensation insurance, disability benefits, social security, and other similar taxes now in effect or hereafter imposed. The Association shall reimburse the Management Company for all salaries paid to on-site Association employees and for all taxes and expenses related to the employment of said employees and other payments made by the Management Company in behalf of the Association.

(10) The Management Company shall establish and maintain in a bank whose deposits are insured by the Federal Deposit Insurance Corporation or the Federal Savings and Loan Insurance Corporation, and in a manner to indicate the custodial nature thereof, separate bank accounts as agent of the Association for the deposit of the monies of the Association with authority to draw thereon for any payments to be made by the Management Company to discharge any liabilities or obligations of the Association incurred pursuant to this Agreement, all of which payments shall be subject to the limitations in this Agreement. The Management Company shall deposit all reserve funds provided for in the Declaration Establishing the Condominium and as established by the Annual Budget or as directed in writing by the Board of Directors of the Association.

(11) Those employees of the Management Company who handle or are responsible for the handling of the Association's monies shall, without expense to the Association, be bonded by a fidelity bond acceptable to both the Management Company and the Association.

b. *Maintenance Management.*

(1) Subject to the direction and at the expense of the Association, the Management Company shall cause the building, appurtenance, and grounds of the Condominium and its common areas and facilities to be maintained according to standards acceptable to the Association, including but not limited to, interior and exterior cleaning, painting and decorating, plumbing, steamfitting, carpentry, and such other and normal maintenance and repair work as may be necessary, subject to any limitations imposed by the Association in addition to those contained herein. For any one item of repair or replacement the expense incurred shall not exceed the sum of five hundred dollars ($500) unless specifically authorized by the Board of Directors of the Association by separate writing or by a budget which has been approved by the Board of Directors of the Association; provided, however, that emergency repairs, involving manifest danger to life or property, or immediately necessary for the preservation and safety of the property of the Condominium, or for the safety of the owners, or required to avoid the suspension of any necessary service to the Condominium or to its common areas and facilities, may be made by the Management Company, irrespective of the cost limitation imposed by this paragraph. Notwithstanding this authority as to emergency repairs, it is understood and agreed that the Management Company will, if at all possible, confer immediately with the Board of Directors of the Association regarding every subject expenditure.

(2) On the basis of the budget, job standards, and wage and contract rates previously approved by the Board of Directors of the Association, the Management Company shall hire in its own name, pay and negotiate agreements with, and supervise personnel required for the efficient discharge of the duties of the Management Company hereunder. All such personnel shall be employees of the Management Company and not employees of the Association. All salaries, taxes, and other expenses payable on account of such employees shall be operating expenses of the Association.

(3) Subject to approval by the Association, the Management Company shall negotiate and present to the Board of Directors for approval contracts for maintenance and other necessary services which the Management Company or the Association shall deem advisable. The Management Company shall also place orders for equipment, tools, appliances, materials, and supplies as are necessary to properly maintain the Condominium and its common areas and facilities. All such contracts and orders shall be made in the name of the Association and shall be subject to the limitations set forth in Paragraph b(1) hereof. When taking bids or issuing purchase orders, the Management Company shall act at all times under the direction of the Association, and shall be under a duty to secure for and credit to the latter any discounts, commissions, or rebates obtainable as a result of such purchases. The Management Company shall maintain appropriate records of all such contracts and orders and correspondence relating thereto.

(4) The Management Company shall handle all homeowner calls and complaints by providing a communications center for disbursing information.

(5) Any other provision in this Agreement notwithstanding, the Management Company shall have no authority or responsibility for maintenance or repairs to individual dwelling units in the Condominium.

c. *Administrative Management.*

(1) The Management Company agrees that one of its employees shall be designated as Property Manager for the Condominium. The Property Manager shall, upon not less than 48 hours' notice, attend meetings of the Board of Directors of the Association as requested once monthly.

(2) The Management Company shall be the custodian of the official records and files of the Board of Directors of the Association and of the Association and shall provide access to said records at the office of the Management Company at any time during normal business hours to any member of the Board of Directors of the Association and to any member of the Association upon appointment.

(3) The Management Company shall administer and assist the Board of Directors of the Association in calling and conducting special and annual meetings of the members of the Association, and a representative of the Management Company shall attend one such meeting annually. Attendance of Management Company representatives at additional meetings must be requested in writing by the Association, and all attendance and preparation costs on the part of the Management Company representative shall be reimbursed by the Association.

(4) The Management Company shall cause to be placed and kept in force all forms of insurance needed to adequately protect the Association, its members and mortgagees holding mortgages covering dwelling units in the Condominium as their respective interests appear or as required by law, including but not limited to worker's compensation insurance, public liability insurance, property damage insurance, fire and extended coverage insurance, and any other forms of insurance requested by the Association or required by law. All such insurance shall be placed with companies licensed to do business in the state of _____ and rated at least AAAA-1 by Best's Insurance Guide. The Management Company shall promptly investigate and make a full written report of all accidents or claims for damage relating to the management, operation, and maintenance of the Condominium and its common areas and facilities, including any damage to or destruction of the same, and the estimated cost of repair, and shall cooperate and make any and all other reports required by any insurance company insuring the Condominium and if necessary retain at the expense of the Association the services of a public fire loss adjuster.

(5) Subject to the direction of the Board of Directors of the Association, the Management Company shall solicit, negotiate, and present to the Board proposals and bids for insurance coverage.

4. **Management Fee.** The Association shall pay to the Management Company a fee equal to $375 per month as sole compensation for all services performed under this Agreement. The Management Company fee shall be paid monthly in advance. Costs incurred for mailings of notices, newletters, and official Association business to homeowners for such items as postage, materials, and copies shall be at the expense of the Association.

5. **Association Responsibilities.** The Association agrees to the following conditions and responsibilities which shall become effective on the date of execution of this Agreement.

a. The Association, in performing and acting under this Agreement, shall act through its Board of Directors and its officers. The Management Company, its officers and employees, may and can rely on the directions and authorizations given to it by the Board of Directors of the Association or any of such officers, and the Management Company, in relying and acting on directions and authorizations given by the Board of Directors or officers of the Association, shall not be obligated or required to inquire into the authority of the Board of Directors or of any of such officers; provided, however, that the Management Company and its officers and employees shall not rely or act on any direction or authority which is contrary to the terms and conditions of this Agreement as the same may be amended from time to time as herein provided.

The Association may, by written resolution, designate an officer or director as primary liaison between the Board of Directors and the Management Company. In the event of such designation, the Management Company, its officers, and employees shall rely and act on directions and authorizations given by such individual and shall not be obligated or required to inquire into the authority of such individual. It shall be the responsibility of the Association to terminate by written resolution the liaison responsibilities of such individuals and to advise the Management Company accordingly.

b. The Association is fully responsible for, and the Management Company has no responsibility for, compliance by the Association with the requirements of any ordinance, laws, rules, or regulations of the city, county, state, or federal government or any public authority or official thereof having jurisdiction over the Association, provided, however, that the Management Company shall promptly notify the Board of Directors of the Association of any complaints, warnings, notices, or summons received by it relating to such matters. The Association hereby represents that to the best of its knowledge the Association complies with all such requirements. The Association further agrees to indemnify and hold harmless the Management Company, its representatives, servants, and employees from all losses, costs, expenses, and liabilities whatsoever which may be imposed on the Management Company or any of its representatives, servants, and employees by reason of any present or future violation or alleged violation of such ordinances, laws, rules, or regulations.

c. The Association agrees to hold the Management Company and its officers and employees harmless from and indemnify and defend them against any and all claims for damages or injury to property or persons, or death of persons, involving the Association or occurring on or about the premises of the Condominium except for such claims as arise due to the act or neglect of the Management Company or its officers or employees. The obligations of this Paragraph 5 shall specifically include the payment by the Association of all damages, court costs, litigation expenses, and attorneys' fees. The Association further agrees to carry, at its own expense, public liability and worker's compensation insurance in form, substance, and amount reasonably satisfactory to the Management Company, and further to furnish the Management Company certificates evidencing the existence of such insurance upon request and to inform the Management Company of any change in said policies within ten (10) days of change.

6. **Services.** The Management Company shall have no obligation to perform or render any services beyond, or in addition to, those required of it hereunder. Any additional services shall be performed or rendered by the Management Company only pursuant to a separate written agreement and for additional consideration to be agreed upon and set out in such agreement.

7. **Notices.** Any notice required or permitted hereunder may be served by registered mail or in person as follows:
To the Management Company:
   Community Management Company
To the Association:
   President of the Board of Directors of
   The _____ Association, Inc.
   at his or her home address.

8. **Assignment.** The Management Company shall not assign its interest under this Agreement without prior written approval by the Board of Directors of the Association.

9. **Entire Agreement.** This Agreement shall constitute the entire Agreement between the parties hereto, and no variance or modification hereof shall be valid and enforceable, except by supplemental agreement in writing, executed and approved in the same manner as this Agreement. This Agreement shall inure to the benefit of and constitute a binding obligation upon the parties hereto, their respective successors and assignees.

IN WITNESS WHEREOF, the parties hereto have executed this Agreement the day and year first above written.

The _____ Association, Inc.
By _____
   Its _____
Community Management Company
By _____
   Its _____

142

Appendix E—Condominium Association Articles of Incorporation

Article I

The name of the corporation (hereinafter called the "Association") is _____ .

Article II

The principal office for the transaction of business of the Association is located in the county of _____, state of _____.

Article III

This Association is organized pursuant to the General Nonprofit Corporation Law of the state of _____ .

Article IV
Purposes and Powers of the Association

This Association does not contemplate the distribution of gains, profits, or dividends to its members, and the specific primary purposes for which it is formed are to provide for the acquisition, construction, management, operation, administration, maintenance, repair, improvement, preservation, and architectural control of the Association property within that certain tract of property situated in the county of _____, state of _____, a map of which was filed for record in the office of the County Recorder, and to promote the health, safety, and welfare of all the residents within the above described property and any additions thereto as may hereafter be brought within the jurisdiction of this Assocation for this purpose, all according to that certain Declaration of Covenants, Conditions, and Restrictions (the "Declaration") recorded or to be recorded with respect to said property in the Office of the Recorder of _____ County.

In furtherance of said purposes, this Association shall have power to:

(a) Perform all of the duties and obligations of the Association as set forth in the Declaration;

(b) Fix, levy, collect, and enforce assessments and fines as set forth in the Declaration;

(c) Pay all expenses and obligations incurred by the Association in the conduct of its business including, without limitation, all licenses, taxes, or governmental charges levied or imposed against the Association property;

(d) Acquire (by gift, purchase, or otherwise), own, hold, improve, build upon, operate, maintain, convey, sell, lease, transfer, dedicate for public use, or otherwise dispose of real or personal property in connection with the affairs of the Association;

(e) Borrow money and, only with the assent (by vote or written consent) of two-thirds (⅔) of each class of members, mortgage, pledge, deed in trust, or hypothecate any or all of its real or personal property as security for money borrowed or debts incurred;

(f) Dedicate, sell, or transfer all or any part of the common area to any public agency, authority, or utility for such purposes and subject to such conditions as may be agreed to by the members. No such dedication or transfer shall be effective unless an instrument has been signed by two-thirds (⅔) of each class of members, agreeing to such dedication, sale, or transfer.

(g) Participate in mergers and consolidations with other nonprofit corporations organized for the same purposes, or annex additional residential property and common area(s), provided that any merger, consolidation, or annexation (other than an annexation of additional phases, which shall be allowed according to the Declaration) shall have the assent by vote or written consent of two-thirds (⅔) of each class of members;

(h) Have and exercise any and all powers, rights, and privileges which a corporation organized under the General Nonprofit Corporation Law of the state of _____ by law may now or hereafter have or exercise.

Article V
Membership Voting Rights

The number and qualifications of members of the Association, the different classes of membership, if any, the property, voting and other rights and privileges of members, and their liability for dues and assessments and the method of collection thereof shall be as set forth in the Declaration and bylaws.

Article VI
Board of Directors

The affairs of this Association shall be managed by a Board of seven (7) Directors, who need not be members of the Association, until conversion of Class B memberships to Class A, after which time all Directors must be members of the Association. The number of Directors may be changed by amendment of the bylaws of the Association. The names and addresses of the persons who are to act in the capacity of Directors until the selection of their successors are: (list names).

Article VII
Dissolution

In the event of the dissolution, liquidation, or winding up of the Assocation, after paying or adequately providing for the debts and obligations of the Association, the Directors or persons in charge of the liquidation shall divide the remaining assets among the members in accordance with their respective rights therein, except where the Association holds its assets in trust, in which case the assets shall be disposed of according to the applicable provisions of the State Corporations Code for nonprofit corporations.

Article VIII
Duration

The Association shall exist perpetually.

Article IX
Amendments

The Articles may be amended by the vote or written assent of members representing fifty-one (51) percent of a quorum of the total voting power of the Association and fifty-one (51) percent of the voting power held by members other than the Declarant under the Declaration, provided, however, that the percentage of the voting power necessary to amend a specific clause or provision shall not be less than the prescribed percentage of affirmative votes required for action to be taken under that clause. For so long as two (2) classes of membership exist, amendment of the Articles shall require the vote or written assent of the prescribed percentage of each class of membership.

IN WITNESS WHEREOF, for the purpose of forming this Association under the laws of the state of _____, we, the undersigned, constituting the incorporators of this Association, have executed these Articles of Incorporation this _____ day of _____, 19_____.

State of _____
County of _____

On this day of _____, 19_____, before me, a Notary Public for the state of _____, duly commissioned and sworn, personally appeared _____ known to me to be the persons whose names are subscribed to within the Articles of Incorporation and acknowledged to me that they executed the same.

IN WITNESS WHEREOF, I have hereunto set my hand the day and year first above written.

Notary Public in and for
said county and state

Appendix F—Condominium Purchase Agreement

Dated: _____ , 19 ___

In consideration of the payments and mutual promises set forth in this Purchase Agreement, _____ Corporation, a _____ corporation ("Seller"), agrees to sell, and _____ ("Buyer") agrees to purchase apartment number _____, together with an undivided _____ percent interest in the common areas and facilities, and garage apartment number(s) _____, together with an undivided _____ percent interest in the common areas and facilities, in the _____ condominium, located at _____.

The purchase price of the apartment is $_____ and the purchase price of the garage apartment(s) is $_____, making a total purchase price of $_____, which Buyer agrees to pay Seller as follows:

(a) Buyer has paid as Earnest Money, receipt of which is hereby acknowledged, the sum of......... $_____

(b) Buyer shall pay, no later than _____, the sum of............................. $_____

(c) Buyer shall pay, at the time of closing from the proceeds of a mortgage, the sum of .... $_____

(d) Buyer shall pay, at the time of closing, the balance in the sum of............................. $_____

Total Purchase Price...................... $_____

1. Delivery of Deed. Subject to performance by Buyer, Seller agrees to execute and deliver at the time of closing a Warranty Deed conveying marketable title to said premises subject only to the following exceptions (hereinafter referred to as the "Allowable Encumbrances"):

(a) Building and zoning laws, ordinances, and state and federal regulations.

(b) The provision of (state) statutes.

(c) The provisions of the Declaration establishing the Condominium (hereinafter referred to as "Declaration"), the bylaws of the Association, Inc. (hereinafter referred to as "bylaws"), and the floor plans of the Condominium (hereinafter referred to as "Floor Plans") of record as of the date of closing.

(d) Easements and restrictions of record.

(e) Any mortgage given by Buyer and encumbering the apartment.

2. Use of Buyer's Payments. All earnest monies and downpayments made hereunder will be deposited into a Trust Account and will not be disbursed to Seller prior to the closing cancellation of this Agreement, upon written agreement by Buyer and Seller, or upon a court order.

3. Assessment For Common Expenses. Buyer is obligated and agrees to pay monthly to The _____ Association, Inc., a fractional share of the common expenses attributable to the apartment(s), which fractional share has been established as of the date hereof as $_____. Buyer agrees to pay two of said monthly assessment payments in advance at the time of closing, the first of which payments shall be prorated as of the date of closing. Common expenses, as defined in the Declaration, include, but are not limited to, heat, gas for kitchen range, water and sewer charges, common area repairs and maintenance, upkeep, landscaping, building liability insurance, and management for the condominium property and its common areas and facilities.

4. Real Estate Taxes and Assessments. If the unit purchased is closed in the year of sale, the real estate taxes and installments of special assessments due in the year 19_____ shall be prorated between Buyer and Seller on a calendar year basis as of the date of closing. Subsequently, Buyer shall pay the real estate taxes due in the year 19_____ and unpaid installments of special assessments payable therewith and thereafter. If the unit purchased is closed in the year following the year of sale, each of the above dates shall be advanced one year.

5. The Condominium. Seller will deliver apartment building and other improvements at the address referred to above, which will be part of a condominium substantially as it presently exists, subject to reasonable modifications approved by Seller which do not materially change the size or floor plan of Buyer's apartment nor the extent or nature of the common facilities, to the prejudice of Buyer. Buyer acknowledges that the apartment which he has contracted to buy is being sold unfurnished, but will be equipped with range, refrigerator, dishwasher, disposal, air conditioning unit(s), and carpeting. Buyer further acknowledges and understands that model unit is for display purposes only and does not constitute a representation of items included in the purchase price.

6. Closing and Possession. Seller agrees to deliver possession not later than _____ and the parties agree to close the purchase on or before _____, at a time and place specified by Seller, provided, however, in the event that Seller has not contracted for the sale of at least 15 residential apartment(s) in The Condominium by said closing date, then this Agreement, at the option of the Seller, shall become null and void and all earnest money paid hereunder shall be refunded to Buyer in full without interest. Buyer and Seller agree that pro rata adjustments of utilities and common expenses under the Declaration and bylaws shall be made as of the time of closing. It is expressly understood by the parties hereto that the Seller shall use its best efforts to meet the closing date described herein, and the parties hereto expressly agree that Seller shall not be liable for any postponement in closing.

7. Closing Costs. It shall be the obligation of Buyer to pay closing costs charged by a title insurance company or by a lending institution in connection with Buyer's purchase of the apartment under this Agreement.

8. Destruction of Property. In the event the apartment building or other improvements at the above address are destroyed or substantially damaged by fire or any other cause before the closing date, this Agreement shall be voidable, at Seller's option, and all monies paid hereunder shall be refunded to Buyer without interest.

9. Title. Seller shall furnish a binder for an owner's policy of title insurance in the amount of the purchase price, issued by a reputable title insurance company authorized to do business in _____, insuring a marketable title subject only to allowable encumbrances, taxes, and special assessments to be paid by Buyer pursuant hereto. If any title objection is shown on the policy binder, other than said allowable encumbrances and said taxes and special assessments, Seller shall, within 120 days from the date of said binder, make such title marketable. Pending correction of title, the payments hereunder required shall be postponed, but upon correction of title Buyer shall perform this Agreement according to its terms. Within a reasonable time after closing, Seller shall deliver a final title insurance policy pursuant to said policy binder. Seller shall not be obligated to furnish any abstract, registered property abstract, nor any title evidence other than said title insurance policy, provided, however, at such time as Buyer enters into an agreement to resell said apartment, Seller shall furnish an updated abstract of title or registered property abstract for said apartment at a cost to Buyer not to exceed the then current cost of continuing an abstract or registered property abstract to date.

10. Marketability of Title and Remedies. If said title is not marketable and is not made so within the 120-day period above provided, this Agreement shall be void, neither party shall be liable for damages hereunder to the other, and all money paid hereunder by Buyer shall be refunded without interest, but if title be found marketable, or be so made within said time, and Buyer shall default in any of Buyer's agreements herein, then Seller may specifically enforce this contract or may terminate this Agreement, and upon such termination all payments made hereunder shall be retained by Seller as liquidated and agreed damages, time being of the essence hereof. Buyer recognizes that in arranging this purchase, Seller has incurred numerous expenses relative to sales, model apartment, advertising, etc., and that no method other than that of liquidated and agreed damages would be sufficient to determine precise damage to Seller resulting from Buyer's breach.

11. Condominium Documents. Buyer shall be provided with a booklet of Condominium documents, including, but not limited to the following: (i) Declaration; (ii) Articles of Incorporation of the Condominium Association, Inc., (iii) by-laws; and (iv) Rules and Regulations of The Condominium. Seller reserves the right to modify or amend the above-described documents without the approval or joinder of buyer: provided, however, that no modifications or amendments will materially affect the rights of Buyer of the value or size or floor plan of his apartment. Nothing contained herein shall require Seller to secure Buyer's approval to any change in the prices or terms upon which Seller will sell the remaining apartments in the Condominium, and any such changes shall be at the sole discretion of Seller, Buyer agrees to be bound by all of the terms and conditions of the above described documents and to purchase and hold the apartment pursuant to this Agreement and the said documents.

12. Notices. All notices to the parties herto shall be delivered or mailed by U.S. mail, postage prepaid, to the respective party at his address as shown on the signature page of this Agreement.

13. Personal Property. Seller will equip the Buyer's apartment with a gas range, vent hood, refrigerator, dishwasher, disposal, air conditioning unit(s) and carpeting, and will deliver a Bill of Sale at closing warranting the existing gas range, vent hood, refrigerator, dishwasher, disposal, and air conditioning unit(s) against manufacturing defects for a period of ninety (90) days from the date of closing. If Buyer purchases from Seller a new gas range, vent hood, refrigerator, dishwasher, disposal for said apartment, said new appliances shall be warranted against manufacturing defects for such period as provided by the manufacturer.

14. Limited Common Areas. Certain common areas and facilities shall be designated in the Declaration as reserved for the use of Buyer's apartment to the exclusion of other apartments in The Condominium. Those common areas and facilities reserved for the exclusive use of Buyer's apartment shall be storage locker No. _____.

15. Rental Occupancy. Should Buyer desire to take possession of or occupy the apartment or a similar apartment prior to the closing date provided for herein at a time mutually agreed upon by the parties hereto, Buyer hereby agrees to execute an Interim Rental Occupancy Agreement and to pay the monthly rental of $_____ as provided therein for a period commencing on the date Buyer takes possession of or occupies the apartment through the date of actual closing.

16. Miscellaneous. This Agreement shall not be binding upon Seller until accepted in writing by a duly authorized officer of _____ Corporation.

This Agreement is personal to Buyer and cannot be assigned without the written approval of Seller. The obligations of Buyer shall be joint and several if more than one. This Agreement expresses all agreements between the parties concerning the subject matter hereof and supersedes all previous understandings, oral and written, related hereto.

In the event that this Agreement is cancelled or becomes void under its provisions, Buyer agrees to execute a written cancellation or Quit Claim Deed conveying Buyer's entire interest to Seller.

17. Schedule of Additional Terms. This agreement is subject to and shall be performed in accordance with the terms and contingencies, if any, set forth herein.

_____

I (we) hereby agree to purchase the apartment(s) for the price and upon the terms mentioned above and subject to all conditions herein expressed.

Buyer:_____
Address:_____
Telephone Number: Home_____
                Office_____

Buyer:_____
Address:_____
Telephone Number: Home_____
                Office_____

The undersigned agrees to sell the apartment for the price and upon the terms above mentioned and subject to all conditions herein expressed.

By:_____
      (Agent for Seller)

Accepted by Seller:
By:_____
Its:_____
Date_____

NOTICE TO PURCHASER: YOU ARE ENTITLED TO RESCIND THIS AGREEMENT AT ANYTIME WITHIN FIVE DAYS FROM THE DAY YOU ACTUALLY RECEIVE THE INFORMATION REQUIRED BY LAW. SUCH RESCISSION MUST BE IN WRITING AND MAILED TO THE VENDOR OR HIS AGENT OR HIS LENDER AT THE ADDRESS STATED IN THIS DOCUMENT. UPON RESCISSION, YOU WILL RECEIVE A REFUND OF ALL MONIES PAID.

The Arlington, A Condominium
Decor Selection Sheet

Purchaser: _____ Unit No._____ Unit Type _____

Phone No. _____ Work _____
_____ Work _____

Carpet Selection

	Style	Color	Pad	Price
Living Room	_____	_____	_____	_____
Dining Area	_____	_____	_____	_____
Hall	_____	_____	_____	_____
Steps	_____	_____	_____	_____
Master Bedroom	_____	_____	_____	_____
Bedroom #2	_____	_____	_____	_____
Bedroom #3	_____	_____	_____	_____
Family Room	_____	_____	_____	_____
Den	_____	_____	_____	_____
Other	_____	_____	_____	_____

Subtotal _____

Resilient Selections

	Style	Color	Price
Kitchen	_____	_____	_____
½ Bath	_____	_____	_____
Hall Bath	_____	_____	_____
Master Bath	_____	_____	_____
Family Room	_____	_____	_____
Foyer	_____	_____	_____
Den	_____	_____	_____
Other	_____	_____	_____

Subtotal _____

Appliances

	Model	Color	Price
Refrigerator	_____	_____	_____
Dishwasher	_____	_____	_____
Range	_____	_____	_____
Range Hood	_____	_____	_____
Microwave	_____	_____	_____
Other	_____	_____	_____

Subtotal _____

Countertops

	Pattern	Finish	Price
Kitchen	_____	_____	_____
½ Bath	_____	_____	_____
Hall Bath	_____	_____	_____
Master Bath	_____	_____	_____

Subtotal _____

Vanities

	Size	Base Style	Color	Style	Top Color	Price
½ Bath	____	____	____	____	____	____
Hall Bath	____	____	____	____	____	____
Master Bath	____	____	____	____	____	____

Subtotal _____

Patio

Landscape Package _____

_____

Subtotal _____

Miscellaneous

Description	Price
_____	_____
_____	_____
_____	_____

Subtotal _____

Date: _____   Total _____
_____

_____   _____
Purchaser   Purchaser

By _____
Seller's Agent

The Arlington, A Condominium
Subscription and Purchase Agreement

☐ Original   ☐ Re-Write   ☐ Transfer   Date: _____

The undersigned, hereinafter referred to as "Buyer," hereby offers and agrees to purchase the real property described below and upon the terms and conditions as set forth below and on the reverse side.

THIS SUBSCRIPTION AND PURCHASE AGREEMENT is made and entered, on the above date, between Claremont Apartments, Ltd., and Ohio Limited Partnership (Hereafter "Seller") and

Condominium Unit No. _____ Type _____ The Arlington, A Condominium

                                                                                    Bus.
Property Address _____ Phone _____
                                                                                    Home
Buyer: _____ Phone _____
    First   Middle   Last
Co-Buyer: _____ Relationship _____
    First   Middle   Last
Present Address: _____
            No.   Street   City   State   Zip

Present Home   (Seller reserves the right not to   To Be   Yes ☐
To Sell   ☐ Yes   ☐ No   accept contingency sales)   Owner Occupied   No ☐

WHEREAS, Seller is the owner of a multifamily condominium project known as The Arlington, A Condominium; and,

WHEREAS, the said Condominium has been registered with the Virginia Real Estate Commission under the terms of the Condominium Act; and,

WHEREAS, a Unit Owner's Association to be composed of all the unit owners of the Condominium Units in The Arlington, A Condominium, has been established for the purpose of operating, maintaining, and regulating the common elements of The Arlington, A Condominium.

The Buyer hereby agrees to become a member of the Unit Owner's Association, and hereby agrees to purchase the above-numbered Condominium Unit and the allocated fractional undivided interest in the general and/or limited common elements of The Arlington, A Condominium, appurtenant to the unit.

				Conventional	☐ ___ LTV% ___
Sales Price		**Financing**	Other	☐ _____	
Base Price	$	Total Cost		$	
Extras:		Mortgage (interest rate to be			
Premium location		Amount specified by lender)			
		Downpayment			
				Check # _____	
		Deposit Received		Cash _____	
		Balance of downpayment due on mortgage approval			
		Estimated closing costs			
		Estimated prepaid items			
Total Cost	$	Total Estimated Cash Due Upon Mortgage Approval		$	

Other Conditions: *All agreements must be in writing. Verbal representations are invalid and non-binding. If none, write none.*

_____

_____

Buyer's deposit shall not bear interest and shall, until settlement or other disposition thereof as herein provided, be maintained in a separate escrow account designated as such by Seller, and shall not be commingled with other funds of the Seller.

This offer is subject to acceptance by Seller. If Seller does not accept this offer, Buyer's deposit will be returned and this offer shall become null and void. Upon acceptance by Seller, this agreement shall become a firm and binding contract, subject to the hereinstated terms and conditions.

WITNESS our hand this _____ day of _____, 19____.

                                          _____
                                                            Buyer

By: _____   _____
    Sales Representative   Buyer
The within offer is hereby accepted this _____ day of _____ , 19___, subject to the hereinstated terms and conditions.

CLAREMONT APARTMENTS, LTD.
An Ohio Ltd. Partnership

By: _____

1. **Mortgage Loan.** The Buyer shall make prompt, diligent, and truthful application to a lending institution designated by the Seller, or to such other lending institution as the Seller may approve in writing and shall, without delay, furnish to the Seller, or such lending institution, such information or other materials as may be required by such lending institution in connection with the Buyer's application for a mortgage loan in the amount of $_____ at an interest rate within the legal limits and consistent with current available rates.

In the event the Buyer is unable to obtain approval and qualification for the mortgage loan aforesaid, or if the lender refuses to consummate and make the loan after commitment is issued, the Seller shall have the option to cancel and terminate this Agreement and return the deposit to the Buyer, less any actual expenses incurred in processing the loan application and credit check, unless the Buyer, by prompt written advice to the Seller, elects to perform this Agreement without the benefit of such mortgage loan. In the event the lender refuses to consummate the loan to the Buyer as a result of Buyer's failure to comply with the terms of their commitment, then this Agreement, at the option of the Seller, may be declared cancelled and terminated and the deposit retained by the Seller as liquidated damages. All Buyers will complete and submit all mortgage or credit applications, or other similar forms, provided by the Seller or the lender promptly within fifteen (15) days after being so requested. Should the Buyer fail to do so, then this Agreement, at the option of the Seller only, may be declared cancelled and terminated and the deposit retained by the Seller as liquidated damages.

2. **Expansion of Condominium.** It is understood that the Seller or its assignees or successors in title has reserved the right to subject additional portions of the property more particularly described in Schedules "A" and "B" to the Declaration and contained in the Document Book, to the community known as **The Arlington, A Condominium.**

Until the date of the expansion of the Condominium, the Declaration shall be deemed to be applicable only to that portion of the property described in Schedule "A". Thereafter, the Seller specifically reserves the right to extend the portions of the property subject to the Declaration to all or any part of the property described in Schedule "B". These extensions may be made from time to time until 100 percent of the property described in Schedule "A" and Schedule "B", or such lesser amount thereof as the Seller may determine, is subject to the Declaration. The Seller shall subject additional portions of the property to the Declaration either by means of recording an amendment or supplement to the Declaration and merely amending or supplementing the Exhibits thereto. The right of the Seller to subject additional portions of the property to the Declaration shall be vested only in the Seller, **Claremont Apartments, Ltd.,** or its assignees or successors in title, and no other owner, member, or other person shall have such right. The right reserved herein, to the extent not exercised, shall lapse without further act or deed, and Schedule "B" deemed to be a nullity, if such right is not exercised on or before seven years after the date of recording of the Declaration; provided, however, that the Seller may waive and renounce said right prior to said date by recording an appropriate instrument among the Land Records of Arlington County.

In the event the Seller waives or renounces the right contained herein or said right lapses by failure of exercise on or before seven years from the date of recording of the Declaration, the Declaration shall be applicable only to the portion of the Property described in Schedule "A" and shall be a covenant running with and binding upon the land described in Schedule "A" only.

3. **Unit Owner's Association.** A Unit Owner's Association, all of whose members shall be all of the owners of Condominium Units, has been established for the purpose of managing, operating, and maintaining the common elements of the Condominium. Each owner of a Condominium Unit will be a member of this association and will be fully subject to the provisions of the Declaration of the Condominium and the bylaws and rules and regulations of the Unit Owner's Association.

4. **Alteration of Condominium Documents.** No substantial changes shall be made to the Declaration or bylaws prior to the settlement on the sale of this Condominium Unit without the prior written consent of the Buyer.

5. **Title.** The Condominium Unit is sold free of encumbrance except as aforesaid. Title is to be good, merchantable and insurable at regular rates subject, however, to covenants, easements, conditions, and restrictions or record, including, but not necessarily limited to those appropriate to the establishment of a condominium property regime for the project; otherwise, all sums deposited by the Buyer pursuant to this Agreement are to be returned and this Agreement shall become void and of no effect; but if any defect arises of such a character as may be remedied by legal action, then this Agreement shall terminate only upon the Seller's failure to remedy the defect within a reasonable time, not exceeding thirty (30) months after the date of this Agreement.

The premises are sold subject to easements, if any, created or to be created prior to or after settlement in favor of utility companies, municipal authorities, and for the installation of utilities or street lights, television antenna cable and towers, and/or additional covenant, restrictions, or easements which may be placed on record by the Seller after execution hereof for the benefit of The Arlington, A Condominium, and/or the community of which it is a part.

6. **Display Materials.** Furniture, wallcoverings, furnishings, landscaping, or the like, as shown in or about any model Condominium Unit are for display purposes only and are not considered a part of such unit for purposes of this Agreement.

7. **Custom Finishing.** Items in the nature of "custom finishing" optional items, refurbishing, decorating, repair, or the like which are not standard to the model Condominium Unit, may be affected by and at the cost of the Buyer only with the prior written consent of the Seller, and under such conditions as the Seller may establish. Failure or delay in the installation or completion of any such item which does not materially affect the habitability of the unit shall not be a bar to settlement hereunder or grounds for the postponement thereof, beyond the time otherwise appointed by the Seller in accordance with the provisions hereof.

8. Conveyance of Title. The Seller agrees to convey to the Buyer a good and sufficient special warranty deed to said Condominium Unit.

Within fourteen (14) days after the Seller, or its agents, has mailed to Buyer notice in writing that the Seller will be prepared to tender title and possession of the Condominium Unit, on a day certain, the Seller and the Buyer are required and agree to make full settlement in accordance with the terms hereof at the time and place specified by the Seller. In the event the Buyer shall fail to make full settlement, or shall default in any of the payments of obligations called for in this Agreement, and such default shall continue for fifteen (15) days after notice by the Seller or its agents to the Buyer, then at the sole option of the Seller, this Agreement shall become void and of no effect and any amounts paid toward the purchase price may be retained by the Seller as liquidated damages, or the Seller may elect not to forfeit the deposit, but to pursue any other legal and/or equitable remedies available to it, in which event, it may retain the deposit while pursuing such remedies. Deposit to the Account of the Seller of the aforesaid purchase price, the deed of conveyance for execution, and such other papers as are required of either party by the terms of this Agreement, shall be considered good and sufficient performance of the terms hereof. Time shall be considered of the essence in this Agreement.

In the event Seller does not notify the Buyer that it is prepared to tender title and possession of the Condominium Unit within 24 months of the date hereof, then either party, by delivery of notice in writing to the other, shall have the option to withdraw from this Agreement, whereupon any amounts theretofore paid by the Buyer to the Seller pursuant to the terms hereof shall be returned to the Buyer and all rights and liabilities of the parties hereunder shall cease and terminate. Any delay caused by the act of default of the Buyer shall extend the time for performance hereinabove referred to for the period of such delay. Delays caused by weather, actions of governmental bodies, acts of God, strikes, or other causes beyond the control of the Seller, shall extend the time required for the Seller's performance, but in no event later than thirty (30) months from the date hereof.

At Seller's option Buyer may be permitted to defer settlement not in excess of thirty (30) days after appointed settlement date by payment to Seller of twenty-five dollars ($25.00) per day to defray carrying costs, said added cost per day to be payable at, and as part of, settlement. Requests for deferment must be in writing from Buyer and agreed to in writing by Seller.

Notwithstanding anything to the contrary herein contained, the unit and Buyer's interest in the common elements are to be conveyed subject to: (a) all applicable zoning regulations and ordinances, (b) facts as may be shown by an accurate survey of the premises at the date of delivery of Deed, provided such facts do not render title unmarketable, (c) sewer, water, electric, gas, telephone and other utility easements and consents and other covenants and restrictions, if any, now or hereinafter recorded or granted provided they do not prohibit the use or maintenance of the structure and improvements, (d) all service contracts affecting the property, building, and unit(s) entered into by Seller or Council and which exist at the time of the delivery of the Deed, including contracts for management, clothes washers and dryers, extermination, vending machines and building employees (including union contracts), (e) accrued taxes and municipal charges not yet payable, (f) any leases which Seller may have entered into for the leasehold of any recreational facilities within the common elements of the property. Any and all of the foregoing subject provisions may be omitted from the Deed to be delivered hereunder, but all such provisions so omitted shall nevertheless survive delivery of Deed.

9. Closing and Settlement Fees. Preparation of the Deed of conveyance and cost of state revenue stamps shall be at the expense of Seller. Examination of title, all conveyance costs, including preparation of documents, settlement fees, notary fees, tax certificates and all recording costs, including those for purchase money trust, if any, are to be at the expense of the Buyer.

At settlement, the Buyer agrees to pay to the Unit Owner's Association an initial working capital contribution in an amount equal to two months' condominium assessment and to pay one full month's assessment, plus a pro rata portion of one month's assessment, prorated from the date of settlement. The initial working capital contribution will be in addition to and not in lieu of assessments attributable to the Condominium Unit for common expenses of the condominium as they may regularly occur thereafter.

The settlement shall be conducted by the settlement officer designated by the Seller at the location selected by the Seller.

10. Adjustments. Taxes and assessments for common expenses of the condominium are to be adjusted to the date of closing. Taxes, general and special, are to be adjusted according to the certificate of taxes issued by the Division of Revenue for Arlington County, Virginia, except that assessments for improvements completed prior to the date hereof, if any, whether assessment therefore has been levied or not, shall be paid by the Seller, or allowance made therefore at the time of closing.

11. Risk of Loss. Possession is to be delivered to Buyer at closing. The risk of loss or damage to the Condominium Unit by fire or other casualty, is assumed by the Seller until such date.

12. Destruction of Unit. In the event of partial or total destruction of the unit or any improvements therein, prior to delivery of Deed hereunder, Seller may, at his option, either reconstruct or repair said damages within a reasonable time therefrom in which event delivery of deed and possession shall be deferred for a like period of time, or in his discretion, declare this Agreement null and void without further liability or right by and between the parties hereto except repayment to Buyer of the sums paid by Buyer to Seller prior thereto, without interest except as earned in the escrow account, if any, but without deduction of any kind. In the latter event, Seller may without obligation to Buyer subsequently proceed with construction upon the property or take such other action with respect thereto as he so desires.

13. Assignment. The rights of the Buyer hereunder are not assignable without the prior consent in writing of the Seller. The fact that the Seller refuses to give its consent to an assignment will not give rise to any claim for damages against the Seller.

14. Access or Entry. The Buyer may not have access or entry to the Condominium Unit or the condominium project prior to settlement, nor may he store any of his possessions in or about the Condominium Unit or the condominium project prior to the settlement of this Agreement and delivery of possession to the Buyer.

15. Merger. All understandings and agreements heretofore made between the parties hereto are merged in this Agreement which expresses the parties entire agreement, and no representations, warranties, or conditions or statements, oral or written, not contained herein shall be considered a part hereof. This Agreement may not be altered, enlarged, modified or changed except by an instrument in writing executed by all of the parties hereto. Anything to the contrary herein contained notwithstanding, it is specifically understood and agreed by the parties hereto that the acceptance of the delivery of the Deed at the time of the closing hereunder shall constitute full compliance by the Seller with the terms of this Agreement, that none of the terms hereof, except as otherwise herein specifically provided, shall survive settlement and the terms hereof shall be merged into and extinguished by the delivery of the Deed at the time of closing of the title.

16. Notice. Whenever, by the terms of this Agreement, any notice is required to be given, notice shall be conclusively considered given when deposited in the United States Mail, postage prepaid. Certified Mail, Return Receipt Requested, to any of the parties at the addresses set out herein. Such designation may be changed by any of the parties by notice to all of the other parties.

17. Execution of Documents. In the event the Buyer is a corporation, partnership, or other such entity, it is understood that the principal officers or owners and their respective spouses shall be required to execute mortgages, notes, applications, and other documents generally required of an individual buyer. In the event this Agreement is signed by an individual who is unmarried at the time of execution hereof and at the time of final settlement said individual is then married, the Buyer does hereby agree to indemnify the Seller from any loss or damages that may arise by reason of the failure of the spouse of the Buyer to execute any applications, mortgages, notes, or other documents required by the lender. If the Buyer is married and his or her spouse is not also a buyer under this Agreement, then Buyer shall be responsible for his or her spouse executing the mortgage loan documents and the failure of the spouse to do so shall not relieve the Buyer of the obligations under this Agreement and the Buyer agrees to hold the Seller harmless from any loss as a result of the refusal of such spouse to sign any document.

18. Gender. Whenever the context so requires, the use of any gender shall include all genders and the use of the singular shall include the plural. The words "deed of trust" shall refer to a "mortgage" and vice versa. The word "mortgages" shall include any lender on a deed of trust. Trustees on any deed of trust, where applicable, shall be named by the parties secured thereby.

19. Subordination. This Agreement shall be subject and subordinate to any mortgages now or hereafter encumbering the property of which the unit forms a part, and to any subsequent advances made thereunder, provided, however, that the Seller shall obtain a release of the unit to be conveyed hereunder from the lien of such mortgage.

20. Seller's Unsold Units. Seller reserves the right to lease its unsold Condominium Units, and to make such use of its unsold Condominium Units and the common elements as is necessary for its sales program. Such use, however, shall not unreasonably interfere with the enjoyment of the condominium by the other owners of the Condominium Units. Seller is not required to secure Buyer's approval for any change in the price or terms upon which Seller will sell the remaining Condominium Units in the condominium project. Any changes may be made at the sole discretion of the Seller. Notwithstanding anything to the contrary herein contained, the provisions of this Paragraph 20 shall survive settlement hereunder.

21. Miscellaneous. The laws of the Commonwealth of Virginia shall govern the interpretation, validity, and construction of the terms and conditions of this Agreement. The parties to this Agreement mutually agree that it shall be binding upon them, their and each of their respective heirs, personal representatives, successors, and assignees. The captions of this Agreement are for the convenience of the parties and shall not be considered as a material part hereof. This Agreement may be executed in counterparts, each of which, when so executed, may be considered an original.

22. Condition of Units. Except to the extent that a unit is to be restored or renovated as stated herein the Buyer shall take the Condominium Unit in "AS IS" condition. Seller makes no warranties other than the warranties made pursuant to Title 55 Section 79.79(b) of the Code of Virginia as amended, which warranty is a LIMITED WARRANTY.

23. Receipt of Condominium. BUYER HEREBY ACKNOWLEDGES RECEIPT OF THE CURRENT PUBLIC OFFERING STATEMENT OF THE ARLINGTON, A CONDOMINIUM.

24. Buyer's Right to Cancel. THIS AGREEMENT IS EXPRESSLY AND WITHOUT CONDITION SUBJECT TO CANCELLATION BY THE BUYER WITHIN TEN (10) DAYS FROM THE AGREEMENT DATE, OR DELIVERY OF THE CURRENT PUBLIC OFFERING STATEMENT, WHICHEVER IS LATER IF BUYER ELECTS TO CANCEL. HE MAY DO SO BY NOTICE THEREOF HAND-DELIVERED OR SENT UNITED STATES MAIL, RETURN RECEIPT REQUESTED, TO THE SELLER. SUCH CANCELLATION SHALL BE WITHOUT PENALTY, AND ANY DEPOSIT MADE BY BUYER SHALL BE PROMPTLY REFUNDED IN ITS ENTIRETY.

25. Offer. The parties expressly acknowledge that execution of this Agreement by the Buyer shall constitute a mere offer to buy and this Agreement shall not be binding upon the Seller until executed by an officer of the Seller and delivered to the Buyer. The signature of the sales person hereon constitutes a mere acknowledgement of receipt of the Buyer's offer.

Amendment To Subscription and Purchase Agreement

This is Amendment No. _____ to Subscription and Purchase Agreement No. _____   Unit No. _____

The undersigned hereby desire to amend the aforestated Purchase Agreement as hereinafter described with all other terms, conditions, and provisions of the Purchase Agreement remaining in full force and effect.

Amendment to Purchase Price:		**Amendment to Financing:**	
Base Price:	$_____	Revised purchase price:	$_____
Extras per décor		Revised mortgage amount:	$_____
selection sheet		Revised downpayment:	$_____
Attached hereto and		Deposit:	$_____
made a part hereof:	$_____	Balance of downpayment	
Other:		due on mortgage approval:	$_____
	$_____	Revised closing cost estimate:	$_____
_____		Revised estimate of prepaid	
Revised purchase		items:	$_____
price:	$_____	Revised estimate of cash due	
		upon mortgage approval:	$_____

This Amendment is subject to acceptance by Seller. Upon acceptance thereof, this Amendment shall become firm and binding as part of the Subscription and Purchase Agreement as aforestated, subject to the terms, conditions, and provisions thereof, and as stated hereinabove on this Amendment.

WITNESS our hand this ___ day of _____, 19___.

By:_____   _____
          Sales Representative   Buyer

                                              _____
                                                              Buyer

This Amendment is accepted this ___ day of _____, 19___, subject to the hereinstated terms and conditions.

CLAREMONT APARTMENTS, LTD.
By: _____

Attachment: _____ dated _____

Buyer agrees to purchase these modifications or improvements from **Seller** under the following conditions:

A. To the extent that any modifications or improvements are being made, they will substantially be similar in construction, design, materials, and quality to the samples, specifications, or promotional materials on display in **Seller's** Sales Office, Model Unit, or Décor Center. **Seller** reserves the right to make such changes and/or substitutions in construction, design, materials, or quality because of unavailability of certain materials or labor. Any substitutions or changes shall be substantially equal in cost to the present costs, but the prices set forth herein shall not be decreased by reason of such substitution or change.

B. Where **Seller** is delayed from delivering or installing said modifications or improvements, such delay shall not be cause to postpone the closing of title of the unit and funds equal to the amount charged by **Seller** for such modifications or improvements shall be held in escrow until delivery or installation. In the event that **Seller** is unable to complete said modifications or improvements within one hundred twenty (120) days of the Closing of Title as set forth in the Agreement of Sale, **Buyer** is exclusively entitled to a refund of the sums held by the escrow agent, without interest, and **Seller** shall be released from any obligations to complete said modifications or improvements providing however, that **Seller** shall reinstall the original equipment, appliances, carpeting, and floor covering if they have been removed so as to render the **unit** to the conditions of this date. In the event the delivery or installation of modifications or improvements ordered is delayed by strikes, Acts of God, or other occurrence beyond the control of the **Seller,** the time of delivery may be extended for an additional period equivalent to the duration of such strikes, Acts of God, or other matters beyond its control. In any event, **Seller** shall not be liable to **Buyer** for any damages resulting from delay or non-performance of this rider, except to return any monies deposited hereunder, without interest.